BACKROOMS AND BEYOND

Partisan Advisers and the Politics of Policy Work in Canada

Though they serve in many roles and under many titles, no one doubts that political staffs now wield substantial influence in the making of government policy. *Backrooms and Beyond* draws on interviews with ministers, senior public servants, and political advisers to offer the first detailed Canadian treatment of how that influence is gained and exercised in the policymaking process.

A comparative analysis of case studies from three Canadian jurisdictions, including the federal Prime Minister's Office, two premier's offices, and ministers' offices, the book presents a detailed account of partisan advisers' involvement in policy work and a new theoretical framework for understanding this work and its impact. As Jonathan Craft shows, partisan advisers often engage in policy work with public servants, outside stakeholders, and often in types of policy work that public servants cannot.

Backrooms and Beyond is a rich and rigorous look at an important aspect of contemporary Canadian politics, essential reading for scholars and practitioners, journalists, students of the Westminster system from around the world, and those wanting to understand just how policy is made today.

JONATHAN CRAFT is an assistant professor in the Department of Political Science and the School of Public Policy and Governance at the University of Toronto. He is a former provincial legislative assistant and federal public servant.

IPAC
The Institute of
Public Administration of Canada

IAPC
L'Institut d'administration
publique du Canada

The Institute of Public Administration of Canada Series in Public Management and Governance

Editors:
Peter Aucoin, 2001–2
Donald Savoie, 2003–7
Luc Bernier, 2007–9
Patrice Dutil, 2010–

This series is sponsored by the Institute of Public Administration of Canada as part of its commitment to encourage research on issues in Canadian public administration, public sector management, and public policy. It also seeks to foster wider knowledge and understanding among practitioners, academics, and the general public.

For a list of books published in the series, see page 305.

Palakh,
Enjoy the book! I expect big things from you. All the best, Jonathan April 2016

Backrooms and Beyond

Partisan Advisers and the Politics of Policy Work in Canada

JONATHAN CRAFT

IPAC
The Institute of
Public Administration of Canada

IAPC
L'Institut d'administration
publique du Canada

UNIVERSITY OF TORONTO PRESS
Toronto Buffalo London

© University of Toronto Press 2016
Toronto Buffalo London
www.utppublishing.com
Printed in the U.S.A.

ISBN 978-1-4426-4876-0 (cloth)   ISBN 978-1-4426-2635-5 (paper)

♾ Printed on acid-free, 100% post-consumer recycled paper with
vegetable-based inks.

Library and Archives Canada Cataloguing in Publication

Craft, Jonathan, 1980–, author
Backrooms and beyond : partisan advisers and the politics of policy work
in Canada / Jonathan Craft.

(Institute of Public Administration of Canada series in public management
and governance)
Includes bibliographical references and index.
ISBN 978-1-4426-4876-0 (cloth).   ISBN 978-1-4426-2635-5 (paper)

1. Policy sciences – Canada – Case studies.   2. Political planning – Canada –
Case studies.   3. Political consultants – Canada – Case studies.   4. Canada –
Politics and government – Case studies.   I. Title.   II. Series: Institute of
Public Administration of Canada series in public management and governance

JL86.P64C73 2016   320.60971   C2015-907323-5

This book has been published with the help of a grant from the Federation
for the Humanities and Social Sciences, through the Awards to Scholarly
Publications Program, using funds provided by the Social Sciences and
Humanities Research Council of Canada.

University of Toronto Press acknowledges the financial assistance to its
publishing program of the Canada Council for the Arts and the Ontario
Arts Council, an agency of the Government of Ontario.

Canada Council   Conseil des Arts
for the Arts   du Canada

ONTARIO ARTS COUNCIL
CONSEIL DES ARTS DE L'ONTARIO
an Ontario government agency
un organisme du gouvernement de l'Ontario

Funded by the   Financé par le
Government   gouvernement
of Canada   du Canada

Canadä

For my parents and Zoiey

Contents

List of Tables and Figures xi

Foreword xiii

Acknowledgments xv

Introduction: Partisan Advisers, Policy Work, and the Political
Arm of Government in Canada 3
  Introduction 3
  Enduring Debate 6
  *Political Control and Public Service "Neutral" and "Responsive"
  Competence* 8
  *Partisan Advisers and Currents of Change in Contemporary Canadian
  Governance* 11
  A Core Executives Approach 18
  Main Arguments 19
  Organization of the Study 22

1 A "No Surprises" Environment 24
  Introduction 24
  *Buffers and Bridges, Movers and Shapers: A Framework for the Study of
  Partisan Advisers' Policy Work* 25
  Buffers and Bridges: Partisan Advisers' Policy Advisory Activity 32
  Movers and Shapers: Partisan Advisers' Policy Formulation Activity 37
  Studying Federal and Provincial Partisan Advisers 40

2 Institutionalization, Expansion, and Specialization 44
  Introduction 44
  Partisan Advisers in Ottawa 45
    Harper-Era Advisers in Ottawa 57
  British Columbia 60

      Campbell-Era Partisan Advisers in British Columbia, 2001–9   63
   New Brunswick   67
   Conclusion   70

3 Buffers and Bridges at the "Centre"   71
   Introduction   71
   First Ministers' Office Partisan Advisers' Buffering   72
     PMO Buffering   72
     Buffering from the West Annex   80
     Buffering from the "Centre" in New Brunswick   84
   First Ministers' Office Bridging Activities   86
     Prime Minister's Office Bridging   86
     First Ministers' Office Bridging in British Columbia   92
     First Ministers' Office Bridging in New Brunswick   96
   Conclusion   101

4 Movers and Shapers at the "Centre"   104
   Introduction   104
   Procedural Formulation Activity in First Ministers' Offices   106
     PMO Policy Movers   106
     Moving at (and around) the Centre in British Columbia   116
     Moving at the Centre in New Brunswick   119
   First Ministers' Office "Shaping"   123
     PMO Shapers   123
     First Ministers' Office Shaping in British Columbia   130
     First Ministers' Office Shaping in New Brunswick   136
   Conclusion   141

5 He Said / She Said: Ministers' Office Buffers and Bridges   145
   Introduction   145
   Ministerial Office Buffering   146
     Buffering at the Federal Ministers' Office Level   146
     Ministerial Partisan Advisers' Buffering in BC   154
     Ministers' Office Buffering in New Brunswick   159
   Ministers' Office Bridging   162
     Federal Ministers' Office Partisan Advisory Bridging   162
     BC Ministers' Office Partisan Advisers' Bridging   169
     Ministers' Office Bridging in New Brunswick   174
   Conclusion   177

6 Movers and Shapers Down the Line   183
   Introduction   183
   Procedural Policy Work and Ministers' Offices   185

Federal Ministers' Office "Moving"   185
Ministers' Office "Moving" in BC   196
Ministers' Office "Moving" in New Brunswick   203
Ministerial "Shaping"   207
Federal Ministers' Offices' Substantive "Shaping"   207
BC Ministers' Office "Shaping"   214
New Brunswick Ministers' Office "Shaping"   218
Conclusion   220

7 Conclusion: Core Executives, Partisan Advisers, and the Politics
of Policy Work in Canada   224
Introduction   224
Canadian Partisan Advisers and Advisory System Participation   226
*The Federal Dynamic Advisory System Configuration: Comprehensive-
Differentiated and Layered-Dispersed*   229
*BC: Limited-Dispersed and Integrated Advisory System
Configuration*   232
*New Brunswick Dynamic Advisory System: Limited-Dispersed and
Centralized-Integrated Configuration*   234
Canadian Partisan Advisers as Formulation Participants   238
Process Dimensions of Partisan Advisers' Formulation Activity   238
"Shaping": Beyond Determinations of Political Feasibility   241
*Partisan Advisers, Core Executive Operation, and the Politics of Policy
Work*   243
Conclusion   250

Appendices   253
*Appendix A: Federal Exempt Staff by Department (31 March 2001
to 31 March 2014)*   253
Appendix B: Organization of BC Premier's Office (2001)   256
Appendix C: Organization of BC Premier's Office (2011)   257
*Appendix D: BC Ministers' Office Staff by Department and Classification
1996–2001)*   259
Appendix E: Interview Index   262

Notes   267

References   273

Index   295

Tables and Figures

Tables

I.1   Policy Advisory Systems 13
I.2   Two Idealized Models of Policy Advising in Canadian Government 14
I.3   Resources of Prime Ministers, Ministers, and Officials 18
1.1   Conceptualizing Partisan Advisers' Policy Work 27
1.2   Comparison of Rational (Cold) and Political (Hot) Advice 33
1.3   Partisan Advisers' Policy Advisory Activity 35
1.4   Conceptualizing Partisan Advisers' Policy Formulation Activity 39
2.1   Political Staff and Expenses for the Prime Minister's Office (1962, 1967, and 1970) 48
2.2   Federal Exempt Staff by Department (31 March 2001 to 31 March 2011) 53
2.3   Total Expenditures for Federal Ministers' Office Personnel (2006–13) 60
2.4   Political Staff in British Columbia (1996–2011) 63
2.5   BC Premier's Office Expenses and Staffing Levels (2001–11) 63
7.1   Core Executive Actor Resources 244
7.2   Structural and Operational Criteria of Partisan Advisers' Core Executive Resource Exchanges 247

Figures

1.1   Three Models of Political Advisers and the Machinery
           of Government   25
7.1   Dynamic Ideal-Type Mode   228
7.2   Federal Partisan Advisers and the Dynamic Policy
           Advisory System   231
7.3   BC Partisan Advisers' Dynamic Policy Advisory
           System   233
7.4   New Brunswick Partisan Advisers and the Dynamic
           Policy Advice System   235

Foreword

This volume opens a new dimension to the IPAC Series in Public Management and Governance. Until now, the work of scholars on political staff was only found in journals. Jonathan Craft's work inaugurates a fresh field of practice, and a captivating one at that.

The art of giving partisan policy advice is not new. Think of Niccolò Machiavelli, who worked for many years as a top functionary in early sixteenth-century Florence, but who distinguished himself in giving such counsel. Today's political advisers are sometimes held in the same light as the Renaissance philosopher – seen with suspicion as self-serving agents bent on undermining the work of elected politicians and interfering with the work of the non-partisan civil service. Too often is their good, and necessary, political advice ignored.

Political advisers, specifically the men and women who advise chief elected officers and ministers, have undeniably grown in importance. It was not so long ago that prime ministers could manage their affairs with a few dependable young men. They sought advice widely, among friends, business associates, journalists, and the party activists who organized local clubs to disseminate messages and to feed intelligence back to the provincial capital or to Ottawa.

Things changed slowly but surely. The jarring impact of the Second World War forced Mackenzie King to bring more rigour to the organizing of the prime minister's office. By the 1950s the premiers in most provinces also had political staff simply to manage the increasingly complex demands of accountability and coordination that were thrust upon them by an expanding bureaucracy and the rigours of province-building. Strangely, few thought of themselves as "policy" advisers. In his excellent memoir *A Public Purpose: An Experience of Liberal Opposition and Canadian Government* (1988), Tom Kent, the legendary adviser to Lester B. Pearson, recounted that he had reluctantly accepted the title of "Policy Secretary to the Prime Minister" on the grounds that "policy was for elected people." By the 1970s, numerous advisers were appointed to guide ministers in their management of ever more complex policy files. More and more people were appointed to handle media requests.

The system has never looked back. The demands of modern statesmanship simply command far more hours than a minister, or a first minister, can muster. They must rely on others to ensure that the key initiatives of their departments are evaluated through partisan lenses. Some may chafe at this interference; others will remind them that democratically elected officials in Canada have the final say and that bureaucracy must bend to the will of responsible government.

Staffers now routinely attract more public attention than most members of cabinet, and their views are held with more regard than people elected to legislatures. They have become fixtures in television political dramas and comedies; their stories are seemingly more interesting than those of elected officials.

Jonathan Craft brings a new sophistication to the analysis of the work of political advisers in Canada. He focuses on their policy impact, both at the federal level and at the provincial level, and brings to bear a new theoretical light by which their work can be evaluated. Far from raising spectres of the demise of democracy, he explores their role as an integral part of the new governance of modern states. He brings significance to the topic and compels the reader to the reality that political advisers are an entrenched part of modern governance. His book encourages the student of public administration and governance to think more broadly about what makes the work of political advisers important. The question now becomes one of management and regulation. Should policy advisers be subjected to certain constraints, a clear code of conduct, or even legislation? This ground-breaking work prepares the terrain for mature answers to these questions.

Patrice Dutil
Editor, IPAC Series in Public Management and Governance
Ryerson University
Canada Day, 2015

Acknowledgments

A project like this comes to fruition only with the generous access afforded by its participants. I want to thank the ministers, senior officials, and partisan advisers who gave their time to answer questions, offer candid reflections, and provide insights and context about one of the lesser-known facets of elite policy work in Canada. Some spoke on the record while others preferred to remain anonymous, but all contributed graciously. I have quoted from many participants at length in the following pages. This was a conscious decision to let their words speak for themselves and to allow readers to draw their own conclusions and get a sense for what life is like at the seams of governance.

This study was motivated in part from my own experiences working for the federal public service and later as legislative assistant to my hometown Ontario Liberal Member of Provincial Parliament. This is shared in part to disclose that I have worked as part of the political arm and the public service. More importantly, exposure to the policy process from public service and political perspectives, and critically their intersection, was fascinating and invaluable. These experiences, however, did not always seem to square well with textbook accounts of how policymaking is *supposed* to work. This book continues in the tradition of those who seek richer accounts of the *actual* work of policy.

I want to thank Richard Phidd who, during my time at the University of Guelph, helped me see that I was more interested in politics and public policy than computer science and human psychology. I would also like to acknowledge Herman Bakvis, Graham White, the late Peter Aucoin, Andrew Heard, and Donald Savoie for formal and informal comments along the way. Their work sparked my initial interest in public administration, Cabinets, and political-administrative relations – it also sets a high bar for all of those who follow. I owe the greatest of thanks to Mike Howlett for his support and mentorship, and for his contagious passion and thoughtfulness in the study of public policy.

From the halls of Sidney Smith to those of the School of Public Policy and Governance, I am privileged to work at the University of Toronto. Since joining the faculty I have benefited from world-class colleagues and terrific students. My thanks go to them for providing a warm welcome and encouragement to take deep dives into public policy, administration, and governance. I benefited tremendously from the editorship of Daniel Quinlan at the University of Toronto Press, the able copyediting of Ian MacKenzie, and the thoughtful and constructive feedback from the anonymous reviewers. I also gratefully acknowledge the support of the Social Sciences and Humanities Council of Canada. I would like to acknowledge a few international colleagues: Chris Eichbaum, Richard Shaw, Bernadette Connaughton, Marleen Brans, Anne Tiernan, John Halligan, and Maria Malley. As fellow scholars working on similar puzzles in the Westminster tradition, you have provided considerable advances from which to draw. My hope is that this work is a modest contribution to furthering our shared research interests.

This book is dedicated to my wife and to my parents. Any achievements that I may claim are due in large measure to your encouragement, sacrifices, and support. Any imperfections and shortcomings in the following pages rest, however, with the author alone.

Jonathan Craft
High Park, Toronto
November 15, 2015

BACKROOMS AND BEYOND

Partisan Advisers and the Politics of Policy
Work in Canada

Partisan Advisers, Policy Work, and the Political Arm of Government in Canada

Introduction

This book explores the operation of the political arm of government in Canada. More precisely, it examines the policy work of appointed ministerial political staffs in three jurisdictions. It delves into the "backrooms" of government to examine how political staffs engage in policymaking and the implications of that activity for contemporary executive governance. Typically, in Canada and elsewhere, political staffs receive attention when they are complicit in political or ethical scandals that come to light. The Canadian "sponsorship" scandal and Australian "Children Overboard Affair" are but two prominent examples (Benoit 2006; Tiernan 2007). Questions regarding the appropriate accountability regimes for political staffs have attracted the lion's share of popular and scholarly attention (King 2003; Eichbaum and Shaw 2010). These remain important lines of inquiry to be sure, but this book argues that political staffs also deserve attention as policy workers – that is, as actors whose day-to-day practices in the backrooms but also beyond them may be consequential to policymaking. Based on over sixty-five interviews with ministers, senior public servants, and political staffs in Ottawa, British Columbia, and New Brunswick, this book provides a rich depiction of partisan advisers' policy work, and why it matters for contemporary executive governance.

With privileged access to decision-makers and their resources, political staffs have become influential policy actors. This has been widely accepted in Canadian circles for some time, at least as far as premiers' and prime ministers' staffs are concerned (Bakvis 1997; Doern 1971; Lenoski 1977; Savoie 1999a; White 2001).[1] They also figure prominently in claims that the equilibrium among political and public service elites has shifted over the last forty years. Canadian and international scholars alike have argued the fundamental "bargain" underpinning the political–public service relationship in the Westminster tradition is broken or adapting (Hood, 2000; Lodge 2010; Savoie 2003). Others have gone further, contending that governance arrangements are, in fact, moving towards an altogether different model of "New Political Governance" (Aucoin 2012). These logics suggest the fundamental roles and activities of political and public service elites have been transformed with deleterious consequences for policymaking and governance. Political staffs are included in such claims as actors who have displaced the public service in the policy process and as sources of policy advice. Colourfully styled as the "junkyard dogs" of politics (Weller 2002), the barbarians at the gates (Eichbaum and Shaw 2008), and the "kids in short pants" (Ivision 2012), advisers wield great influence in the halls of government despite their inexperience and unelected status. Indeed, one scholar contends that ministerial political staffs are one of the most significant examples of institutional innovation in Westminster-style systems (Maley 2011). Yet, there is little systematic study of Canadian political staffs. Some excellent studies touch upon their functions and contributions to broader governance (Savoie 1999a; Benoit 2006), but Canadian research lags well behind that of its Westminster counterparts. For example, little is known about the *contemporary* type, nature, and scope of their policy work, their patterns of interaction with other policy actors inside and outside of government, or the implications of their participation in policymaking. The study of Canadian political staffs is also decidedly first minister–centric. The predominant focus on premiers' and prime ministers' offices has led to little study of ministers' office staffs (White 2005). More importantly, there is a paucity of comparative intra-Canadian scholarship that systematically attends to all political staffs located throughout political executives. What then exactly goes on in the backrooms of ministerial offices? What policy work do political staffs actually undertake?

A glimpse was provided in 2013 when an email sent from the Prime Minister's Office (PMO) to ministers' offices was leaked. The email requested that political staff prepare a transition binder in advance of an impending Cabinet shuffle, to help orient new ministers to their new departments and files. This practice is common in transition periods (Zussman 2013). Binders were to include "sword" and "shield" issues – those that would equip ministers with policy issues they could use to promote the government agenda and attack opponents, along with those useful to deflect criticisms and defend the government. Also to be included, an update on departmental specific policy "to-do" lists, called a mandate letter, along with a lay of the land of what new ministers should know, and advice on with whom they should interact or avoid. The full checklist included:

1. What to say at Question Period
2. What to expect soon, hot issues, legal actions, complaints
3. What to expect later, longer-term forecast
4. What to do, status of mandate items, off-mandate items
5. What to avoid: pet bureaucratic projects
6. Who to avoid: bureaucrats that can't take no (or yes) for an answer
7. What to attend: upcoming events, meetings and Federal/Provincial/Territorial meetings
8. Who to appoint: outstanding Governor in Council [appointments] and hot prospects
9. Who to engage or avoid: friend and enemy stakeholders
10. Private Members Bills – lines and Caucus packages (CBC News 2013)

It provides a sense of the breadth of what political staff do and who the players are who are involved in governing, but also alerts ministers to who their *friends* and *enemies* are in a policy and political sense. This last feature is telling in that it openly reveals the tensions that can exist at the political-administrative nexus. It is striking in that it details that ministers should guard against not only stakeholders – the paid and unpaid advocates and lobbyists from organizations and policy sectors *outside* of government – but also the public service. As this checklist makes plain, they can all be perceived enemies of the government with particular policy preferences or pet projects of their own. The email attracted significant attention and consternation from various circles and provides a rare snapshot into the functions of political staffs during times of ministerial transitions, but also their day-to-day policy work.

It is crucial at the outset to recognize that political staffs are not a homogeneous group. As their titles suggest– chiefs of staff, executive assistants, ministerial assistants, press secretaries, legislative assistants, constituency assistants, and policy advisers – all serve different functions (White 2001; Treasury Board 2011). This book focuses on only a single subset of appointed political staffs termed *partisan advisers*,[2] who serve in officially recognized policy capacities. This is an important distinction in that it narrows the scope of the study of political staffs who deal primarily with policy matters. Discerning observers of Ottawa and the provincial legislatures might wonder why political staffs' communications work is not examined, particularly given the prominence of blame avoidance, "spin," and heightened message control prevalent in modern governance (Hood 2010; Thomas 2010). The answer as chronicled here is that focused examination of partisan advisers provides important insights that improve our understanding of the political arm of government, and the politics of policy work in Canada.

Enduring Debate

The Canadian Public Service Employment Act is the latest in a line of federal legislative acts that allows elected officials to appoint staffs from outside the normal public service hiring channels.[3] The rationale for these appointments is spelled out clearly in the 2011 Privy Council Office (PCO) *Guide to Ministers and Ministers of State*. Political staffs are made available to ministers to provide them with "advisors and assistants who are not departmental public servants, who share their political commitment, and who can complement the professional, expert and non-partisan advice and support of the public service. Consequently, they contribute a particular expertise or point of view that the public service cannot provide" (Privy Council Office 2011, 45).

For introductory purposes it must be emphasized that while they are established, the normative utility and functions of partisan advisers remains hotly debated. Two opposing views on what political staffs *should* do were articulated as far back as the late 1960s, and the debate endures. The prescient exchange was limited to the federal order of government but is equally apt for the provinces as well. On the one hand, in one of the earliest scholarly assessments of Canadian "exempt" staffs, Professor Mallory concluded the trend of increasing political staff in Ottawa was an affront to the Westminster-style Cabinet-parliamentary system. Writing in the wake of a political scandal involving political staffs, he put it plainly: "It is clearly undesirable that a considerable number of persons not a part of the civil service should be interposed between a Minister and his department" (Mallory 1967, 32). He went on to surmise, "Not only do these functionaries wield great power because they control access to the Minister and can speak in his name, but they may wield this power with ludicrous ineptitude and in ways that are clearly tainted with political motives" (ibid.). This perspective stands in stark contrast to the above official rationale of the PCO, which contends political staffs share their ministers' "political commitment" and provide a form of "expertise" that the public service cannot. Should ministers' offices employ political staff? If so, should they engage in *political* forms of policy work or instead be relegated to basic administrative support or communications functions? Mallory clearly favoured the latter, with policy work to remain the exclusive purview of the professional non-partisan public service. He did, however, allow for political staffs to serve as buffers "between a busy Minister and his constituents and political followers of all sorts" (Mallory 1967, 34). However, this function was exclusively political, in that it was not extended to their interposing themselves between ministers and the public service.

A year later, Paul Tellier would provide an alternative perspective. Tellier, who would eventually serve for seven years in the public service's most senior role, clerk of the Privy Council, began his Ottawa career in the 1960s as an assistant to the Minister of Energy, Mines, and Resources. Tellier argued that ministerial political staff tended to engage in precisely the types of work Mallory outlined, but that they should be better used to provide advice to ministers. This work was not to be "political" per se, but rather the utility of a more robust ministerial office could be found in the new perspectives and greater contestation, or challenge function, that political staff could bring to bear. Tellier saw political staff as part of a new laudable trilateral political-administrative arrangement, when properly used. In her excellent study of federal political exempt staffs, Benoit (2006, 158) characterized the debate that endures as "a battle of two opposing philosophies framed on the one hand by Mallory, the champion of the emasculated Westminster model of the ministerial office, and Tellier on the other, whose approach would see Ministers bulwarked by a hand-picked cadre of young operatives ready and willing to ensure that the machinery of government marches to the tune of the democratically elected drummer." Not only is this debate germane to normative questions of what political staffs ought to do, but it also strikes at the heart of broader questions about the division of labour among political and administrative elites in policy work, and the fundamental tension between political control and public service neutral competence in Canada.

Political Control and Public Service "Neutral" and "Responsive" Competence

The debate may endure but there is consensus on why political staffs were introduced in Canada in the first place. Partly, it was a function of the increasingly complex nature of policymaking and the growing demands on Cabinet and ministers. This extends equally to the demands of their serving as ministers of the Crown and their functions as elected officials and partisans (Savoie 2003; Aucoin 1995a, 2010). A readily available example includes simply tending to basic executive correspondence. Until about the 1930s, Canadian prime ministers were essentially able to deal with their own correspondence. In contrast, millions of pieces of mail are now sifted, sorted, and responded to by the Prime Minister's Office. A comparison of the size and annual budgets of both federal and provincial governments makes clear that differences in contemporary government extend not only to scale, but also scope and complexity (Dunn 1995, 2010; Bernier, Brownsey, and Howlett 2005).

The advent of partisan advisers, however, extends beyond issues of capacity. It is also linked to a broader set of public management reforms aimed at strengthening political control and securing public service responsiveness (Aucoin 1990; Politt and Boukaert 2011; Savoie 1983; Di Francesco 2000). This is well captured by the above email leak confirming that ministers need to guard against self-interested public servants. This is not a new phenomenon nor one restricted to Canada. Indeed, across a number of Anglo-American systems in the late twentieth century, the public service had fallen out of favour. A shared concern emerged among politicians that the public service was at best unable and at worst unwilling to accept and follow the policy preferences of politicians (Rhodes, Wanna, and Weller 2010). It stood accused of being "bloated, expensive, unresponsive, a creation of routine deliberately resistant to changes, and largely incapable of dealing with new challenges" (Peters and Savoie 1994, 419). In short, the public service was perceived to have become unresponsive and for some, even obstructionist. Concerns about the degree of political control and public service responsiveness highlight a tension that flows from Canada's adaptation of central Westminster features and traditions – responsible government and a permanent or "career" non-partisan public service (Aucoin 1995a).

Simply put, the principle of responsible government by individual and collective ministerial responsibility ensures that all public officials – politicians and public servants alike – are held accountable to the democratic will of the people through Parliament. As Mallory put it, "The power of the official is derivative, that of the minister inherent in his office. The minister is constitutionally responsible and he therefore has the right to make the final decision, even if it is against the advice of his officials" (Mallory 1984, 137). The public service is therefore in principle subservient to the elected will of the people, as embodied through the actions of ministers, who are (almost always) elected members of Parliament. However, responsible government alone is not sufficient to constitute a system of governance. Responsible government requires more than just political input and decision-making, and a professional, non-partisan, public service is a hallmark of the Westminster family of ideas and traditions (Aucoin 1995a; Rhodes, Wanna, and Weller 2010).

As the aphorism goes, politicians propose and public servants dispose. For some time now in the scholarly literature there has been some debate as to whether the fundamental principles of a Westminster-style professional non-partisan public service, with its "expertise" and years of experience, is "neutrally" competent in governing and policymaking (Montpetit 2011). Neutral competence has been defined as "the ability of career officials to do the work of government expertly, and to do it according to explicit, objective standards rather than to personal or party or other obligations and loyalties" (Kaufman 1956, 1060). This neutrality suggests that the public service exercises a degree of independence in the disposition of its work. That is, the public service has a constitutionally distinct "personality" from the government of the day (Savoie 2006), with obligations and responsibilities over and above those duties and obligations owed to whomever forms the government. Some contend that with this distinct constitutional "personality," and its independent, non-partisan, and permanent nature, the public service has a custodial role as "guardians of the public interest" (Sossin 2006). The implications from a policymaking perspective are that the public service then plays an important counterbalance or contestation function in the policy process. It protects the long-term public interest of citizens from being unduly compromised by potentially uninformed decision-makers, or partisan short-termism (Dawson 1922; Sossin 2006). This is often captured by the notion in public policy literature that the public service must "speak truth to power" (Wildavsky 1979). As Westminster scholar John Wanna has put it, "There are grounds to accept an independent, neutral, career civil service as an important attribute of Westminster and an institutional counterbalance to the majoritarian concentration of power in the executive – especially on independent, professional policy development and frank-and-fearless advice" (Wanna 2005, 175). Others of course vehemently disagree with this normative reasoning of a public service "platonic guardianship" of the public interest (Rhodes and Wanna 2007) and point to the difficulties associated with operationalizing the principle in practice (West 2005; Aberbach and Rockman 1994).

In contrast, "responsive competence" consists of public servants having "an appreciation of the reality of politics in policy-making and governance (and the status of the electoral mandate in shaping the policy programme of the government of the day)" (Eichbaum and Shaw 2010, 9). From this perspective, public servants are not understood to be "neutral" or "detached," but rather motivated by organizational or self-interest (Moe 1989; Peters and Pierre 2004). Among the Anglo-American countries, neutral competence was perceived by some to have led to unduly influential public servants, with too much discretion and reduced commitment to the policy objectives of their democratically elected counterparts (Savoie 2003). The use of partisan advisers has emerged as a common tool by which elected governments have sought increased political and policymaking responsiveness in governance (Dalhström, Peters, and Pierre 2011; OECD 2011; Savoie 1983). Comparatively, Canada is noteworthy in that its experimentation with an expanded policy function for partisan advisers predates that of other Westminster systems. Subsequent to Canada, Australia, New Zealand, and the United Kingdom all moved in some measure towards an expanded systematic use of partisan advisers to secure policymaking responsiveness (Aucoin 1990, 1995b; Kemp 1986).

There is, however, an acknowledged risk in seeking to ensure responsiveness. When deployed correctly, partisan advisers may beneficially add policy capacity to the political arm of government vis-à-vis the permanent public service (Aucoin and Savoie 2009; Peters 2001; Tiernan 2011; Savoie 1983). However, if used inappropriately, they may politicize the public service by impeding its ability to provide "free and frank" non-partisan policy advice, or colour and contaminate the content of that advice (Aucoin and Savoie 2009; Eichbaum and Shaw 2007a, 2007b). Following Eichbaum and Shaw (2010), the use of political staffs may thus be viewed as an institutional change designed to "effect movement" along the continuum from neutral to responsive competence. Finding and holding the equilibrium on that spectrum is an abiding concern for scholars and practitioners alike.

Partisan Advisers and Currents of Change in Contemporary Canadian Governance

Two significant trends in contemporary Canadian governance are linked to attempts to strengthen political control and secure responsiveness in policymaking. Both also involve partisan advisers and have emerged to varying degrees across the Westminster family of systems. The first is that dramatic changes have taken place in the types and nature of public sector policy advice. In particular, the perceived public service policy advisory monopoly has been eroded, and the practices of policy advice have themselves been transformed. The second is that power has accreted towards the "centre," particularly the political-administrative apparatus around the first minister.

The public service in Westminster systems had traditionally been the primary adviser to governments (Savoie 2015; Zussman 2015; Rhodes and Weller 2003). Breaking this perceived monopoly was a key means by which the political arm of government sought to reassert control and the primacy of politics in policymaking. Partisan advisers were a conscious, institutional adaptation designed to provide the political arm with its own politically attuned supply of policy advice. As Aucoin puts it, in seeking to avoid being captured by their public services' policy preferences, political executives "had to end the bureaucracy's monopoly position in giving advice to ministers by bringing in political staff as alternative or competing sources of advice" (Aucoin 2008a, 25). In short, partisan advisers were to be used as "counterstaffs" for the political arm of government to challenge policy advice from *various* sources (Peters 2001, 246). Their ability to contest policy advice is, however, unique in two respects. They are able, if not expected, to engage in partisan-political contestation that non-partisan public service counterparts cannot. In addition, as political appointees in ministers' offices, advisers have unique access to decision-makers and the policy process that others simply do not. In his review of advisers in Organization for Economic Cooperation and Development (OECD) countries, Zussman captures these trends succinctly: "They provide a challenge function and an element of contestability within the policy development cycle. Many other actors play this role as well, but only political advisers have the advantage of operating at the very centres of power. The norm is now for a minister to welcome and demand multiple channels of policy advice and political advisers are one manifestation of this trend" (2009a, 35).

It is important to recognize that the contestation functions and expanded use of partisan advisers is only part of the story. A general proliferation of other advisory sources has contributed to weakening any public service monopoly on policy advice (Rhodes and Weller 2001; Campbell and Wilson 1995). Studies of Westminster-style systems now characterize the modern executive advisory landscape as a complex web of policy advisory sources, many of which exist outside of government. Think tanks, consultants and lobbyists, political parties, international organizations, academia, and a host of others are ready suppliers of policy advice (Dobuzinskis, Howlett, and Laycock 2007; Rhodes, Wanna, and Weller 2010). This is not to suggest that these developments have rendered the public service obsolete, but rather that a greater plurality of suppliers exist from which the executive may draw.

Given this plurality of suppliers, it is useful to conceive of partisan advisers as one component in an overall *policy advisory system* – that is, an interlocking set of actors with a unique configuration in each sector and jurisdiction, who provide information, knowledge, and recommendations for action to policymakers (Halligan 1995). Such systems are now acknowledged to be key parts of the working behaviour of governments as they go about their policy formulation and governance (Seymour-Ure 1987; Weaver and Stares 2001; Scott and Baehler 2010). Table I.1 depicts the conventional advisory system as one that includes some combination of a public service, political, and exogenous supply of policy advice. These may be configured differently by jurisdiction and policy sectors, and may change over time (Craft and Howlett 2013; Prince 1983; Tiernan 2006a). The Canadian advisory system follows this conventional format, including a compartmentalized "political" and public service stream of policy advice along with external suppliers. While their particular configurations may vary, federal and provincial Cabinets, as a general rule of thumb, "receive both partisan – Prime Minister's Office (PMO) type – and policy/technocratic – Privy Council Office (PCO) type" input (Dunn 2010, 92).

The advisory system concept is useful in that it maps where advice is generated versus where it is interpreted for consumption by policymakers, and arranges and categorizes suppliers. As originally depicted, advisory systems relied on a control-autonomy approach. Influence within such systems was understood as a product of the location of the supply and its proximity to government, as well as the degree of control governments could expect to exert over them, relatively speaking. The

Table I.1. Policy Advisory Systems

Location	Government control	
	High	Low
Public service	Senior departmental policy advisers Central agency advisers / strategic policy unit	Statutory appointments in public service
Internal to government	Political advisory systems Temporary advisory policy units (ministers' offices, first ministers' offices) Parliaments (e.g., a House of Commons)	Permanent advisory policy units Statutory authorities Legislatures (e.g., U.S. Congress)
External	Private sector / NGOs on contract Community organizations subject to government Federal international organizations	Trade unions, interest groups, etc. Community groups Confederal international communities/ organizations

Source: Adapted from Halligan (1995)

second control dimension was not specified, but barring the extremes set out above, and from a traditional textbook perspective, the elected government of the day was expected to be able to "control" public service supplies. Advisory systems are also quite useful in that they allow some analysis and categorization of shifts in components over time. Its original articulation was offered as a means to review Anglo-American systems and trace changes in such systems, the conclusion being that across the jurisdictions the overall trend was that "the internal government category has expanded at the expense of the internal public service. But, in turn, the rise of external forms has been at the expense of internal mechanisms (Halligan 1995, 159).

The advisory system concept is less useful in explaining the relationship of the components to each other. In a thoughtful and comprehensive reflection on the state of policy advice in Canada, Prince (2007) echoes similar temporal shifts but goes further. His retrospective analysis contends that in Canada, it is not only the supply and demand dynamics that have evolved but also the basic practices of policy advice. Both have undergone dramatic changes in concert with broader societal developments and evolving governance arrangements, the key argument being that Canada has shifted from a policy advisory mode characterized as "speaking truth to power" (Wildavsky 1979) to one consisting of "sharing truths with many actors of influence" (Prince 2007). The former has direct linkages to notions of neutral competence, reviewed above, which has been a mainstay of Canadian policy analysis for scholars and practitioners (Doern and Phidd 1992; Good 2003; Savoie 1999a). Fundamentally, it characterizes policy advice in bilateral terms, with expert informed non-partisan policy advice flowing from public servants to democratically elected decision-makers. Elected political actors are seen to be the bearers of legitimate power flowing from democratic elections, while a "truth," however contentiously defined, is provided by a professional public service with its years of experience, expertise, and technocratic mastery of government process. Table I.2 classifies these and other broad trends, contrasting important

Table I.2. Two Idealized Models of Policy Advising in Canadian Government

Elements	Speaking truth to power of ministers	Sharing truths with multiple actors of influence
Focus of policymaking	Departmental hierarchy and vertical portfolios	Interdepartmental and horizontal management of issues with external networks and policy communities
Background of senior career officials	Knowledgeable executives with policy-sector expertise and history	Generalist managers with expertise in decision processes and systems
Locus of policy processes	Relatively self-contained within government, supplemented with advisory councils and royal commissions	Open to outside groups, research institutes, think tanks, consultants, pollsters, and virtual centres
Minister / deputy minister relations	Strong partnership in preparing proposals with ministers, trusting and taking policy advice largely from officials	Shared partnership with ministers drawing ideas from officials, aides, consultants, lobbyists, think tanks, media
Nature of policy advice	Candid and confident advice to ministers given in a neutral and detached manner. Neutral competence	Relatively more guarded advice given to ministers by officials in a more compliant or preordained fashion. Responsive competence

Elements	Speaking truth to power of ministers	Sharing truths with multiple actors of influence
Public profile of officials	Generally anonymous	More visible to groups, parliamentarians, and media
Roles of officials in policy processes	Confidential advisers inside government and neutral observers outside government Offering guidance to government decision-makers	Active participants in policy discussions inside and outside government Managing policy networks and perhaps building capacity of client groups

Source: Adapted from Prince (2007, 179)

differences in the types and methods by which policy advice is used and shifts in the policy process.

The contemporary "sharing truths with multiple actors of influence" model operates within a different context and on different terms. It recognizes that where and how governments govern has little resemblance to the traditional model of public administration within which the "speaking truth to power" mode prevailed. Globalization, increased complexity and interconnectedness of policy issues, the media, advanced communications technologies, and a seemingly endless number of non-state actors now complicate the milieu in which government governs (Zussman 2015; Conteh and Roberge 2013; Savoie 2015). Canada is not alone in having to grapple with these currents of change, with noted scholars of public administration and management arguing that governing has evolved through three dominant modes: the traditional public administration and management, New Public Management, and New Public/Political Governance (Aucoin 2012; Gow 2004; Osborne 2006). The various modes and their associated characteristics fill volumes and will not be reviewed at length here. Suffice it to say that in the generally accepted narrative there is a slow drift from traditional public administration characterized by Weberian notions of hierarchy and command and control, to modes of "governance,"[4] the latter consisting of a greater interactivity and exchange in policymaking involving various combinations of interactions, processes, and values that extend beyond government to also involve the participation of civil society, the private and non-profit sectors, and citizens. In such a context, policy advisory activity is more accurately understood in dialectical terms, as "sharing," "weaving," or "making sense together" (Hoppe 1999; Parsons 2004). Prince notes, from a Canadian policy advisory perspective, this raises implications for neutral competence, supply and demand dynamics, and indeed the way by which policy is made. Partisan advisers are not examined in detail in his retrospective, but the general picture he paints is one of a policy process and advisory system that is considerably more interactive, contested, and porous.

A second key trend also involving partisan advisers is the purported concentration of power to the "centre" of government or what has been termed "court government" (Savoie 1999a, 2008). The "centre" consists of courtiers including "key advisors in [the prime minister's] office, two or three senior cabinet ministers (notably the minister of finance), carefully selected lobbyists, pollsters and other friends in court, and a handful of senior public servants" (Savoie 1999b, 635). The key contention is that over the course of the twentieth century there has been a steady erosion of the tenets of responsible government due to the displacement of the Canadian Parliament by the Cabinet, followed by the displacement of the Cabinet and governance by prime ministers and their courtiers. Concerns of overly powerful first ministers in Canada are by no means new, with similar worries having been articulated in the past and in other Westminster Cabinet-parliamentary systems (Smith 1970; Rhodes, Wanna, and Weller 2010). Canada is, however, suggested to be even more susceptible to this development than most, given the particularly limited constraints facing the executive and prime minister (Aucoin 2010; Bakvis and Wolinetz 2005; O'Malley 2007). Not only does court government raise sweeping implications for the traditional Canadian public administration and responsible government, but Savoie contends it also produces a bifurcated policymaking reality – that is, one where a first typical or "housekeeping" track operates in a "textbook" fashion, with the machinery of government, including public service and political components, operating through the standard channels and processes. The second atypical or "lightning bolt" track prevails for the key policy priorities of the court and is characterized by less-to-no formality, expeditiousness, and far fewer policy actors and therefore is not subject to the typical accountability standards, practices, and safeguards (Savoie 1999a). For their part, partisan advisers may be able to engage in both tracks. The logic of powerful first ministers running the show also resonates provincially in Canada, with provinces long characterized as "premiers' government" (Dunn 1995; White 2001; Young and Morley 1983). Careful analysis has, however, found a more uneven pattern of centralized first-minister-centric governance among the provinces (Bernier, Brownsey, and Howlett 2005; Lewis 2013). Critics of the centralization thesis more generally have pointed to historical examples of powerful first ministers predating Savoie's courtier period, and institutional constraints such as federalism, the Charter of Rights and Freedoms, and the sheer improbability of single-handed governance, in the face of overwhelming complexity (White 2005; Bakvis 2000).

Canadian public administration scholar Peter Aucoin (2001) argued that the quest for political control and policy responsiveness extends beyond courtier style governance, reaching an apogee in the form of the New Political Governance (NPG). In addition to a centralization of power, NPG consists of an enhanced number, role, and influence of political staff; increased personal attention by the prime minister to the appointment of senior public servants; increased pressure on the public service to provide a pro-government spin on government communications; increased expectation that public servants demonstrate enthusiasm for the government's agenda; and finally the integration or emergence of a permanent campaign style of governing.[5] Testing either the enduring nature of court government or the emergence of New Political Governance is beyond the scope of this study. Rather, this book's aim is to offer a better understanding of how partisan advisers contribute to policy work itself. It is crucial, however, to recognize that NPG represents the first analytical attempt to explicitly align changes in modes of governance to the *systematic* functions and influence of partisan advisers. Aucoin contends, much like Savoie, that the current state is one where "the most trusted political staff are as influential, if not more influential, with the prime minister in the determination of government policy as senior ministers or senior public servants" (Aucoin 2008b, 15). NPG goes further than the court government thesis in that one of its central contentions is that partisan advisers *throughout* the executive, not just in first ministers' offices, are reshaping policy-making and executive governance (Craft 2015b). Together, shifts in the types and nature of policy advisory practices along with broader shifts in modes of executive governance suggest growing policy influence for partisan advisers. Importantly, these trends also highlight that partisan advisers are not simply a source of policy advice but are policy workers as well (Howlett and Wellstead 2011; Craft 2015a). That is, they may engage in policy activity that includes, and extends beyond, the provision of policy advice to include a plethora of advisory and non-advisory forms of policy work.

A Core Executives Approach

Students of Canadian politics and public administration have focused attention on particular sets of actors or institutions such as Cabinets, prime ministers, or public service mandarins (Aucoin 1991; Dunn 1995; Granatstein 1982; Punnett 1977). Alternatively, some approaches have compared the perceived health of Canada's adaptation of the Westminster system to that of its British, Australian, or New Zealand counterparts (Campbell and Wilson 1995; Peters, Rhodes, and Wright 2000; Peters and Savoie 2000a; Rhodes, Wanna, and Weller 2010; Savoie 2008). There are also excellent accounts of the elite Canadian political-public service relations and analysis of the workability of the traditional model of public administration (Savoie 2003, 2015). This book adopts a *core executive* approach. The approach recognizes that the institutions of the executive are not limited to the prime minister and Cabinet alone, but also include ministers and their departments. Core executives consist of "all those organizations and procedures which coordinate central government policies, and act as final arbiters between different parts of the government machine" (Dunleavy and Rhodes 1990, 4). The concept was advanced to move away from understanding executive power as fixed and positional (e.g., Cabinet versus first ministers) towards a functional, contingent, and a relational understanding (Bevir and Rhodes 2006; Dunleavy and Rhodes 1990). Core executives are characterized by resource dependence and exchange. The primary research questions are "who does what?" and "who has what resources?" (Rhodes 2007, 1247). Table I.3 provides an illustration of the types of resources that core executive actors might possess and exchange.

Table I.3. Resources of Prime Ministers, Ministers, and Officials

Prime Minister	Ministers	Officials
Patronage	Political support	Permanence
Authority	Authority	Knowledge
Political support / party	Department	Time
Political support / electorate	Knowledge	Governance network
Prime Minister's Office	Policy networks	Control over information
Bilateral policymaking	Policy success	Keepers of the constitution

Source: Adapted from Smith (1999, 32)

Some have sought to revise the purely contingent and relational nature of core executives espoused by Rhodes and colleagues, contending instead that those resources and power dependencies are asymmetrical – subject to differences in the persons occupying particular offices and structural or institutional conditioning (Heffernan 2003; Marsh et al. 2003). The thinking is that some core executive actors benefit from personal or institutionally based resources that others do not. For example, one may have particular reputational resources or substantive expertise while others possess other or no resources at all, given that "not all Cabinet ministers are created equal" (Savoie 2008, 233). Institutionally, the asymmetrical approach suggests that location within the core executive may also produce differences in resource allocation or exchange dynamics. For example, actors in a central agency may require or wield types of resources that are different from those working within a line department.

The core executive approach is well suited to an analysis of partisan advisers, and some previous Canadian studies have adopted it and included limited reference to political staffs (Bakvis 1997; White 2005). The approach improves depictions and accounts of partisan advisers' contributions to policy work by focusing on their policy-based resource exchanges, power dependencies, or how partisan advisers *themselves* may be resources to be used by other core executive members. Resources include, for example, money, legislative authority, or expertise (Rhodes 1997, 203). As it was originally stated and subsequently revised,[6] partisan advisers outside of first ministers' offices are not explicitly included as core executive members. The evidence presented in this study of Canadian partisan advisers, along with a growing corpus of Westminster findings (Eichbaum and Shaw 2010; Rhodes, Wanna, and Weller 2010; Maley 2011; Rhodes and Tiernan 2014), suggests the time has come to do so – that their inclusion should be *systematic* and extend beyond an exclusive focus on first ministers offices (Craft 2015b).

Main Arguments

Four main arguments are introduced here and developed throughout the book. The first and overall argument is that partisan advisers should no longer be *assumed* to be mere "political operatives." Rather, their policy practices suggest that in some cases they are policy workers – actors who contribute to policymaking and its outcomes (Colbatch 2006;

Colebatch, Hoppe, and Noordegraaf 2010a, 2010b). Partisan advisers can be conceived of as policy workers with partisan links – or, as Campbell styled them, *amphibians* – who "exhibit the operational traits of policy professionals – expertise and knowledge of how to negotiate through the bureaucratic maze" but maintain explicit partisan ties (Campbell and Peters 1988; Campbell 1988). A subsidiary contention is that their policy practices may extend beyond advisory activities typically associated with determinations of political feasibility to include a broader array of policy work. The study uses four concepts – *buffering*, *bridging*, *moving*, and *shaping* – to more clearly set out and understand advisers' policy work. Together they facilitate examination of the provision (buffering) and circulation (bridging) of policy advice, and their procedural (moving) and substantive (shaping) contributions to *formal* policymaking. Chapter 1 develops this analytical framework in detail.

A third and related argument is that policy work should not be conceived exclusively as non-partisan or the sole ambit of non-partisan public service officials. The non-partisan professional policy work of public services is, of course, essential to policymaking and governance. Elected politicians will continue to depend on the public service's expertise, policy knowledge, and experience to govern effectively. Many first- rate texts detail the numerous theoretical approaches and methods, and provide rich empirics on the policy process. Most of them often emphasize the central function of the public service in the policy process (Miljan 2008; Hill 2012). Typically, such tomes broadly acknowledge the constraining and enabling functions of "politics" and the role of elected officials in the policy process (Howlett and Cashore 2014). It is widely recognized that policy, "rational" or otherwise, is created and unfolds within a political context. Yet, much less attention has been paid to how the political arm of government participates in policy work, despite the fact that the very notion of policy work was advanced to recognize the broad range of policy actors and practices that are consequential to policymaking (Colebatch 2006; Colebatch, Hoppe, and Noordegraaf 2010, 2010b). The analytical framework and empirical findings presented in ensuing chapters not only detail precisely the types of policy work reported in three Canadian cases, but also those that advisers could more generally undertake. This specifies advisory system and core executive operation, providing a fuller and more contemporary understanding of the political arm of government's policy work.

It is essential to be clear that this book is certainly not a wholesale defence of partisanship in executive governance, but rather acknowledges that policy work involves partisan elements. Canadian and Westminster-style systems around the world provide ample examples of "hyper" or reckless partisanship having done disservice to responsible government and policymaking (Bakvis and Jarvis 2012; Aucoin 2012; Peters and Pierre 2004). New Political Governance and concerns about rabid partisanship and concomitant public service politicization are important and must be taken seriously. However, partisanship remains an essential component of a healthy Canadian system of responsible government rooted in party government (Aucoin, Jarvis, and Turnbull 2011). At their worst, partisan advisers are neophytes – the "kids in short pants" who lack the maturity and requisite experience, knowledge, or understanding of their function within core executives (Ivision 2012). At their best, they may contribute to improved policymaking and core executive governance, even protecting the essential non-partisan nature of the professional public service (Aucoin 1995b; Axworthy 1988; Brodie 2012). Part of what makes partisan advisers unique as policy workers is their potential to undertake "boundary-spanning" policy work. Their policy work can be expected to occur in concert with other partisans, non-partisan public servants, ministers and caucus members, and a host of non-governmental actors (Tushman and Scanlan 1981; Williams 2002; OECD 2011; Eichbaum and Shaw 2010). In addition to widely recognized "political" functions, their interactions with non-partisan policy actors necessitate that they engage in non-partisan forms of policy work that are "technical," "operational," "programmatic," or "administrative," such as facilitation of the circulation of public service or external stakeholder policy advice within advisory systems, or substantive content-based contributions to the development or specification of formal public service policy proposals. Studies from a range of Westminster systems have provided evidence of multiple "role types" that reflect the range of policy activities undertaken by partisan advisers (Connaughton 2010a; Maley 2000; LSE GV314 Group 2012). How then do Canadian partisan advisers stack up?

Astute readers will have discerned that several of the concepts and themes introduced above are linked to location. Notions of proximity and insider-outsider logic animate advisory systems; courtier-style governance attributes greater policy influence to the "centre," and core executives originally eschewed positional interpretations of power in favour of functional ones. The fourth and final argument advanced in this book is that institutional location can mask how policy-based influence is gained and exercised within core executives. Part of this argument was set out above in that ministers' offices are argued to be important but often overlooked components of core executives. They too may be consequential to resource exchanges with the constellation of actors inside *and* outside of core executives. Location must, however, be qualified. Clear differences were apparent across the cases in this study regarding the policy instruments partisan advisers, at various locations, could wield. Further, advisers' patterns of interaction with other policy actors, how they were configured within core executives, and the type of advisory and non-advisory policy work they undertook also varied. These differences are explored in detail in this book. The main point to be emphasized here is that these factors are crucial to understanding how partisan advisers gain and exert policy-based influence but are apparent only when analysis shifts from ideal-type classification schemes, and spatial attributions of influence, to analysis of advisers' actual policy work.

The overall purpose of *Backrooms and Beyond*, particularly given the currents of change noted above, is to offer improved conceptual and empirical accounts of policy work through analysis of Canadian partisan advisers. The intention here is not to overstate advisers' policy functions or influence, but rather to recognize that in many cases they have become established systematic features of the core executive. This book provides a nuanced comparative examination of advisers' policy work and its intersection with that of other policy workers, at various locations within the core executive.

Organization of the Study

The book proceeds through seven chapters and is broadly divided into two sections that focus on partisan advisers' policy advisory activity and non-advisory policy work. These are in turn examined in relation to first ministers and ministers' office partisan advisers respectively. This structure was adopted to facilitate comparisons of partisan advisers based on their location within the core executive and to draw attention to the diversity of potential types of policy work partisan advisers can engage in.

The first part of the book develops the analytical framework and provides context. Chapter 1 operationalizes the key concepts and theories, and provides basic descriptive details on the size of Cabinet, public service, partisan advisers, and the prevailing governance arrangements in each case. Chapter 2 provides a historical examination of how partisan advisers evolved, arguing that in general all three cases demonstrate a pattern of institutionalization, expansion, and specialization of political staff. Key historical texts and documents are combined with new data to detail the pattern in each case.

The second part of the book shifts to examine advisers' contemporary policy work. Chapter 3 examines first ministers' offices' partisan advisers as policy advisory system participants. It examines their contribution as direct content-based suppliers of policy advice (buffers), and functions in the circulation of *other* sources of policy advice (bridging) within advisory systems. Important distinctions emerge with respect to PMO and Premier's Office partisan advisers' advisory activity, with whom it occurs, how, and with what impact for core executive operation. Chapter 4 continues to focus on first ministers' partisan advisers, but examines the types and nature of their non-advisory policy work. It examines them as movers and shapers, to assess their functions as contributors to the process-based and substantive aspects of policy development respectively. Chapters 5 and 6 then focus exclusively on ministers' office partisan advisers as policy workers. Chapter 5 examines their functions as buffers and bridges, comparing their policy advisory system participation to one and another, as well as to that of their first ministerial counterparts. Chapter 6 then uses the notions of moving and shaping to focus on ministers' office non-advisory work. Here too important differences in practice emerge among the cases, but also with the policy work of first ministers' offices as well.

The concluding chapter distils the findings with a focus on the implications they raise for the configuration and operation of core executives, advisory systems, and policy work itself. The findings detailed in this study offer opportunities to sharpen and reappraise important questions about the intersection of partisan politics and public service, from a policy perspective, and better detail how partisan advisers gain and exert policy influence within backrooms, and beyond them.

Chapter 1

A "No Surprises" Environment

Introduction

Interviews with politicians, their advisers, and senior public servants revealed an emphasis on the importance of fostering a "no surprises" environment. Nothing could be worse than a surprise decision, not having consequential political information, or being caught off-guard by the work of one's minister, department, or government. This is not to say that unexpected events or differences of opinion would not still be a fact of life. Simply, optimal policymaking was the product of an environment with as few surprises as possible. This type of environment requires considerable resource exchanges. In fact, many respondents commented on the volume and types of information circulating within government along with the challenges of managing it and putting it to use effectively. It was not only about information but also the interdependence on others for their knowledge, expertise, and ability to secure desired policy and governance outcomes. What did the minister think about a certain policy proposal? What was the deputy's advice about how to proceed with a certain policy? Was the Cabinet committee on board with suggested policy options, or did they have concerns? What was the caucus reaction and feedback? Had the proposal been reviewed by central agency officials and other departments that would be affected? What was the stakeholder input? Was there money to do it? As a "third element" in the traditionally bilateral executive relationship (Wicks 2003), partisan advisers are pertinent to inquiries of these sorts and policy-based resource exchanges.

This chapter does two things. It develops a framework to understand partisan advisers' policy work using the four concepts of *buffering*, *bridging, moving,* and *shaping*. The framework is then used to elaborate two subsidiary frameworks to examine partisan advisers' policy advisory and policy formulation activities respectively. In addition, background information is provided on the three cases. This includes details on the size and types of machinery of governance and an overview of who was interviewed for the study. This context is helpful, given that a principal aim of this book is to compare partisan advisers, at work, at different institutional locations within the core executive, and in different jurisdictions. The federal, British Columbia, and New Brunswick cases differ in some important respects that must be laid bare, given their pertinence to the evolution and contemporary policy functions of partisan advisers.

Buffers and Bridges, Movers and Shapers: A Framework for the Study of Partisan Advisers' Policy Work

Zussman's (2009) review of "political advisers" and the machinery of government in Organization for Economic Cooperation and Development (OECD) countries is an excellent point of departure. It usefully situates partisan advisers within the overarching political-administrative relationship and implicitly presents three versions of how they engage in policy-based resource exchanges. As illustrated in figure 1.1, advisers can be conceived of in three ideal types: collaborative, gatekeeper, and triangulated.[7] Keep these three models in mind, as they provide a baseline against which the descriptive and analytical assessments in the ensuing chapters can be understood and compared.

Figure 1.1. Three Models of Political Advisers and the Machinery of Government

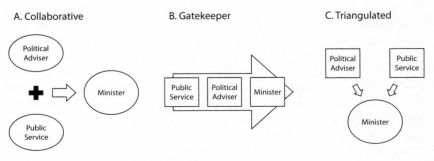

Source: Adapted from Zussman (2009)

First, the collaborative model hinges on a cooperative relationship between professional public servants and politically appointed partisan advisers, with advice jointly tendered to the minister. In this configuration, political advisers and public servants consciously and collaboratively combine their forms of expertise, with collaboration occurring frequently in advisory, political strategy, and managerial contexts (Zussman 2009, 14). This ideal type involves partisan advisers playing strong roles in policy development and advice, including representing ministers at various stages of policy processes, speaking in the name of the minister, and even holding the right to sign official documents on the minister's behalf. However, in most cases, this is done through informal influence, with political advisers having no official authority over their public service counterparts (Zussman 2009). From the core executive perspective, this ideal type requires considerable resource exchanges that necessitate content- and process-based coordination for policy development (Craft 2015b; Shaw and Eichbaum 2014; Weller, Bakvis, and Rhodes 1997).

Second, the gatekeeper ideal type consists of partisan advisers interposing themselves between the two sets of elites, as represented in figure 1.1.B. As an institutional arrangement, it is suggested to frequently manifest itself through "occasional bursts" rather than in any permanent fashion (Zussman 2009, 15). The gatekeeper model, with advisers potentially blocking officials from accessing ministers, raises questions about public service neutral competence and independence, essential to a healthy Westminster system (Eichbaum and Shaw 2007b). It is also germane for thinking about policy-based resource exchanges, in that in this model partisan advisers can preclude and limit such exchanges.

Third, the triangulated model represented by figure 1.1.C, under which Canada is said to generally operate, involves public servants and partisan advisers acting as independent sources of advice flowing to the minister. Zussman (2009, 14–15) explains that this approach is rooted in a belief that ministers benefit from "neutral" public service advice, as well as political advice in the discharge of their duties. In keeping with the advisory system logic, these two streams of advice are presented as compartmentalized and separate, combining only when mutually beneficial but typically confined to their respective spheres of expertise. Most often, this suggests two discreet policy-based resource exchanges in parallel within core executives. A fourth "hybrids and outliers" category also exists for instances and configurations that do not fit the three main ideal types.

This typology draws attention to distinctions in how partisan advisers are configured vis-à-vis other elites, and sets out corresponding implications for their policy work. Two key issues are, however, apparent in that the emphasis in these ideal types rests almost exclusively upon their advisory activity. Second, in a similar fashion to both courtier and NPG modes of governance, little if anything is said of interactions with policy actors outside of government, despite considerable evidence of partisan advisers engaging in such policy-based interactions and characterization of contemporary policymaking as porous, interactive, networked, and polycentric (Bingham, Nabatchi, and O'Leary 2005; OECD 2007, 2011).

Using the four concepts of *buffering, bridging, moving,* and *shaping,* table 1.1 introduces the conceptual framework that anchors this study. An initial step towards an improved analytical approach can be taken by recognizing that partisan advisers' policy work can consist of substantive and procedural practices, including advisory and non-advisory forms of policy work (Craft 2015a). This basic distinction figures prominently, implicitly and explicitly, in most approaches to the study of partisan advisers (Connaughton 2010a, 2010b; Eichbaum and Shaw 2010; Maley 2000, 2011). Eichbaum and Shaw (2008) use it to great effect in their analysis of political appointees and the potential for public service politicization in New Zealand. They posit that procedural politicization occurs when partisan advisers intervene in the minister–public service relationship or when partisan advisers' activity is "intended to or has the effect of constraining the capacity of public servants to furnish ministers with advice in a free, frank, and fearless manner" (343).

Table 1.1. Conceptualizing Partisan Advisers' Policy Work

	Type of policy activity	
Nature of policy interactions	Substantive "Content-oriented"	Procedural "Process-oriented"
"Advisory" One of many other sources of policy advice	*Buffers* Content-based provision of policy advice	*Bridges* Integration/preclusion of policy advice from disparate sources
"Non-advisory" policy work Actor with special access to decision makers and policymaking	*Shapers* Content-based Non-advisory policy work	*Movers* Process-based Non-advisory policy work

Substantive politicization is suggested to occur when the actual substance of public service advice is "coloured" with "partisan considerations" (343–4).

This distinction is argued to be useful beyond examinations of politicization to broader analysis here of the advisory and non-advisory policy work of partisan advisers. These are not mere analytical constructs, as there is significant evidence of partisan advisers engaging in procedural activities such as coordinating, steering, delivering, monitoring, and gatekeeping (Maley 2000; OECD 2011; Eichbaum and Shaw 2010; Rhodes and Tiernan 2014). Similarly, ample substantive policy activities have also been documented, including advisers' provision of policy advice and the specification, calibration, and contestation of policy in development (Anderson 2006; Benoit 2006; Connaughton 2010a, 2010b; O'Connor 1991; Maley 2000, 2011; Walter 1986). Buffering and bridging are used to account for advisers' potential "pure" policy advisory functions – that is, as one of many participants in advisory systems who supply and exchange policy advice on policy issues at various conjunctures in policymaking. In contrast, moving and shaping facilitates depictions and analysis of partisan advisers' unique access and ability to participate in content- and process-based non-advisory policy work, as actors with special access to decision-makers and policymaking (Gains and Stoker 2011; Walter 2006; LSE Group GV314 2012).

Policy work is a term that captures both the applied practice of policy – what it is that policy professionals actually do – as well as a theoretical lens or the field of research for its study. The term was advanced to capture the variety of tasks and activities that policy actors engage in the work of policy. In part this was a reaction to disconnections between expository accounts and empirical findings of those who actually engaged in the work of policy. Understanding policy work involves more than simply policy analysis in structured authoritative decision-making contexts but rather the construction and maintenance of relations among stakeholders, policy diplomacy, and the creation and use of "policy knowledge" (Tenbensel 2006; Colbatch 2006). A comprehensive study of partisan advisers' non-advisory policy work is beyond the scope of this book.

Applying a policy cycle or "stagist" approach helps define and parse salient conjunctures at which partisan advisers may be particularly influential. A policy cycle is a heuristic devise that disaggregates and presents policymaking as a process. This typically includes discreet and sequential stages linked to applied problem solving (Howlett,

Perl, and Ramesh 2009). It conceives of policymaking as an essentially rational and linear process involving a combination of stages, including issue identification, suggestions and deliberations on policy options (formulation), decision-making, implementation of the selected course of action, and monitoring or evaluation of outcomes (Bardach 2009; Laswell 1971). The approach is an acknowledged simplification of the complexity of policymaking in practice. It has certainly been subject to some trenchant critiques, including its inability to model the role of power in shaping the policy process, path dependence or oversimplifications, and overlaps among supposedly discreet "stages" within the cycle (Sabatier 2007; Jann and Wegrich 2007). Nevertheless, it persists as a useful heuristic for accounts of policymaking, given its ability to provide much-needed conceptual and organizational clarity, and its utility in examining individual and combined stages or entire "cycles" of policymaking (Althaus, Bridgman, and Davis 2013; Hill 2012).

Each stage in the policymaking cycle involves a range of actors, both inside and outside of government. The formulation stage is the only stage that is examined in this book. It was selected in part to narrow the scope of the study, but also because it is particularly germane to investigations of partisan advisers' policy work. Formulation involves the identification and assessment of potential solutions to policy problems, and trade-offs that may include the political, technical, financial, and capacities required to determine policy objectives and the instruments to achieve them (Craft and Howlett 2012; Jordan Turnpenny 2015). Crucially for the purposes of this book, formulation, unlike most other stages of policymaking, is restricted to a smaller group of actors with the requisite knowledge and/or authoritative decision-making powers to generate feasible policy options to be presented to decision-makers (Sidney 2007). Formulation is devoted to "generating options about what to do about a public problem" (Howlett 2011, 29), and in a Cabinet parliamentary context this means that ministers, partisan advisers, and public service elites typically dominate.

Scholars have sought to clarify how options are considered and why some advance while others do not, by subdividing formulation into a series of distinct sub-phases, including appraisal, dialogue, formulation, and consolidation (Howlett, Perl, and Ramesh 2009; Thomas 2001). The *appraisal* sub-phase consists of the identification, creation, collation, and appraisal of data and information on the policy issue at hand and development of potential policy options in response. At this sub-phase, government and/or non-government actors may take stock of policies and official positions on an issue and set a loose structure for its parameters. The *dialogue* sub-phase consists of potential structured or unstructured communications between the policy actors on the issue and solutions, and again this dialogue can occur both within and outside of government. This sub-phase can involve town halls, stakeholder engagement meetings, or more formal presentations from experts or consultants. At the *formulation* sub-phase, public officials interpret the advice and information garnered from the previous sub-phases. A more pronounced role for the political context is taken into consideration, and initial options or responses to policy issues developed. These options may take the form of draft legislation, regulations, or adoption of other policy instruments. The *consolidation* sub-phase is the final sub-phase of policy formulation, whereby dissent to the initial policy options may be vetted through formal or informal channels. These sub-phases help to break formulation down into its subsidiary components and provide further nuance for comparative assessment of partisan advisers' potential involvement in that type of policy work.

Importantly, as noted above, formulation is also considered a highly political conjuncture in the policy process. As Birkland notes, formulation is "the process by which policies are designed, both through technical analysis and the political process, to achieve a particular goal" (2001, 150). Formulation has thus long been acknowledged as a key point for assessment of what options may be most politically feasible and acceptable (Althaus 2008; Majone 1975; May 2005; Weber 1986; Öberg, Lundin, and Thelander 2015). Given that this book is interested in how partisan advisers, as partisans, engage in policy work, readers may wonder where the partisanship is in this framework and how it will be operationalized. The use of the term *partisan* is suggested to better specify the *type* of political policy work that is undertaken by actors within the political arm of government. It is argued to more accurately capture policy activity that is not just "political" but rather partisan-political.[8] Students of government have long recognized that senior public service officials are engaged in political activities, broadly conceived, given that policymaking is itself an intrinsically political exercise (Campbell and Szablowski 1979; Campbell 2007; Heclo and Wildavsky 1974; Peters 2001; Plumptre 1987). As the eminent Canadian scholar Ken Kernaghan aptly summarizes it, "Partisan politics should be separated from the administration of government policies and programs. In practice, a very large number of public servants are

unavoidably involved in politics in the broad sense of the authoritative allocation of scarce resources. This involvement takes the form of
providing policy advice to political superiors and making discretion-
ary decisions in policy implementation. Thus, in the normal course of
conducting government business, politicians and public servants cannot easily separate politics from administration. This kind of political
involvement is not, however, politics in the partisan sense. Partisan politics can more easily be separated from administration" (1986, 642–3).

The argument here is that there is a distinction between the administration of policy and its formulation – that policymaking itself can,
and in party-based systems undoubtedly does, include some measure
of partisanship. This aspect of policymaking should remain distinct
from the administrative aspects of policy formulation that require non-
partisan public service detachment in keeping with Westminster traditions and principles. To suggest policymaking should be devoid of
electoral alignment considerations seems unrealistic and to an extent
undemocratic. Cabinet and legislatures have long been institutional
settings hospitable to partisan-political considerations (White 2005;
Bakvis 1991); the point here is that so too is the policy process. In short,
the policy process includes "positive" politicization or the integration
of the partisan-political calculus as it relates to the initial policy direction and questions of ongoing alignment. Crucially, however, the public service must not be politicized in the discharge of its duties in the
policy process. The devil is, however, in the details in that this has to be
operationalized. Following Kemp (1986), some general parameters can
be set out that will be further specified for advisory and formulation
activities in the subsidiary frameworks below. Kemp postulates that
partisan politics in a governance context involves:

- "The preservation of the decision-capacity of the leadership
  either as individuals or as representatives of a political party. This
  includes maintaining the necessary organizational frame, interest,
  and public support to win elections.
- The expression and implementation in policy of the values, beliefs,
  and objectives of the party or its leadership. This value-setting
  component of partisan politics may involve the determination
  of priorities among subjects of policy; the supervision and
  monitoring of the implementation process for developed policies;
  the development of new policies in response to changing
  circumstances, including the consequences of past policies; and

the integration or coordination of policy fields to ensure that the policies of government harmonize in coherent programs.
• The use of leadership to provide purpose and direction to the policy process, to coordinate the activities of government, and to communicate to and persuade those whose support is necessary for policy success and the maintenance of decision-capacity that the government's policy course is correct." (Kemp 1986, 57–8)

These functions resonate with many of the capacity, political control, and policy responsiveness imperatives that gave rise to the institution-alization of partisan advisers. They also raise implications for the function of partisanship from a policy process perspective, inasmuch as that process includes substantive ideational values-based policymaking imperatives as well as procedural aspects. The following section suggests that these considerations and their implications for policy work can be further operationalized in advisory and non-advisory categories.

Buffers and Bridges: Partisan Advisers' Policy Advisory Activity

The Privy Council Office guide and the review of advisory systems examined in the introduction make clear that partisan advisers are recognized suppliers of policy advice. The PCO guide implicitly paints their advisory activity as political and not "administrative" in stating that advisers provide advice that is distinct from that of the "expertise" provided by the non-partisan public service. However, the guide later suggests that the advisory role of partisan advisers includes a blend of both "traditional" policy advisory functions as well as politically oriented policy work. It lists a range of activities such as "reviewing briefings and other advice prepared by the department; assisting the Minister in developing policy positions, including those that reflect the Minister's political perspective" (Privy Council Office 2011, 45). Similarly, 2011 Treasury Board Secretariat (TBS) guidelines for ministers' offices detail that a ministerial director of policy "is also responsible for advising and briefing the minister on all relevant policy issues" (Treasury Board Secretariat 2011, 66). This guidance suggests that partisan advisers can engage in policy advisory functions that include but also go beyond simply the provision of "political" advice to the provision of policy advice as traditionally conceptualized. As noted already, this is further supported by the acknowledged nature of partisan advisers' interactions with public servants and other potential non-partisan policy actors, including stakeholders and the like.

In his study of policy advisory practices in Australia, Prasser (2006, 36) sets out the characteristics of what he conceives as short-term "hot" (political) and longer-term "cold" (rational) forms of policy advising (see table 1.2). Although Prasser categorizes advice in two distinct categories of "political" vs "rational," the general situation he describes is one in which neither partisan nor civil service actors have a monopoly of one type of advice over the other. These categories are useful in that they attend to the potential reasons why policy advice can be provided, and suggest that the provision of policy advice can be for reasons beyond those associated with the rationality often claimed by some proponents of policy analysis (Majone 1989; Plowden 1987).

Prasser suggests that policy analysts may in fact engage in "hot" or political forms of policy advice, or "rational," "cold," or what is termed here "administrative-technical" policy activity. The latter is expected as a product of advisers' policy-related interactions with non-partisan policy actors, such as but not limited to public servants or in cases where there is no prevailing partisan-political policy agenda. The term *partisan-political policy advice* is introduced here to set out a separate and distinct partisan-political form of policy advice that partisan advisers are uniquely able to provide, which involves the explicit and purposeful application of a political lens to policy analysis (Head 2008; McConnell 2010a; Esselment, Lees-Marshment, and Marland 2014) – that is,

Table 1.2. Comparison of Rational (Cold) and Political (Hot) Advice

Rational (cold) advice	Political (hot) advice
Information based	Relies on fragmented information, gossip
Research used	Opinion/ideology based
Independent/neutral and problem solving	Partisan/biased and about winning
Long term	Short term
Proactive and anticipatory	Reactive / crisis driven
Strategic and wide range / systematic	Single issue
Idealistic	Pragmatic
Public interest focus	Electoral gain oriented
Open processes	Secret / deal making
Objective clarity	Ambiguous/overlapping
Seek, propose best solution	Consensus solution

Source: Reproduced from Prasser (2006, 36)

policy advice that differs from the traditionally conceived policy advice involving non-partisan, bureaucratic, rational policy analysis (Head 2008; Radin 2000).[9] It is posited to consist of the provision of policy advice to elected officials by financially remunerated actors involving *input of new, or commentary upon existing, courses of policy (in)action by way of judgments/analysis of such activity based on its political feasibility, desirability, and consistency with stated partisan-political objectives, commitments, and/or anticipated political/operational consequences.* This advisory activity is an attempt to flesh out the types of partisan-political policy tasks suggested by Kemp (1986) as components of policy work. There is a range of actors who could engage in advisory activities of this sort: political consultants and strategists, lobbyists, friends, and "kitchen Cabinets" (Bakvis 1997; Plowden 1987; Howlett et al. 2014). This book looks only at politically appointed partisan advisers, working within the offices of ministers, at the executive level of government. These actors benefit from privileged access to resources and decision-makers that others, such as those potential alternative suppliers listed above, generally do not.

The advisory framework set out in table 1.3 includes these two forms of direct policy advice provision, or buffering, that partisan advisers may engage in. It also includes process-based bridging to account for their potential functions in the integration or preclusion of *other* sources of policy advice within advisory systems. At a basic level, partisan advisers are well positioned to serve as channels for the brokerage of policy advice among political and administrative spheres. The PCO *Guide to Ministers* describes precisely this type of process-based policy advisory activity, explaining that while partisan advisers have no statutory authority to delegate or direct public servants, "it is normal for ministerial staff to transmit instructions or gather information on behalf of the Minister" (Privy Council Office 2011, 44). The 2011 TBS guidelines detail that partisan advisers engage in "liaison activities" with departmental officials, the first minister's office, and external stakeholders (Treasury Board Secretariat 2011, 66). Zussman comes to similar conclusions in his study of OECD advisers, underscoring that public servants can benefit from positive working relations with partisan advisers. He suggests that partisan advisers serve as a vehicle for officials to access the minister (or ministerial thinking), that advisers are able to "shed greater light on the priorities, mind-set and expectations of the Minister. The political adviser has the advantage of a close working relationship with the minister and it is often easier for a public servant to gain access to the political adviser rather than the minister" (Zussman 2009, 22).

Such bridging thus involves "administrative-technical" dimensions in that it may facilitate the development of non-partisan public service policy advice. For example, partisan advisers may advise departmental officials that their minister has recently undertaken unofficial consultations with experts, international counterparts, or stakeholders (Craft 2013; OECD 2011). Partisan advisers may share policy advice that was proffered by any number of actors to the minister. Advisers are not directly providing their own advisory content but instead are bridging by integrating policy advice from *other* sources within the advisory system. Bridging of this kind informs the public service of the sources (and content) of policy advice the minister may have received and may in fact benefit development of official departmental policy advice. The 2011 TBS guidelines for ministers suggest exactly such integration, referencing "liaison" activities that partisan advisers may undertake with endogenous or exogenous actors. For example, the guidelines explicitly document that minister's office *"policy advisers"* "should liaise with key stakeholders in order to inform and/or consult on important policy initiatives within the minister's purview" (Treasury Board Secretariat 2011, 68).

A second form of "partisan-political bridging" can also be theorized relating to integration involving inputs from other partisan advisers

Table 1.3 Partisan Advisers' Policy Advisory Activity

Policy advisory activity (One of many sources of policy advice)	Nature of policy advisory activity	
	Partisan-political	Administrative-technical
Buffering (Direct content-based provision of policy advice)	Partisan-political policy advice Provision/contestation of policy advice by partisan advisers based on partisan-political criteria	"Administrative" "program" policy advice Provision/contestation of policy advice based on "technical," "program," or "evidence-based" criteria
Bridging (Process-based integration or exclusion of advisory inputs)	Partisan-political policy advice integration Integration/preclusion of partisan-political sources of policy advice	Non-partisan policy advice integration Integration/preclusion of "evidence-based," "technical," or "program" policy advice

or political actors within advisory systems. Again, this would involve unidirectional/bidirectional integration but in this instance relate to partisan-political policy advice, as defined above, such as integrating partisan-political policy advice within a minister's own office where there is more than one partisan adviser, or among partisan advisers in different offices within the core executive. This type of activity is well supported by empirical findings detailing precisely such a function, including those related to regional political implications of policy advice, or in relation to determinations of prospective Cabinet support (Maley 2011; OECD 2011; Weller 1987; Craft 2013; Eichbaum and Shaw 2010). Bridging also has exclusionary potential in line with the notions of gatekeeping and "funnelling." Here too empirical studies of partisan advisers have examined the screening or removal of policy alternatives to meet anticipated political criteria (Eichbaum and Shaw 2007a; Walter 2006). Most have found mixed results with such practices occurring in some cases but in others public servants considering advisers to be of net benefit to the overall policy advisory capacity (Connaughton 2010b; Eichbaum and Shaw 2008, 2010; Craft 2015a). Providing, facilitating, or impeding the exchange of policy advice speaks directly to the notion of resource exchange and dependence central to core executives. It is also quite clearly linked to notions of political control and public service responsiveness. Buffering may contribute to strengthening political control through greater contestation of policy advisory inputs for ministers, and broadening the availability of alternative sources and content of policy advice. Bridging may also diversify the availability of administrative-technical or partisan-political sources of policy advice, and increase political control through avoidance of potential "bureaucratic capture." Bilateral bridging among political and administrative spheres facilitated by partisan advisers may also strengthen political control. It may facilitate avoidance or reduction of information asymmetries as well as increase or improve interactions in areas where political and administrative actors necessarily overlap (Svara 2006; Osbaldeston 1987).

Conversely, buffering provided through partisan-political policy advice may also strengthen discreet forms of core executive resource exchange. That is, it may safeguard the non-partisan and independent values and policy work of Westminster-style public services. While seemingly counterintuitive, given that partisan advisers may pose a risk for public service politicization (Peters and Pierre 2004), studies have found evidence supporting the "insulating effects" of advisers (Aucoin

2010; Eichbaum and Shaw 2007b). Aucoin among others has argued that partisan advisers are useful to the public service "to the extent that they attend to matters of political management that are beyond the scope of a nonpartisan public service" (Aucoin 2012; see also Axworthy 1988). Buffering and bridging are therefore useful for assessments of policy advisory related resource exchanges important to core executives, but tell only part of the story.

Movers and Shapers: Partisan Advisers' Policy Formulation Activity

A central argument of this study is that, as policy workers, partisan advisers' non-advisory policy work is also important to how they may exercise influence in policymaking and core executives. Contemporary studies, almost exclusively federal, are generous in their interpretations of Canadian partisan advisers' influence in the policy process. One analysis of federal ministers' office staffs found that they "can, and often do, exert a substantial degree of influence on the development and in some cases on the administration of public policy in Canada" and that "by virtue of their political relationship with the party in power and/or the minister they serve, are well placed to influence both the bounce and bobble of bureaucratic-political interface and the pace and progress of public policy in Canada" (Benoit 2006, 146). Others have also underscored their non-advisory based policy activity and influence (Aucoin 2010; Thomas 2008, 2010; Zussman 2013). A range of studies in other Westminster jurisdictions have also provided comprehensive accounts detailing non-advisory activity flowing from partisan advisers' interactions with their counterparts located in the executive, public servants, and even non-governmental actors and stakeholders (OECD 2011; Eichbaum and Shaw 2010; Craft, 2015a; LSE GV314 2012; Maley 2015). While acknowledged, how they engage in policy activity or what makes it influential typically goes underspecified.

Official Canadian government documents also recognize partisan advisers' non-advisory policy work. Here, again, the federal government is the most useful as an illustration, given the greater comparative documentation of the role and functions of political "exempt staffs." Treasury Board Secretariat guidelines detail that ministers' offices' *"directors of policy"* are "responsible, in collaboration with the department, for overseeing policy development on behalf of the minister"

(Treasury Board Secretariat 2011, 66). Some of the policy functions ascribed to partisan advisers include that they:

- Work closely with the Prime Minister's Office and other ministers' offices to coordinate development of policies and programs within the government;
- Must ensure that policy development within the minister's responsibilities is consistent with the broad policy goals of the government, as laid out in key documents, such as the Speech from the Throne and the budget;
- Should work closely with the department to ensure that policies and policy development are consistent with the minister's objectives and the government's mandate; and
- Should liaise with key stakeholders to inform or consult on important policy initiatives within the minister's purview. (Treasury Board Secretariat, 2011, 66)

To what degree and with what consequence such activities are *actually* occurring in contemporary policy development remains empirically untested. As styled in table 1.4, the concepts of movers and shapers capture the procedural/substantive and partisan/"administrative-technical" dimension noted above but add vertical (intra-ministerial) and horizontal (extra-ministerial) dimensions of formulation. Westminster studies have long noted that partisan advisers could extend policy options, "pay attention" to the policy agenda, act as policy "mobilizers" in the face of policy vacuum, or play a "catalyst" role (Walter 1986). Others have noted a range of substantive and procedural types of policy activities undertaken by partisan advisers with actors both within and outside of government (Connaughton 2010a; Eichbaum and Shaw 2010; Maley 2015; OECD 2007, 2011). Procedural and substantive categories have been used explicitly in the analysis of partisan advisers' policy activity (Eichbaum and Shaw 2011; Maley 2000, 2011; Campbell 1988), as well as in studies of policy formulation more generally (Colebatch 1998; Matheson 2000; Howlett 2000).

Moving and shaping are again argued to potentially span partisan-political and administrative or technical categories and have clear and potential implications for core executive resource exchanges and policy responsiveness. Moving potentially strengthens political control through process-based formulation such as monitoring, "steering," sequencing, or coordination of multiple policy actors during

Table 1.4. Conceptualizing Partisan Advisers' Policy Formulation Activity

Policy activity and orientation		Nature of formulation activity	
		Partisan-political	Administrative-technical
Shapers (Substantive non-advisory contributions to policy formulation)	Intra-ministerial	Vertical partisan-political shaping, e.g., aligning substance of departmental policy with electoral platform	Vertical administrative-technical shaping, e.g., substantive contributions to departmental public service policy development such as program or technical specifications
	Extra-ministerial	Horizontal partisan-political shaping, e.g., calibration of content of policy for partisan political purposes with other ministers' offices	Horizontal administrative technical shaping, e.g., technical or programmatic policy content calibration undertaken with central agencies or extra-departmental officials
Movers (Procedural non-advisory contribution to policy formulation)	Intra-ministerial	Vertical partisan-political moving, e.g., policy process coordination or management with a minister or advisers from one's own office	Vertical administrative-technical moving, e.g., policy process, coordination/ management with one's own departmental officials
	Extra-ministerial	Horizontal partisan-political moving, e.g., partisan-political policy process coordination/ management with first minister's office	Horizontal administrative technical moving, e.g., policy process coordination/ management with central agencies

formulation. Process-based formulation is a key vehicle by which partisan advisers can increase public service "responsiveness" and strengthen political control (Dahlström, Peters, and Pierre 2011; Eichbaum and Shaw 2007a, 2007b; Brans, Pelgrims, and Hoet 2006). On content or substantive grounds, shaping has clear and direct linkages with attempts to "align" governmental policy formulation with the substantive policy direction or preferences of ministers/government – that is, the degree to which priorities and policy are consistent throughout different levels of an organization (Di Fracesco 2000; Kellermanns et al. 2005; Andrews et al. 2012).

For example, it may involve administrative-technical calibration or refinement of options in development based on evidentiary or consistency preferences. Alternatively, partisan-political shaping may increase political control through improved alignment of government policy with stated partisan-political preferences communicated during elections, in platforms, or with key political "stakeholders." Partisan advisers' influence, as Aucoin (2010, 82) reminds us, stems not only from their functions as sources of advice but also "because they operate at a level where substantive policy, policy process and policy implementation expertise is either challenged or outweighed by political expertise relating to other things." This again raises the importance of potential non-advisory policy work and resource exchanges that are partisan-political during formulation. These are precisely the types of policy work that are aimed at, for instance, initial appraisal of what is politically feasible or ongoing calibration and alignment of policy in concert with Cabinet, its committees, and caucus, or involving partisan advisers or policy actors. Lastly, extra-core executive resource exchanges are also of interest. That is how partisan advisers engage with other actors outside of the core executive and subsequently "move" their inputs into core executives. For example, stakeholder consultations on specific pieces of legislation could involve either or both programmatic or technical aspects or be of a partisan-political nature.

Studying Federal and Provincial Partisan Advisers

This book is based on information from a variety of sources: government reports and secondary sources, as well as unstructured interviews. The goal was not to draw out generalized findings that apply to all potential cases or at all periods in time. Given the paucity of studies examining Canadian partisan advisers' policy activity, particularly in the provinces,[10] this study is exploratory (Stebbins 2001; Brady and Collier 2004). The choice of the federal and two subnational cases was motivated by the practical realities of field research, including the cost of doing fieldwork in all Canadian cases, and particularly the potential difficulty in securing the agreement from "elite" respondents. Access has been cited as a key issue in the study of appointed political staffs (Maley 2002; Tiernan 2006b). With this in mind, the initial selection of cases was informed by tentative agreement from a significant number of political and administrative elites in the three cases.

The cases were also chosen to facilitate examining partisan advisers in small to large institutional settings and with different political-administrative arrangements. In the Canadian context, institutional size is important, because differences both of Cabinet and the public service size affect patterns of interaction among political and administrative elites (White 1990). This has direct implications for their respective policy formulation activities and core executive resource exchanges. One contention is that smaller institutional settings are characterized by frequent and unmediated interaction between ministers and their deputy ministers. In larger institutional settings, for example with large Cabinets, a greater number of political staff can result in a mediated interaction pattern (ibid.). Including the federal case was thus an easy decision, as it is by far the largest and most institutionally complex. Cabinet and public service departments are comparatively larger in personnel and budgets than any subnational government. It also employs the greatest number of Canadian political staffs and has long been noted to have the most sophisticated political machinery of government (Bernier, Brownsey, and Howlett 2005; White 2005). The two subnational cases of British Columbia and New Brunswick also provide variance on this front. British Columbia represents a mid-sized provincial government in Canada offering a level of institutional complexity and Cabinet size that fell in between the smaller case of New Brunswick and the federal case with the largest Cabinet size and larger plurality of partisan advisers both at the centre and in ministers' offices. New Brunswick's inclusion allows for the analysis of a jurisdiction characterized by a very small machinery of government and thus "intimate" political-administrative space within which partisan advisers operate (Hyson 2005; Bouchard 2014). Also, in New Brunswick there are typically a limited number of Cabinet committees, and ministers historically employ one partisan adviser in their ministerial offices.

The three cases have also been characterized differently in their governance arrangements. That is, they differ in their perceived degree of centralization of power and the influence of partisan advisers. The federal order of government has given rise to the courtier governance and NPG theses, and is characterized by high levels of centralization, and prominent policy functions and influence of partisan advisers as detailed above. Provincially, a recent and authoritative study of the Dupré-Dunn-Savoie thesis of evolving modes of Cabinet government in Canada suggests a differentiated pattern among the provinces. Specifically, that the pattern towards courtier-style post-institutionalized Cabinet governance is "much more pronounced in the largest Canadian jurisdictions, with pronounced moves in this direction over the last decade at the federal level and in Ontario, Alberta, and British Columbia. Most of the smaller Canadian provinces retain a system of institutionalized cabinets" (Bernier, Brownsey, and Howlett 2005, 11). The selection of New Brunswick therefore offers a case where court government has yet to be fully entrenched with a smaller machinery of government and expectation of accessibility to political actors, including the first minister, serving as key constraints (Hyson 2005; Bouchard 2014). The British Columbia case allows for the examination of partisan advisers' policy functions in a more centralized provincial jurisdiction (Ruff 2005). Lastly, the cases also feature differences in how long the administrations had been in office and their parliamentary status. While interviews were conducted in 2010–12, the Graham government in New Brunswick was a first-term majority government, while British Columbia was in the final days of a three-term Campbell majority government, and the federal case included two Harper minority governments and a majority government.

Within each case, four departments, including one central agency and three "line departments," were targeted but will not be specified to ensure anonymity of participants[11]. The "line departments" were selected for literal replication among cases and for control of variance along sectoral policy lines. Over sixty-five in-depth semi-structured interviews were carried out. These typically included four ministers, four deputy ministers, and four chiefs of staff (or provincial equivalent) per case. Interviews were also completed with first minister's office staff in each case and central agency officials in the federal and BC cases. The federal case included a greater number of interviews, given its comparatively larger complement of partisan advisers in the PMO and ministers' offices. In that case, additional interviews were conducted with directors of policy and "junior" partisan advisors in ministers' offices and the PMO. Additional interviews were also carried out in that case with former PMO and PCO staff to confirm differences in contemporary organization and practice that emerged from early interviews.

Having set out some basic characteristics of the three cases along with a framework to better evaluate what policy work partisan advisers undertake, chapter 2 turns to an examination of how partisan advisers, as a subset of political staffs, emerged in each case. It is more historical in nature than any of the other chapters that follow. Those who wish to move directly to the first-hand accounts of the three cases may want to skip ahead to chapter 3. However, attention to the evolution of partisan advisers as a subset of the broader category of appointed political staffs is important. It contextualizes the evolution of these actors as part of the political arm of government and participants in the politics of policy work.

Chapter 2

Institutionalization, Expansion, and Specialization

Introduction

Those who govern have always had access to many potential sources of counsel. Advisers exist in many guises, from employed staffs, to colleagues, friends, and "kitchen Cabinets" (Bakvis 1997; Goldhamer 1978; Plowden 1987). Appointed political staffs are a relatively new *formal* addition to the Westminster machinery of executive governance. This chapter combines readily available historical analysis pertaining to Canada with new figures and findings made available when this book was being completed. It is not intended to provide a comprehensive historical account (though one is needed). Rather, this chapter traces key milestones in the historical evolution of partisan advisers as a subset of political staff in Ottawa, British Columbia, and New Brunswick. The chapter begins with a review of the federal case, covering PMO and ministers' offices, followed by British Columbia and New Brunswick. Where possible, new data on their contemporary numbers and officially stated policy functions are provided.

The main argument of this chapter is that partisan advisers, as a subset of appointed political staffs, are the product of a three-step pattern of institutionalization, expansion, and specialization. Though this pattern is not identical in the cases, each demonstrates a pattern of bureaucratic growth (Meyer 1987). As a class of institutionalized government actors, partisan advisers have become subject to much greater "rationalization," specialization, and hierarchical organization. The second and third stages of their evolutionary pattern can be thought of as part of a larger overarching professionalization and bureaucratization of the political arm of government (Fawcett and Gay 2010; Evetts

2003a, 2003b). This study examines in detail one aspect of that professionalization and specialization – the advent of partisan advisers as formal participants in policy work.

Partisan Advisers in Ottawa

The PMO continues to be the largest and most well resourced "political office" in financial and human resource terms in Canada. Meeting the needs of various first ministers, and the contexts within which they governed, has yielded innovations in the structure and function of the political arm. Most have occurred first in Ottawa and have subsequently been adopted or emulated by the provincial governments, chief of which has been a shift from the primary use of seconded public servants to more systematic appointment of "exempt" partisan-political staffs. By all accounts, from Confederation until the 1950s, the PMO was successively managed by prime ministers themselves, assisted by a small but growing coterie of seconded public servants (Punnett 1977; D'Aquino 1974; Lalonde 1971). An early guide developed by public servants for the Privy Council Office suggests that the PMO "emerged as an identifiable unit in the early 1920s with the appearance of staff preforming other than clerical functions" (Privy Council Office 1968a, 476). These other functions are, however, not clearly spelt out. Indeed, until the 1960s, prime ministers had no PMO partisan advisory entourages or policy "shops" to assist them or apply a political lens to policymaking. At the ministers' office level, prior to 1950, it was even more skeletal, with one private secretary, a couple of stenographers, and a "secretary to the executive" on staff (Mallory 1967, 27–8). An Order in Council in 1950[12] raised the allowable number of ministerial staff to eight, and in 1958 a new category of "special assistant" was created for "press officer" duties (Mallory 1967). Other students of the minister's office have noted that a "typical" minister in the St Laurent government (1948–57) "seldom had the services of more than a single political confidant" (Lenoski 1977, 166). Cabinet records indicates that from 1957 to 1960 the number of ministerial staff had risen from forty to seventy, but Cabinet discussion itself noted the problem of compiling such numbers as the result of classification changes (Privy Council Office, 1960a, 1960b). Without providing a concrete figure, Lenoski cites government phone directories as evidence of growth in the number of political staffs in ministers' offices during the Diefenbaker (1957–63) administration (167).

Political appointees serving in an official and formal policy capacity were first implemented in the PMO when Tom Kent was appointed as "special policy adviser" to Prime Minister Pearson in 1963 (Doern 1971). Pearson followed in the British tradition of employing a seconded public servant as principal secretary (D'Aquino 1974), but the additional use of a politically appointed staff laid the groundwork for an architectural and functional redesign of the PMO. In a description that is apt for today's PMO, an early account suggested that the PMO serves three main functions linked to the political arm's desire for capacity, political control, and policy responsiveness: "Firstly, secretarial and administrative capacity; secondly, a source of political advice to the prime minister of the day; and, thirdly, it provides a supply of factual information about the affairs of government, to enable him to face his ministers from an informed base. If he is to be free from dependence on departmental civil servants, this factual information can only come from a private bureaucracy" (Punnett 1977, 74–5).

How PMOs undertake these three functions has changed considerably to accommodate the needs and preferences of prime ministers and the context in which government governs. The potential for dramatic changes to the complements of political staff working in ministerial offices was made possible through the exclusion of the minister's private office staff from the 1963 Civil Service Act. Importantly, the Public Service Employment Act (1967) codified the "special assistant" category of exempt staff and the classification of other positions in a section dealing with the ministers' exempt staff.[13] In general, budgets for ministerial offices, out of which exempt political staff are paid, increased in the 1960s. While growth in ministerial office staff budgets is often attributed to the Trudeau administration taking office in 1968, Cabinet records[14] reveal that the ministerial office budget was, in fact, first set at $72,000 and subsequently rose to the $78,000 limit in 1966 under Pearson. These limits were strictly upheld with a 1967 Cabinet conclusion detailing the minister of justice having to seek Cabinet approval to retain an additional long-serving political staff (PCO 1967). Pearson opened the door to a politically appointed partisan policy staff in Ottawa, but it was indeed the subsequent Trudeau government that would, in the late 1960s, oversee their institutionalization and expansion within the executive.

Trudeau explicitly aimed to build up the PMO as part of a more robust executive. He famously stated, "One of the reasons why I wanted this job, when I was told that it might be there, is because I felt it very important to have a strong central government, build up the executive, build up the Prime Minister's Office" (Radwanski 1978, 146). Trudeau formally institutionalized partisan advisers into the PMO in 1968 with a shift to appointed political staffs as principal secretary, regional "desks," and a policy team – a structure and functional arrangement that remains (Savoie 1999a; Schacter 1999, 6). As Trudeau's former principal secretary wrote, "A new category of official was created – the political adviser. Their role was different from that of public servants who had for years served Prime Ministers they would advise on the interaction of policy and politics and not be subject to the formal rules of the public service" (Axworthy 1988, 258).

The Trudeau PMO reforms of the 1960s were an attempt not only to build up executive capacity in response to policy complexity but also to support the empowerment of the Cabinet and PMO over departments as part of a broader attempt to "rationalize" policymaking and management (French and Van Loon 1984; Doern 1971). An elaborate system of Cabinet committees and processes were put in place with the intention to empower Cabinet and central agency coordination. This paradigm of rational management even extended to the political arm of government, with the PMO asked to "co-ordinate the activities of the senior political staff of ministers in order to promote adherence to the political objectives of the government as a corporate body" (Aucoin 1986, 11). Savoie, among others, has argued that the actual result was the empowerment of the PMO and eventual development of courtier-style governance (Savoie 1999a). As summarized in table 2.1, the PMO grew over this period, not only in staffing but also in its overall budget. By his last year in office 1983–4, the Trudeau PMO was twice the size of Pearson's, with a budget of approximately $4.2 million and a staff of eighty-seven (Axworthy 1988, 258; Punnett 1977, 77). It is important to note that the majority of new Trudeau PMO staff were categorized as clerical, with only twenty or so considered senior advisers (Axworthy 1988, 258). This, however, clearly represents an initial institutionalization and expansion of partisan-political policy capacity in the PMO.

Given the attempt to systematically "rationalize" the policy process, ministers' offices were reorganized and the political arm expanded and specialized. In the late 1960s the special assistant category of ministerial political staffs was subdivided to include parliamentary relations, constituency relations, and legislative assistant. This ushered in the period of specialization of political staff with clear and discrete functions (if in

Table 2.1. Political Staff and Expenses for the Prime Minister's Office (1962, 1967, and 1970)

PMO staff	1962–3	1967–8	1970–1
Principal secretary	–	1	1
Executive assistant	1	1	1
Special assistant	4	3	10
Press office	2	4	6
Correspondence	15	22	41
Regional desks	–	–	7
Secretaries	7	8	17
Private secretary	1	1	1
Constituency office	–	–	1
PMO staff total	30	40	85
Total budget (salaries, contracts, and travel expenses)	$181,550 (approx.)	$331,585	$900,839

Source: Adapted from Lalonde (1971, 532). Figures are for fiscal years 1 April 1 to 31 March. Lalonde notes that the figures do not include seconded public servants working in the PMO.

title only). It should also be noted that ministers' office budgets were also increased to $83,500 under Trudeau in 1968–9 (PCO 1968b). Citing the growth of ministerial duties writ large as a principal cause, Lenoski (1977, 170) explains adviser specialization:

> The continuing diversification of responsibilities assumed by ministers in large measure has accounted for greater role specialization on the part of their bigger staffs. Whereas the executive assistant at one time could take care of virtually everything single-handedly, the necessity of providing additional assistants for varying reasons has led to a fairly strict differentiation of duties amongst many minister's staffs. Moreover, together with the executive assistant and several special assistants for designated purposes, the staff complement backing up a representative minister at the present time, will include some research, administrative and/or departmental assistants. Under these latter, and still other, classifications can be subsumed political operatives who concentrate on anything from press relations to speech preparation, policy analysis and a host of other requirements which must be met to help the minister fulfil his various duties.

What emerges, however, from Lenoski's characterization of exempt staff at the federal level until the 1970s is one marked by expansion, and the onset of increased role specialization. Tellingly, the normative debate between Mallory (1967) and Tellier (1968) extended beyond the confines of scholarly journals to a topic of discussion at the Cabinet table of the day. A 1971 Cabinet meeting echoes the academic debate with the official Cabinet conclusion stating,

> The following points arose during discussion:
> (a) It was the view of *some ministers* that ministers should not be limited in the salaries they could pay within their exempt staff budget; the point was made in this connection that the salary ceilings prevented ministers from hiring competent staff, particularly in the advisory capacity, at a higher salary.
> (b) It was the view of some others that ministers should rely on their departmental officials as advisers, not on highly paid assistants in their own offices. (PCO 1971; emphasis in original)

Those ministers in favour of looser guidelines and higher salaries are recorded as having won the day. Such Cabinet deliberation reveals that the ongoing tension of exempt staff and departmental officials as sources of policy advice is anything but new. During a Cabinet discussion in 1973, exempt staffs were recommended to be included under the existing conflict-of-interest guidelines because "not infrequently people in that category exercised a great deal of influence over decision making and had access to highly classified information" (Privy Council Office 1973).

By 1978 ministers' office budgets had increased to $175,000 and were intended to cover a larger contingent of ministerial staff, often in addition to seconded public servants (Williams 1980). However, ministers were quite capable of circumventing established budget limits through "personal service contracts," which would allow ministers to secure additional staff with expertise or skills found outside the public service (ibid.). The frequently cited example is of Minister of Transport Lloyd Axworthy, whose ministerial office in the 1980s was staffed by 100 employees, of which approximately 20 were exempt staff and the remainder seconded or term public servants (Bakvis 1988, 555). Responding to requests for greater flexibility and in an attempt to curtail the "personal services contract" phenomenon, Cabinet approved the new exempt position of "special assistant – policy adviser" in

1978 (Williams 1980, 219). From available Cabinet documents and secondary sources, this appears to be the first explicit recognition of the partisan-political policy advisory role. It certainly confirms the further specialization of Canadian political staff towards that of partisan advisers.

Such historical examples are useful reminders that greater caution is needed in attributing influence solely to the fact that partisan advisers are in place. For all the attention that this new and more muscular PMO received, its policy influence was fairly constrained. As Campbell (1988, 269) notes, during its first term (1968–72) the Trudeau PMO lacked a formal policy unit, with only Lalonde and others having senior policy functions. Even when such a unit was established in the later majority government, its ability to effectively provide policy capacity was meagre. Key limitations included the limited number of policy specific PMO staff, strong ministers whose policy advice Trudeau trusted, and his reliance on various sources of advice, including strengthened central administrative agencies staffed by his chosen close associates (Aucoin 1986; D'Aquino 1974). PMOs have hovered around the 100 staff-member level since the late 1970s, but the advisory capacity of the PMO has fluctuated and been organized in various ways.

The next wave of major changes came with the election of Brian Mulroney and the Progressive Conservatives. During the course of the Mulroney years (1984–93), several important changes were introduced at both the PMO and ministers' offices. The PMO expanded in 1985–6 with a budget of $6.6 million and a staff complement of 117 (Axworthy 1988, 258). Part of this increased cost can be explained by the explicit emphasis that Mulroney placed on shoring up the policy capacity of the PMO. With a 50 per cent larger budget than in the final Trudeau year in office, the Mulroney PMO staff grew by a single staff person. However, the number of PMO staff with explicit policy functions increased. The strengthened PMO policy function is suggested to have been partly a consequence of attempts to support Mulroney's transactional brokerage decision-making style and also as part of the concerted efforts to reduce the role of other central agencies, notably the PCO (Aucoin 1986). The principal secretary position remained the top political staff position in the PMO filled by Bernard Roy during the majority of the first Mulroney mandate but was replaced with that of chief of staff with the appointment of Derek Burney in March 1987. In his memoirs, Burney (2005, 106–7) provides a summary of what he saw as the key functions of the PMO chief of staff: "The major task for the chief of staff is to focus the prime minister's time and his message on key issues and to ensure consistency between the message and the delivery of government action. As well, there is a major control function, resolving or containing disputes and crises as they inevitably but unpredictably arise in government. The proactive element, giving shape and direction to the prime minister's agenda, was challenging; the firefighting or crisis management was often frustrating but also stimulating."

In addition, the creation of a Deputy Prime Minister's Office (DPMO) was another innovation.[15] It was first headed by Minister Eric Nielson and then Minister Donald Mazankowski, whose prominent role and influence in the Mulroney administration, for example in chairing key Cabinet committees, has been well documented (Aucoin 1986; Savoie 1994). Overall, the size and the cost of the PMO increased under Mulroney, who has the dubious honour of running the most expensive PMO since 1975, at $8.8–12 million per year in inflation-adjusted dollars (Davis 2010).

Like Trudeau before him, Mulroney's organizational preferences extended to the ministers' offices as well. While no Cabinet documents are yet available on the matter, the figures (Bakvis 1989) make clear that a growth in Cabinet had concomitant implications for "exempt staffs" across government. The longstanding practice of some PMO involvement in overall political staffing reached new heights in the Mulroney PMO. The PMO was insistent that appointments be cleared with them, though the practice eventually fell by the wayside (Plassé 1994, 25). The executive assistant position was replaced by the chief of staff position in ministers' offices, a change that had consequences beyond that of simply title. Chiefs were classified at a rank comparable to that of deputy minister, with accompanying increases to the level of pay, and signalled to the bureaucracy that increased political control was the order of the day. As Savoie (2003, 124) bluntly puts it, "Mulroney's decision had one purpose – to check permanent officials' influence on policy." Indeed, the explicit intent of the reclassification was to shore up political control and avoid bureaucratic capture (Bourgault 2002).

With an expanded Cabinet including forty ministers, the number of ministerial staff increased correspondingly. It was not uncommon to find a group of thirty to forty people working in a minister's office under the direction of a chief of staff (Larson 1999, 57). Such changes were considered revolutionary. Overall, by 1990–1 the total number of exempt staff sat at 460, of which 99 served in the PMO (Aucoin 2010, 71).

This expanded contingent of exempt staff was rolled out in ministers' offices across government to ensure a more muscular overall political management and to provide greater political and policy advisory capacity to ministers (Bakvis 2000, 78). As O'Connor explains, the chief of staff position was created to "offer policy advice over and above that provided by the department he or she could achieve this in part by soliciting opinions different from those held by the departmental advisers" (1991, 23–5). This is squarely in line with the notion of diversification of available advisory sources, greater contestation of public service policy advice, and speaks directly to the notion of resource exchanges that fuel core executives (Prince 2007; Craft 2015b; Shaw and Eichbaum 2014, 2015). In a telling description O'Connor later also makes clear the intended use of partisan advisers was to secure greater political control and responsiveness: "The chief of staff is, first and foremost, the senior political adviser to the minister. He or she is also the director of operations and controller for the minister's office. The chief of staff must provide leadership and coherence to the operations of the minister's office, and should bring sound knowledge to both governmental decision-making and the policy process. A key role of the chief of staff is to ensure that ministerial directives are carried out within the department. In this way, the chief of staff assists in increasing ministerial control and accountability" (O'Connor 1991, 24).

Plassé's (1994) study of Mulroney chiefs of staff found that chiefs self-reported their most frequent duties to involve providing advice to the minister, managing the office, liaising with the minister, and review of departmental policies. Mulroney chiefs perceived themselves as participating in decision-making such as departmental management committees and projects, and advice to the minister on all matters (70). The assessments were, however, that the attempt to use partisan appointees, particularly in ministers' offices, had essentially failed to achieve its original intentions. While it did provide some degree of coordination and a political policy capacity within ministerial offices, advisers were found to generally lack the expertise to provide substantive policy advice, and little of this advice appeared to be of a long-term strategic nature (Plassé 1994; Bakvis 2000). The mixed reviews of chiefs have been suggested to be heavily dependent on the qualities and capacity of each individual appointee. In general, the attempt to use partisan advisers was deemed a failure, one where "many chiefs of staff took a dim view of the competence of permanent officials, who took an equally jaundiced view of them" (Savoie 2003, 124).

With the election of the Chrétien governments (1993–3), another prime minister put his stamp on the structure and operation of the PMO. As a long-serving parliamentarian and Cabinet minister in various portfolios in the Pearson and Trudeau administrations, Chrétien brought first-hand experience to the job. Chrétien's PMO has been the subject of detailed treatments by journalists and students of public administration (see Savoie 1999a, 2003, 2008; Simpson 2001; Goldenberg 2006). As detailed in table 2.2, the size of the PMO and the contingent of total appointed political staffs was reduced when Chrétien took office, but would increase during his final mandate.

The PMO had no principal secretary but long-time senior Chrétien aide Edward Goldenberg performed the same general functions but

Table 2.2. Federal Exempt Staff by Department (31 March 2001 to 31 March 2011)

Year	PMO exempt staff complement	Total exempt staff – PMO & ministers' offices
1990–1	99	460
1994–5	76	427
1999–2000	80	525
2001	83	461
2002	81	461
2003	77	488
2004	64	428
2005	68	461
2006	65	194
2007	79	414
2008	92	442
2009	94	487
2010	112	532
2011	99	520
2012	95	536
2013	101	570
2014	96	566

Source: The data presented for 1990–1 and 1994–5 are drawn from Treasury Board Secretariat (2006). All other years are drawn from appendix A.

under the title of senior policy adviser. He had served in the principal secretary capacity when Chrétien was leader of the opposition. In his aptly titled book *The Way It Works*, Goldenberg dismisses the popularized accounts of "court government," preferring to characterize the PMO role as one of "oversight" and "coordination," "advice giving and communication," and "gatekeeping" (Goldenberg 2006, chapter 5). Goldenberg explained that in addition to responsibility for overall political strategy, Prime Minister Chrétien "expected me to focus on his major policy priorities, and to work with cabinet ministers and deputy ministers to implement them" (96). From a policy perspective, his account makes clear his self-perceived role as policy actor in select files of interest to the prime minister or himself. The PMO policy team, he explained, "were responsible for how the PMO managed and coordinated government policy priorities and that the policy director and their staff took responsibility for making sure that all the cabinet ministers followed through on election campaign commitments; they also carefully monitored the agendas of all cabinet committees, identified problems between departments and ministers, offered advice, and worked to fix problems" (96).

When consulted as part of this study, senior Chrétien PMO staff explained that approximately seven policy advisers typically staffed the "policy shop" structured along policy lines (social policy, economic policy, etc.), and reported to the PMO policy director. Their job was, as mentioned above, one of monitoring, liaising, and coordinating between the PMO and ministers' offices.[16] Former senior PMO partisan advisers confirmed that PMO staff provided their policy advice via oral briefings, either within PMO up to the prime minister or in consultation with the PCO who would subsequently draft up "clerks notes" or other written memoranda for the prime minister. Those consulted from that era characterized the overall PMO policy advisory function as oral and informal. This resonates with the published accounts as presented by Goldenberg (2006, chapter 5; Jeffrey 2010; Savoie 1999b). Consultations with former PMO staff and published accounts confirm a self-perceived degree of policy capacity within the PMO but that policymaking was "textbook." In most instances, it was produced collaboratively but with the public service as lead pen on *all* documents. This is important, in that this policy process involves the public service consulting with and, to a degree, integrating partisan advisers' feedback into formal policy advice presented to the prime minister and Cabinet. This is not to suggest that the PCO staff were not providing their "free and frank" policy advice up the chain, but that there was "signal-checking" or informal discussions with PMO staff as the PCO prepared their policy work. While PMO staff assumed the lead in some policy files, it was less common (Goldenberg 2006; Savoie 1999a). As this study details, this practice remained in place throughout the Harper years, with PCO and PMO policy staff engaging in discussions and informal signal-checking, but this was supplemented by a parallel formal written PMO policy advisory system.

Cabinet was significantly reduced when Chrétien took office, decreasing from forty to twenty-three ministers, with corresponding across-the-board reductions in political staff complements (Kernaghan and Siegel 1995, 382). Ministers were initially restricted to ten exempt staff, including secretarial support. This restriction was a response to growing criticisms of excessively influential and unelected political staff (particularly PMO staff), as a signal to renew trust in the public service, and a commitment to expenditure reductions that included the political arm (Aucoin 2010; Bakvis 2000). Despite a reversion to the use of executive assistants rather than the chief of staff title, their functions changed only marginally (Savoie 2003). A decade later, 2003 Treasury Board guidelines provided a budget allotment of $828,000 per year for exempt staff in ministers' offices, with an additional $480,000 for the secondment of public servants.[17] These funds were to be used by ministers to hire staff and configure their office as they saw fit within the broad TBS guidelines. Studies point to significantly reduced PMO involvement in the selection of ministers' staff, at least until the latter years of his final mandate when tensions with party leadership rival, and his minister of finance, Paul Martin escalated. Before then the Chrétien PMO retained the authority to veto ministers' chief of staff selection but engaged in such practices only a couple of times in its first two mandates (Jeffrey 2010, 450). After a forty-year parliamentary career, Chrétien retired in 2003, thus ending the prolonged and increasingly acrimonious leadership battle with Paul Martin, who became Canada's twenty-first prime minister.

After being returned with a minority government in 2004 through the thirty-eighth general election, the Martin administration (2003–6) implemented its approach to the organization and operation of the political arm. Accounts of the Martin years emphasize the impact of the large group of close Martin advisers known as "the board," a close group of hardened Martin partisans who had in many cases worked with him over several years in various capacities. This large group of advisers went from running a prolonged leadership quest to running the Martin PMO. Some board members took formal positions within government while others remained in the private sector. The Martin PMO organization and management practices have been described as much more horizontal and "flat" than those of PMOs past, due to Martin's own style as well as the working practices of the board and given that Martin appointed four deputy chiefs of staff for the PMO (Wells 2006; Jeffrey 2010). This is a stark contrast to the much more hierarchical organizations that have long prevailed in PMO. A consultation with Tim Murphy, who served as PMO chief of staff for the entirety of Martin's prime ministership, confirmed this flat horizontal structure.[18] Murphy also confirmed that the PMO and ministerial partisan-political policy advisory process continued to be largely informal and oral. While some written notes were produced, they tended to focus on media or event management and were not of a policy nature. In short, the public service continued to carry the pen on all written policy advice going to the prime minister. Partisan-political inputs and context from senior PMO advisers was informally sought out by senior public servants and then integrated into that advice. Accounts describe the policy advice and policymaking process in the Martin PMO as fluid, chaotic, disjointed, and quite simply unorganized (Wells 2006; Jeffrey 2010). As one board member bluntly put it, "For sure, at a minimum we never got the policy function right" (Jeffrey 2010, 454). The Martin PMO was assessed overall to be light on policy capacity. Its policy leads were seen as less capable then those of PMOs past, with its principal secretaries playing more limited roles. The flat organizational structure also resulted in "board members" weighing in on policy items, creating a loss of policy coherence and influence flowing from the policy shop (Jeffrey 2010).

Martin also created a political Cabinet committee that formally included partisan advisers as formal members. Martin's chief of staff, principal secretary, and senior PMO deputy chief of staff (operations) participated in addition to regional political ministers on the committee chaired by the prime minister. This committee was designed primarily to deal with the political positioning and strategizing rather than policymaking per se, but formal inclusion and reliance on partisan advisers is another striking organizational departure (Jeffrey 2010, 451). While former PMs undoubtedly used external sources for policy advice, Martin's board institutionalized outside advisers as key PMO sources of policy advice; of note were long-time advisers like Elly Alboim, John Duffy, and David Herle (Jeffrey 2010). The policy advisory system thus included a much more overt exogenous political component that was formally integrated into the PMO advisory "court." Finally, reverting to practices introduced in the Mulroney years, the PMO was described as much more involved in the staffing of ministerial offices. Some discretion for staffing was provided but selections were to be from approved lists (Jeffrey 2010).

In putting its own stamp on the political arms, the ministerial office reverted to the chief of staff in favour of the executive assistant model. As Benoit (2006, 164) notes, a PMO spokesperson of the day reported that the change and accompanying pay increases were a consequence of the increased responsibilities falling to ministerial offices in general. As the spokesperson put it, advisers "are being asked to do much more, dealing with parliamentary secretaries, dealing with parliamentarians, the whole role is enhanced." As per table 2.2, the Martin government (2003–6) saw a reduction in PMO staff but an increase in the overall number of political staff, with the exception of the 2006 election year.

Harper-Era Advisers in Ottawa

The interviews used to underpin this study were completed during the mandates of Stephen Harper's ministry (2006–2015). Structurally, the PMO was originally organized in a traditional fashion, despite the government's initial parliamentary minority status (2006–8, 2008–11). Many features introduced during the Martin PMO era were immediately scrapped when Conservative party executive and political scientist Ian Brodie was appointed PMO chief of staff in 2006. Brodie was given the task of organizing the first Conservative PMO in over a decade. Several interviews with Harper PMO staff described the early days as chaotic. The team were finding their footing and processes were being put in place. A former PMO partisan adviser explained that Stephen Harper having been leader of the opposition was helpful, as several positions and processes could simply be transferred or slightly amended at the PMO. Much of Harper's opposition office staff migrated over to PMO jobs or were dispatched to staff ministers' offices.[19]

The PMO was immediately organized in a traditional hierarchical manner, with all staff reporting through the PMO chief of staff. There was no principal secretary during the first minority government. Ray Novak, Harper's long-time executive assistant, was promoted to principal secretary in 2008 during Guy Giorno's term as PMO chief of staff and would eventually become the fourth and final Harper PMO chief of staff in 2014. Significant changes were introduced to the communications team structure of the Harper PMO; however, they are not covered in this overview, as they are outside the scope of this study. The newly elected Conservatives assembled a policy team under the direction of Mark Cameron, a former Liberal exempt staffer. Interviews with Cameron and others from the early Harper PMO revealed that its structure and processes, as well as staffing, were left largely to Cameron.[20] The policy team was assembled along orthodox lines, with PMO policy staff assigned to support the four existing Cabinet committees representing broad policy sectors (i.e., economics, social affairs), as well as the powerful Operations (OPs), and Priorities and Planning (P&P) committees.

A watershed reform was the deployment of a formal, written, partisan-political, PMO policy-briefing note system, in direct contrast to oral and informal partisan-political policy advisory practices that prevailed in PMOs past (Giorno 2009; Goldenberg 2006; Jeffrey 2010). This system was implemented over time within the PMO and eventually ministerial offices as well. It involved formal, written, partisan-political policy advice being provided *separately* from official PCO or departmental policy advice.[21] Ministers and the prime minister received two types of written policy advice, one partisan-political and one non-partisan public service. Another substantial change introduced was the staffing of the PMO foreign policy adviser through partisan appointment, a position that had traditionally been occupied by seconded public servants.[22] The workings of the PMO policy shop and its policy processes are detailed in subsequent chapters, but essentially more junior PMO policy advisers would manage and coordinate policy for their Cabinet committee and/or various policy sectors. This was described by those interviewed as involving significant interaction with their PCO counterparts (at the level of assistant secretaries to Cabinet), as well as policy directors and advisers in ministers' offices. Administrative-technical and partisan-political policy advice was coordinated and managed by the PMO director of policy, who reported to the PMO chief of staff.

It is important to note there have been changes to both the organization and operation of the Harper PMO as two chiefs of staff have headed up the PMO over the course of two minority governments (2006–8, 2008–11). Subsequently Nigel Wright, himself a former Mulroney-era PMO staffer and Toronto investment banker, served as chief of staff from 2011 to 2013. He was shown the door in the wake of his involvement in the personal repayment of Senator Mike Duffy's expenses. Long-time PMO staffer Ray Novak, who until then had been serving as principal secretary, replaced Wright. Several individuals have staffed the PMO director of policy position since 2006, and the policy team has also employed a number of staff. Despite these changes, Harper's PMO continued to involve itself in the staffing of ministers' offices. Popular accounts often portray it as having an iron grip, vetoing any and all appointments it wished. There are certainly instances of this, with the PMO vetoing Graham Fox from becoming chief of staff to Minister Peter MacKay, reportedly the result of Fox's previous public critiques of Harper (Martin 2006). Interviews conducted for this study confirmed heavy but not universal involvement. One PMO chief of staff explained that certain ministers would not have allowed PMO interference. More importantly, however, the practice of PMO oversight in ministerial exempt staffing was formally codified in TBS government documents in 2008. TBS guidelines were amended to explicitly include PMO sign-off on ministerial chiefs of staff as well as any appointment of a regional affairs director (Treasury Board Secretariat 2008, 5). Harper and his various chiefs of staff, like those before, have left their mark on the organization, process, and policy development and advisory practices of the PMO. Comparisons with the staffing and budgetary numbers of PMOs past are complicated by changes to reporting procedures. At the time of writing in 2014, the most recent published public accounts document a PMO personnel budget of $7.5 million for 2012–13. Treasury Board Secretariat officials provided data that the PMO employed ninety-six exempt staff in 2014.

The 2014 figures included in table 2.2 indicate that, at the time of writing, 566 political staff worked in federal ministerial offices. Increases to ministerial office budgets from which exempt staff are funded continued in large measure since the Trudeau administration. With the passing of the Federal Accountability Act, ministers have (since 2006) been forced to disclose their ministerial office budgets. As reported in the published Public Accounts and presented in table 2.3, the expenses of ministerial offices have recently been in flux.

The Harper government expenditures for ministerial office budgets saw a reduction in 2011–12 compared to previous years. In addition, as mentioned above, a clear evolution towards much greater specialization and division of labour within ministers' offices can now be observed. This is formally articulated through the Treasury Board Secretariat's classifications of potential positions included in the 2011 *Policies for Ministers' Offices*. The document includes a variety of positions by which ministers can organize and classify their exempt staff, many

Table 2.3. Total Expenditures for Federal Ministers' Office Personnel (2006–13)

Year	Total $ (personnel only)
1990–1	22.4M
1994–5	20.5M
1999–2000	28.4M
2006–7	N/A
2007–8	46,549,071
2008–9	48,226,012
2009–10	55,959,472
2010–11	51,556,842
2011–12	47,699,514
2012–13	51,019,729
2013–14	48,510,929

Source: Compiled from the annual Government of Canada's Public Accounts, volume 3, "Additional Information and Analyses" section for the years in question. Years 1990–1, 1994–5, and 1999–2000 are "personnel salaries" for all exempt ministerial staffs drawn from Treasury Board Secretariat (2006).

of which have explicitly stated policy functions, such as policy advisers, senior policy advisers, directors of policy, and the chief of staff.[23] Contemporary ministers' offices have thus become much more sophisticated in their internal division of labour and exempt staff specialization. Of particular relevance for this book is the inclusion of exempt staff with clear policy and advisory related functions. As per table 2.2, the number of political staff overall has increased throughout the Harper government in minority (2006–8, 2008–11). The most recently published Public Accounts (2013–14) indicate that the total budget for ministers' office personnel for all categories of ministers' offices over that year was 48,510,929.

British Columbia

The development of the "political arm" in British Columbia evolved more slowly than its federal counterpart. It wasn't until the 1980s that the use of politically appointed staff in the Premier's Office and ministerial offices began institutionalization, expansion, and specialization.

The history of BC's administrative style has been characterized as "laggard insularity" (Ruff, 2005, 226). Until the 1970s, BC premiers governed in a less complex system of government that facilitated personal governance through the premiers themselves. The long run of the W.A.C. Bennett government (1952–72) was an administration characterized by the "unaided" Cabinet style (Tennant 1977), including a simple structure with few standing committees; limited collegiality, in that the first minister is dominant and serves as an "architect of personal choice"; departmental autonomy; few Cabinet-level public service support staffs; and limited Cabinet-led planning functions (Dunn 1995, 11–12). BC was much slower to adopt the Cabinet committee system and strong central agencies that are the hallmark of the "institutionalized Cabinet" that had emerged federally and in other larger provinces (Dunn 1995). Public service central agencies were meagre by today's standards with credit for the "institutionalized Premier's Office" accorded to W.A.C. Bennett with the remuneration of L.J. Wallace (211). Wallace was listed as the deputy minister to the premier and, starting with the 1970–1 public accounts, was paid by the Premier's Office appropriation and not the Public Service Department of the provincial secretary. Wallace was, however, a public servant with partisan aides assuming the principal secretary role a decade later. Young and Morley sum up W.A.C.'s Premier's Office as consisting of skeletal staff, not even including an executive assistant, and where the premier "received his political advice from outside advisers and public relations experts" (1983, 63).

On the political side of the ledger, until the 1980s, the Premier's Office served as a personal support office and played little policy or advisory role. However, some administrations laboured under dictatorial leadership styles and the highly centralized Premier's Office models (White 2005, 2001). It is the Bill Bennett administration (1975–86) that is credited with modernization of the political and administrative "centre" of government in British Columbia, which included creation and use of Cabinet committees, establishment of an Office of Intergovernmental Relations, creation of a Treasury Board Secretariat, and establishment of a deputy minister to the Premier's Office (1981). The Premier's Office was restructured along the lines of the Ottawa PMO, with an eye towards overall policy coordination (Ruff 2009, 211), which included the first-ever appointment of a principal secretary from outside the public service who essentially performed the chief of staff function, a title he would later adopt. The intention was to institutionalize an Ottawa PCO-PMO-style governance arrangement, with the premier's deputy minister to serve in a PCO-like policy coordination function and a principal secretary later to be termed a chief of staff to "perform the PMO function, namely, partisan input" (Dunn 1995, 249). This dual institutionalized structure of a chief of staff and deputy minister to the premier would last through nine successive governments over the last twenty-five years (Ruff 2005).[24]

The 1990s were characterized by more frequent changes in the Premier's Office with each successive premier bringing their administrative style and mark to the design and operation of government. The frequency of change consequently led to higher turnover and varied use of the chief of staff to the premier,[25] with its office holders playing a less significant policy role during the Clark (1996–9) administration, as a result of the close working relationship between the premier and his deputy minister (Ruff 2009). Strong central administrative units like the Cabinet Policy and Communications Secretariat were key sources of support to the Harcourt and Clark administrations. Continued development of central agency institutions and expansion of the role of the Premier's Office during the 1990s has led some to argue that by the 1990s, BC, like its federal counterpart, was "governed from the centre" (Ruff 2009, 205). The decade-long Campbell administration saw the role and activities of partisan advisers continue to evolve. Comprehensive review of the evolution of BC's political arm is difficult, given that there are fewer accounts for ministers' office advisers. Attempts to secure historical information on the number of political staff in British Colombia were met with mixed success. As per table 2.4, figures were provided only for the 1996–2011 period because there was a change in how that data are collected and maintained by the British Columbia Public Service Commission. This data is supplemented with information from secondary sources providing as comprehensive an account as possible on the use of ministerial political staffs more generally.

BC ministers' office staffs also demonstrate a pattern of growth and specialization. The 1983 government of W.R. Bennett featured ministerial offices allotted an administrative staff of five and a complement of three political staff, with an overall budget of approximately $75,000 (Marley 1997). Those levels and structure were reportedly maintained for the subsequent Vander Zalm (1986–90) and Harcourt governments (1991–6) (Morley 1993, 201; Marley 1997, 6). The ministerial office budgets were $115,000 in 1986 and $158,000 under Harcourt in 1991 (Marley 1997, 7). In the selection of their ministerial political staff, Harcourt ministers were given free rein, but the Premier's Office maintained

Table 2.4. Political Staff in BC (1996–2011)

Year	1996	1997	1998	1999	2000	2001	2002	2003	2004	2005	2006	2007	2008	2009	2010	2011
Total Staff	108	97	101	115	140	159	109	105	101	101	96	109	114	119	112	100

Source: Adapted from a table provided to author 8 November 2011 by the BC Public Service Commission. For the full table with departmental breakdown and classification, see appendix D.

Table 2.5. BC Premier's Office Expenses and Staffing Levels (2001–11)

Year	Number of staff (FTE)	Expenses ($000)
2001–2	470	2,882
2002–3	35	2,818
2003–4	35	2,818
2004–5	35	2,786
2005–6	41	3,104
2006–7	40	3,549
2007–8	40	3,676
2008–9	40	3,810
2009–10	40	3,319
2010–11	39	2,878

Source: Compiled from department service plans, Office of the Premier. Unless otherwise indicated, revised and final figures as presented in subsequent service plans were used for accuracy.

The staffing figure for 2001–2 includes five other central administrative agencies and secretariats in addition to the Premier's Office. No figures were available for Premier's Office staff alone. Revised figures drawn from 2002–3 service plan, Office of the Premier. The staffing level for the Premier's Office is reported as estimated in the 2009/10–2011/12 Premier's Office service plan. Figures for 2009–10 and 2011 were not listed, even as estimates in the yearly service plans, likely due to a change in premiers. This figure was listed as "planned" in the 2009/10–2011/12 Premier's Office service plan.

a veto over such appointments, although it was seldom exercised (Morley 1993, 201).

Campbell-Era Partisan Advisers in British Columbia, 2001–9

Incremental increases to the political arm of government, particularly the Premier's Office, were undertaken after the 2001 election of the

Campbell government, which dramatically reorganized the public service and political arm of the Premier's Office. The traditional design of one deputy minister to the premier was altered with the appointment of a second deputy minister to the premier (Ruff 2005, 229). These positions are noted in the BC case, as opposed to the federal and New Brunswick cases, because even though the deputy ministers are physically located elsewhere, they are considered part of the BC Premier's Office. One deputy minister retained the traditional role of secretary to Cabinet and the other was charged with leading a "core services review" of government-wide restructuring. That deputy was given the title of deputy minister, corporate planning and restructuring. As per table 2.5, in its inaugural year the Campbell Premier's Office appears to have a much larger in staff than in subsequent years as a result of inclusion of the executive council office and large Public Affairs Bureau staff. In 2001 it included 470 staff and a budget of $2,882,000 for the operation of Premier's Office staff proper.

Considerable reorganization of the Premier's Office was also undertaken with the chief of staff position maintained but significantly expanded in scope. Campbell appointed Martyn Brown, his chief of staff, who would remain in that position for the decade in which Campbell served as premier – the longest tenure for a provincial chief of staff in recent Canadian history.[26] Brown performed the traditional role of strategic adviser and "firefighter" but was assigned the additional responsibilities of caucus liaison and management as well as external stakeholder management (Ruff 2005, 229). The organization of the Premier's Office went through three acknowledged iterations in the office's "service plans." A minister of state for intergovernmental relations directly under the premier, between the chief of staff and deputy ministers, was in place in 2001 but was subsequently removed in the 2005 and 2011 Premier's Office service plans. All three designs offer a clear illustration of the chief of staff / deputy minister to premier configuration. Additional policy advisory capacity was introduced from outside the public service through the twin additions of the Premier's Technology Council and the British Columbia Progress Board. As per a revised version of the organizational chart for the Office of the Premier, these bodies were included in the policy advisory system available to the premier in addition to the usual suspects.[27]

While such changes allow insight into how the Premier's Office structured the sources of policy advice, they are less informative on the substantive "content" dimensions of that advice. The office certainly benefited from the policy coordination and advisory services of these new non-governmental advisory bodies, and the continued presence of the twin deputy ministers located within the Premier's Office. The revised 2002 Premier's Office service plan organizational chart documents the removal of the minister of state for intergovernmental affairs from the Premier's Office and also sets out new direct accountability relationships to the premier for the premier's chief of staff and twin Premier's Office deputy ministers. Staffing levels and the Premier's Office budget were fairly consistent, with 2008–9 the most expensive year for the Campbell government. By 2011, estimates of the Premier's Office indicated a staff of thirty-nine and an overall budget of $2,878,000. Organizational charts and budgets are useful for tracking major organizational or resource allocation shifts but are less informative about the actual policy functions of partisan advisers "at the centre."

Further clarification can be gained through the 2010/11–2012/13 service plan that provides for the third and final organizational diagram, included as annex C. It also detailed the "purpose" of the Premier's Office and continues to use the language of previous service plans outlining the functions of the Premier's Office:

• Articulates government's goals, commitments, and priorities;
• Works with ministries and Crown agencies to ensure communications of those goals, commitments, and priorities and to track and monitor their implementation;
• Leads the public service and, with the Deputy Minister's Council, leads implementation of the corporate human resources plan for the BC Public Service, Being the Best;
• Provides support for the operation and decision-making processes of Cabinet and its committees; and
• Works directly with the federal government and with all ministries and Crown agencies to ensure that relations with federal, provincial, municipal, territorial, and international governments advance British Columbia's interests. (Office of the Premier 2010, 8)

Also of note, the revised Premier's Office organizational chart included in the 2011 provincial budget (see annex C) provides a more detailed breakdown of the Premier's Office staff. Germane to this study, the chart lists the deputy chief of staff for issues management and policy coordination. This partisan adviser was the point person who provided policy and legislative advice along with coordination for Cabinet and ministers (Ruff 2009). During interviews with senior Premier's Office staff, this role was explained as ongoing since 2001 but the policy coordination was added to the issues management title in more recent descriptions of the Premier's Office staff structure. Senior partisan advisers in BC also reported active participation in Cabinet committee business but explained that their roles were as "unofficial members" of such committees as representatives of the premier.[28] This stands in contrast to recent practices in both the federal and New Brunswick cases where first minister's office partisan advisers were at times formal Cabinet committee members.

An additional position of "senior coordinator, issues management" is also represented, reported to have also existed for several years. It includes some policy coordination, and was designed to assist the deputy chief of staff and permit greater attention to strategic issues management and policy coordination. The chief of staff also engages in policy coordination and oversight and ensures that communication and messaging is aligned with the partisan political perspective of the governing party (Ruff 2009, 213). These three political staff positions are *the* policy positions within the Premier's Office. The historical expansion of the use of political staff, particularly at the Premier's Office level in their role in the policy and Cabinet process is underscored. As Ruff concludes in a review of the dominance of the executive in BC, the Premier's Office is a commanding force: "The premier is in every sense the first minister, and his office and its staff visibly dominate the policy direction and management of provincial government" (208). This study is aimed at understanding how that dominance is achieved from a policy perspective. What role do partisan advisers in the Premier's Office play in policymaking? How are partisan advisers involved in policymaking or policy advice at the ministerial office level?

While previous governments may have played a role in the recruitment or placement of political staffs at the ministers' office level, the Campbell government explicitly documented such practices. In a 2001 letter of instructions to all ministers, the Campbell government advised ministers on their staff and its relationship to the political and administrative actors in the system. The letter, similar to that issued by the Chrétien government elected in 1993, emphasized "lean" and efficient government. It set out how ministers' offices should be organized and configured, including the allotment of a single ministerial assistant (partisan adviser) and single executive assistant (clerical). It also detailed ministers' and advisers' expected comportment with other offices, including senior public service and Premier's Office staffs, and details regarding the Cabinet and Cabinet committee structure and operation (Ruff 2005, 234).

The classification of political staff underwent a change in 2006, the result of an overhaul to the pay scales for political staff. A press release issued by Premier Campbell's office detailed that increased salary levels for "senior political staff" were intended to ensure wages were competitive with other jurisdictions to attract and retain qualified staffs (Office of the Premier 2006b). These new categories included: Band A – representing ministerial assistants with a salary range of $66,150–$94,500; Band B – executive assistants with a salary range of $51,300–$68,400; Premier's Office chief of staff and deputy chief of staff captured by Band C (range $146,361–$185,390) and Band D ($108,000–$144,000), respectively (Office of the Premier 2006a). By the final year of the Campbell government in 2011, the political arm in British Columbia consisted of approximately forty staff in the Premier's Office and a complement of twenty-six ministerial assistants who served as partisan advisers to ministers.[29]

New Brunswick

The final case examined is the government of New Brunswick, with interviews completed during the Graham government (2006–10). The smallest of the three cases in provincial population, size of government, and "political staffs," New Brunswick provides an interesting comparative case. The province had but three premiers from 1960 to 1999, including Robichaud (1960–70), Hatfield (1970–87), and McKenna (1987–97). Since then it has seen frequent leadership changes, including the premierships of Frenette (1997–8), Terriault (1998–9), Lord (1999–2006), Graham (2006–10), Alward (2010–14), and Gallant (2014–). Compared to the two other cases, there is little scholarly assessment of provincial politics or the core executive in New Brunswick. Savoie (1989, 2000) underscores that Premiers Robichaud and Hatfield respectively went to great lengths to ensure the development of a professional public service in New Brunswick. For example, they looked to leading professionals from other jurisdictions and recruited them to key public service positions. Savoie's (2000, 277) characterization of the various governments from Robichaud to Lord is that of a group of political elites who worked with the public service, seeing them as a solution, not a problem. A review of the literature on New Brunswick's political arm and political-administrative relations paints a picture of a very small and intimate executive governance style. Savoie's (1989, 37) previous characterization that "relations between politicians and administrators are much more intense and frequent than they are in larger governments, where cabinet ministers are compelled to delegate considerable decision making authority to their departmental officials" appears equally apt for the contemporary governance of the province.

New Brunswick's political arm is first and foremost quite small. In historical terms, for most of the early twentieth century the Premier's Office consisted of just one secretary. Arthur Doyle documents the first full-time executive secretary having been appointed in 1935 (Doyle 1984, vii, viii). One can infer that ministers' offices during the same period would have been even more basic. For most of late twentieth century, ministers' offices operated with only two political staff, one executive assistant and a secretary. One close observer characterizes the small and relatively untrained modern political arm in New Brunswick as resulting in a category of political staffs who in no way "rival" the deputy cadre (Bouchard 1999, 104). Rather, they are described as concerned primarily with the ministers' constituency issues. The exception is first minister's office partisan advisers who are noted as influential sources of advice and policy formulation, particularly the chief of staff (Bouchard 2014).

Whereas the evolution of the political arm in BC as well as the federal government includes clearly demarcated expansionary and specialization phases, neither is completely discernible in the New Brunswick case. While there has been a small increase in the number and specialization of first minister's office political staff, the same cannot be confirmed for departmental ministerial offices. Detailed historical or contemporary data on first ministerial or ministers' offices are simply not available. Correspondence with senior human resource officials was met with the simple pronouncement that such data were not available, and resource constraints prevented any research to generate such data, if even possible. An official was able to confirm that, as of September 2006, there were twenty-two executive assistants and twenty executive secretaries at the beginning of the Graham administration.[30] As of November 2011, the same official confirmed the new Alward government employed eighteen executive assistants and fifteen executive secretaries.[31] The official explained this continued longstanding practices of ministers employing a ministerial executive assistant and a secretary.

While official figures are not available, scholarly and biographical documents have noted sources of politically appointed policy advice. For example, a strong role for political appointees as sources of political and policy advice has been reported in the Hatfield and McKenna administrations (Hyson 2005; Savoie 1989). More recently, Dunn (2006, 242) found that under the Conservative Lord government, partisan advisers were official members of Cabinet committees in a similar fashion to Prime Minister Martin's organization. Dunn noted that the executive committee included the premier, his chief of staff, the secretary to Cabinet, secretary to Policy and Priorities Committee, president of the Regional Development Corporation, eight ministers and their deputies, and the deputy minister of intergovernmental affairs. Interviews completed for this study confirmed a somewhat similar arrangement existed under the Graham government. Ministers, deputy ministers, and the chief of staff all participated as official members of an ad hoc Cabinet committee.[32] A long-time student of New Brunswick public administration notes the important policy functions that rest with first minister's partisan advisers, notably the chief of staff, that deputies receive their policy mandates and subsequent requests for policy development from Premier's Office advisers, and that "traditionally, when seeking policy direction, Deputies turn to the Chief of Staff who represents the ideal route for accessing the Premier and who is authorized to speak for him" (Bouchard 2014, 111). This account of their policy function highlights the important substantive and procedural advisory and formulation activity attributable to first minister's office partisan advisers. A policy function is also explicit in the New Brunswick Civil Service Act section 27.2(1),[33] which sets out that those working in a central agency (e.g., Premier's Office) who are "politically restricted employees" have duties and responsibilities such as "providing advice, opinions, proposals, recommendations, analyses or policy options to the Premier, a Minister, Executive Council, a member of Executive Council, a committee of or a member of a committee of Executive Council or a deputy head." Bouchard's most recent characterization of the deputy minister–minister relationship in New Brunswick points to the political control exercised by the premier as the only viable means for responsiveness. On the basis of interviews, he claims, "Deputies come to view the Minister as a work colleague at best, sometimes an employee, a spokesperson for the Department, but very rarely do the Deputies view their Minister as a supervisor" (Bouchard 2014, 109).

Conclusion

This chapter has argued that partisan advisers in these cases have evolved through a three-stage process of institutionalization, expansion, and specialization. New data has been presented on the number of "political staff" in two cases, as well as a few federal Cabinet conclusions that have gone unreported in existing studies. The evolutionary phase was clearly discernible in the federal and British Columbia cases. The pattern is, historically, varied on two important fronts. The record suggests that in the federal case this institutionalization, expansion, and specialization began in the late 1960s and has progressed more intensively than in the two subnational cases. In the latter, limited expansion and more recent but restricted specialization date only from the 1980s. Careful review also indicates that the pattern can also vary within governments. The political arm itself can be configured in different ways with degrees of expansion and specialization varying at ministerial and first ministers' office locations with concomitant implications for core executive resource exchanges. This is precisely what scholarly and historical accounts suggest has occurred in New Brunswick (Hyson 2005; Bouchard 2014). Strikingly, the federal case reveals that the overall growth in the total complement of ministerial staffs has been in ministers' offices. This chapter sets the scene for those that follow in foreshadowing differences in function, organization, sophistication, and institutional location. These will be useful for improved depictions of partisan advisers' policy work and its implications for core executives and governance.

Chapter 3

Buffers and Bridges at the "Centre"

Introduction

Prime Ministers' and Premiers' Offices provide a unique vantage point to explore and better understand partisan advisers' policy work and core executive operations. They are widely agreed to be influential, with disagreement relegated to questions of the extent and manner by which they exercise that influence (Bernier et al. 2005; Bakvis 2000; Savoie 1999a). This chapter uses the buffering and bridging concepts to explore how that influence is rooted in advisers' policy advisory activity. It was clear in all cases that first ministers' office partisan advisers, as buffers, engaged in directly providing policy advice. Across the cases it was also described as activity that was at times partisan-political and at other times administrative-technical. The latter was typically reported as part of their interactions with senior public servants but extended to varying degrees to activities involving Cabinet, ministers, and other actors in the advisory system. For their part, senior public service officials across all three cases explicitly recognized partisan-political policy advice as a legitimate part of policymaking. In keeping with international findings, some officials, and even some political actors as well, suggested that first ministers' office partisan advisers were considered a viable means to contain such activity to the political sphere of government (Eichbaum and Shaw 2008; Aucoin 2010). This insolating property was reported in all three cases but was particularly acute in the federal and New Brunswick cases.

Advisers' central location also raises important potential implications for their bridging functions within advisory systems and the core executive. Here too partisan instances of partisan-political and administrative-technical types of bridging were reported, consisting of the integration and synthesis of disparate sources of policy advice. This was important to core executive resource exchanges, as it increased, and in some cases decreased, advisory inputs for decision-makers (Craft 2013). Bridging was frequently described in conjunction with policy advisory activities *beyond* those of formal policy development, such as involving the integration of policy advice on current political and international events and tied to policy issues that were short-, medium-, or long-term in nature. In all three cases, bridging was consistently characterized in predominantly endogenous terms, with First Minister's Office advisers explicitly stating a general preference and practice of "pushing out" stakeholder bridging to ministers, their advisers, or departments. This chapter details how partisan advisers at the centre shared similar perspectives on their advisory functions. However, important differences are also detailed involving how advisers participated in advisory systems, with whom they interacted, and how they sought to exercise policy-based influence. These differences provide nuance for improved understanding of the ways by which this set of actors engages in core executive policy-based resource exchanges, the types of resources they exchange, and how the political arm seeks to secure political control and policy responsiveness (Craft 2015b; Elgie 2011; Savoie 1983).

First Ministers' Office Partisan Advisers' Buffering

PMO Buffering

A range of interviews conducted with PCO and Harper PMO staff revealed an increasingly formal policy advisory system involving significant input and integration from parallel partisan-political and public service policy advisory sources. PMO partisan advisers described their buffering as the provision of partisan-political policy advice that increased the availability of that form of policy advice for the prime minister and Cabinet. It was explained that when it was being set up, the Harper PMO policy advisory process was chaotic, informal, and primarily oral. Many recounted a bumpy transition period when the policy shop was established but spoke of its maturation and capacity development over time. They benefited from an experienced initial director of policy, Mark Cameron, who had served as a partisan adviser to ministers in a previous Liberal government in Ottawa. The policy shop, then numbering five junior policy advisers and a director of policy, divided policy areas along broad themes (i.e., economics and social affairs) and Cabinet committees similar to accounts of how other recent PMOs were organized (See Goldenberg 2006; Savoie 1999a; Jeffrey 2010). The more "junior" of the PMO advisers interviewed explained their policy purviews included several policy areas at times numbering eight or more. They worked with ministers' office partisan advisers on policy in these areas. They also worked, typically in conjunction with the PMO director of policy, with senior PCO staff for policy work tied to the powerful Priority and Planning (P&P) and Operations (OPs) Cabinet committees.

Multiple respondents at various levels of seniority described the partisan policy advisory process as consisting of a mix of oral and written advice. However, there was universal agreement that the great majority of policy advice provided to Prime Minister Harper was in writing. This finding came very much as a surprise. PMOs have historically relied solely on oral advisory practices. Practitioners and students of the Canadian political executive have argued this to be a consequence of increased media scrutiny and a growing emphasis on transparency and access to information legislation (Savoie 1999a, 2003). It was explained by several participants that the development of the formal written briefing system was to ensure that the PMO could directly provide the prime minister with written partisan-political policy advice without it being interpreted or passed through the PCO.[34] Senior PMO policy staff emphasized that all policy items flowing up to the prime minister included a written policy advisory overlay from the PMO policy shop. In fact, those interviewed detailed a systematic attempt to coordinate the flow of written policy advice flowing through the PMO, typically in response to PCO "clerk's notes" or formal written policy advice going to the prime minister. This involved a daily "policy advice tracking sheet" and two binders – a "policy advice tracking binder" – and a "decision binder" that included all policy advice received (PMO and PCO) on which the prime minister had already signed off. The tracking sheet was the coordination mechanism indicating if the PMO had responded to the PCO note, when a response was expected. The prime minister could, of course, respond to PCO policy documents such as decision notes, information notes, and the like without having the PMO policy overlay – but those interviewed made it clear that Harper wanted both. Similarly, one senior PMO staff recounted that the prime minister had made it known that he was *never* going to make decisions without PCO policy advice. Again, the prime minister or a minister could certainly discount or ignore the public service's advice in favour of a more politically sensitive analysis or option(s). However, by all accounts Harper's clear preference, and the entire PMO-PCO advisory system, was configured to ensure that both streams of policy advice were available for consideration in tandem, the key distinction being that at the PMO-PCO level this involved PCO notes going to the prime minister *directly* and his holding those notes until PMO overlays were provided. As is detailed later, ministerial offices saw both streams of notes provided to the minister *concurrently*. The PMO/PCO system was updated daily with outstanding notes tracked, and therefore attempted to synchronize the flow of advice for the prime minister's consideration. Everyone interviewed made it clear that policy advice was also frequently provided verbally, typically within the PMO policy ranks up to the chief of staff, or as required, by senior PMO officials directly to the prime minister. Senior PMO partisan advisers often provided that advice during regularized morning meetings and via more ad hoc policy meetings. This more informal oral advisory process is in keeping with the practices of PMOs past (Campbell and Szablowski 1979; Jeffrey 2010; Savoie 1999a, 2010, 2011).

Advisers candidly acknowledged they understood themselves to be only one of many sources of policy advice sought out and used by Prime Minister Harper or other core executive actors (e.g., ministers, senior officials, other partisan advisers). Various PMO partisan advisers described their advisory activity, regardless of method, as aimed at "adding value." Buffering was predominantly described as challenging policy advice to ensure its "fit" with political goals and objectives. However, many also noted that they would challenge policy advice flowing to decision-makers on technical aspects or with respect to its logic or comprehensiveness. A response from a PMO director of policy illustrates his perceptions of policy advice as well as the type and nature of his policy advisory activity:

> Their advice [public service] is more technical and it's deeper in terms of the policy specifics. As I say, we wouldn't try to out-bureaucrat the bureaucrat. They would write an analysis of we should do this or that based on … it would be a technical argument. They would have all the information on what was done before and what was done elsewhere and all of that stuff. They would put it all together into, you know, a detailed analysis. Then we would come along and say much more superficially, you know, "Yes, we agree with this and we should proceed." Or, you know, "No, we don't, and here are the reasons why." Sometimes our comments would be

technical or what we saw as deficiencies in their analysis and sometimes it would be more political. That's a great factual analysis, they're recommending a course of action but it doesn't take into account, like I said, "Last week the minister said we were going to do something else," or even more, "Last week the prime minister said we were going to do something else." Or, you know, this is not the way the election platform happened to go. Or, you know, this is going to throw a whole region of the country out of work and that might not be the best thing to do. (P13)

Senior PMO partisan advisers described their policy advisory practices as providing an extra voice that was more political and tantamount to ensuring consistency with the stated partisan-political agenda and electoral mandate. The emphasis in the Harper PMO was on providing ongoing written and oral policy advice for the prime minister to consider among other sources of advice he consulted. This involved the communication of advice flowing up from the PMO policy shop or from PMO chiefs of staff on any number of policy items. Junior PMO partisan advisers reported that their policy advice to the prime minister was almost always conveyed via the formal briefing system. The more informal oral types of advice were generally restricted to the PMO chief of staff or director of policy. When asked to comment on whether policy advice was written or oral, all senior PMO policy staff were unequivocal – it was written. As one former PMO policy director described it,

The Privy Council office has 1000 people working with the departments to generate notes, so there was an unending flow of stuff to deal with. There was opportunity for … the prime minister typically sought a lot of informal input and he was also very detailed, and if he didn't get formal input from you on something, he might put you on the spot in a meeting and say, "By the way, I've been waiting on your note for this for three days where is it, and what do you have to say about it?" (P12)

This is a point worth emphasizing. The written partisan-political policy advisory system implemented speaks to the professionalization and specialization argument. It represents a more sophisticated, institutionalized, and – most strikingly – separate channel for written policy advice for first ministers. It marks a significant departure from established practice of previous PMOs but also potential divergences at the political-administrative nexus, one where the political arm is moving towards written and documented advice, while the public service is headed in the opposite direction of an oral advisory culture (Savoie 1999a, 2003, 2008). The political arm benefits from the exemption of ministerial offices from the provisions of access to information, while the public service is subject to the act. This point was not lost on the prime minister's senior policy staff. Many, having spent enough time around Ottawa, or having done homework on previous arrangements, were clear about key differences in the organization and operation of the Harper political arm of government. One PMO director of policy interviewed noted that he had read many leading accounts such as those of Savoie (1999a, 2003) and Goldenberg (2006). He remarked that their reviews of the Chrétien years seemed to emphasize the verbal culture and practices of policy work of PMO staff, but he painted the opposite picture when characterizing the Harper PMO: "We didn't have a lot of time to sit around and chat with PM Harper. I mean that's kind of not the way he does things. I mean we would certainly have meetings and talk to him in person, but we, you know, would certainly send him notes on most things. That tended to be the ways things were done" (P13).

Many of the advisers interviewed explained that as a rule of thumb, this type of system and practice extended equally to how they worked with ministers. It was not that policy advice was not provided verbally, it certainly was, but the logic was that it was best to have *written* policy advice included in a minister's "night package." These are the binders that ministers take home with them that allow them the opportunity to review policy advice, in detail, at their convenience. The written partisan-political policy advice was created knowing that a PCO note on the subject had been created or was in the works. The PMO note was then to be provided so the prime minister could read it at the same time and benefit from both types of advice. The PMO's own advisory process was described in very bureaucratic and systematized terms. Junior PMO partisan advisers, with their particular files and policy responsibilities, would typically draft their policy advice, which was then reviewed and formalized with the PMO policy director. When deemed ready, it would then move up the chain of command and ultimately, in most instances, be provided to the prime minister, who already had the public service policy advice from the PCO. These written, formal, routinized partisan-political policy notes were reported to accompany virtually *all* policy advice from the public service. The process was initially managed by the PMO director of policy but was subsequently transferred to a deputy chief-of-staff-level PMO partisan adviser. This written policy advisory system was supplemented by oral briefings, which occurred formally in a daily morning meeting, or as needed. Multiple PMO chiefs of staff and policy directors interviewed reported providing verbal policy advice *during* Cabinet meetings, at times to supplement previously provided written policy advice or in an ad hoc fashion when requested. Those who detailed such accounts character-ized the experience as being at times somewhat terrifying, given they were being put on the spot to provide additional information, clarifica-tion, or advice. This same system implemented in the PMO was subse-quently instituted at the ministerial office level as well. There seemed, however, to be a bit more variance in how rigidly the system was adopted or followed. Former PMO chief of staff Ian Brodie outlined the genesis of the written briefing system, explaining, "PCO would prepare a note for signature by the clerk to go to the PM. And in parallel to that, PMO staff would produce usually a shorter note, that we would usu-ally try and time it so they would both reach the PM's overnight read-ing binder at the same time. It took some time to work that out, a little more than a year."

Two former PMO chiefs interviewed explained that while they did provide written briefings to the prime minister, they also frequently provided advice orally. On the totality of PMO policy advice, however, both were unequivocal that the majority of advice provided by the PMO was through the written and formal advisory system. For instance, Guy Giorno, when asked about PMO advisory practices, responded, "I can simply say that the primary vehicle for providing advice in the Prime Minister's Office under me and right now under Nigel Wright is writ-ten." PMO directors of policy queried on their policy advisory practices presented more mixed results. Mark Cameron, the first PMO policy director, was clear that the majority of his advice was provided orally, as the written briefing system was still being developed. Conversely, other directors of policy interviewed described predominantly pro-viding formal written policy advice. When asked if the policy shop's advice-giving was oral or written, one PMO director of policy gave a sense of the volume of activity involved, explaining "The latter. I might have written, myself personally, maybe 300 to 400 notes during the time. But that's actually a fairly small proportion of the notes that went through" (P12).

Both PMO and ministerial partisan advisers, in addition to depu-ties, noted the importance of understanding the advisory preferences of ministers. Some were "readers" who preferred to receive written briefs, while others wanted to sit and talk through policies or operational issues. In the case of Prime Minister Harper, all respondents universally described his preference for written advice. Many commented on his mastery of policy files as a consequence of his desire and ability to read through all briefing materials, originating from his political team as well as the public service. One senior PMO partisan adviser recounted how a Cabinet minister, after a Cabinet meeting, could not believe that the prime minister was even very familiar with Cabinet "annex items."[35] In addition, PMO staff interviewed all stated that there was a significant amount of oral policy advice but that it was more informally provided, and that on substantive policy files or major political issues there would be more ad hoc advice-giving. One PMO policy director explained that the advisory practices often involved bringing together the affected parties from the public service and the political arm. The PMO policy director would call a meeting, and whether it was a particular policy issue or a Cabinet agenda, the relevant actors would go through the item. It was explained that the PMO policy director would chair the meeting and ask a series of questions. As the adviser recounted, "What's your perspective on this, what's your perspective on that, what's your perspective on this and try and sort out any difficulties and let them know where the prime minister is coming from on these things as well" (P13). This and many other responses underscored multilateral advisory-based resource exchanges that often involved central agency, departmental, and PMO and ministerial partisan advisers as needed.

It was explained that the desire of then Clerk of the Privy Council Kevin Lynch to give his (and PCO) advice without integration of political advice from the PMO, as had traditionally occurred, was in fact a precipitating reason for the development of a PMO-written advisory system. Lynch was widely respected as a seasoned and capable public servant and worked effectively with former Harper PMO chief Ian Brodie. Political-administrative relations were, however, contentious and strained under PMO Chief Giorno.[36] When asked about his dealings with the PCO, Giorno responded,

There was also a desire to centralize everything [at the PCO]. Well I don't think that governments or any organization work well when everything is funnelled through one person. When that was changed [Wayne Wouters was appointed clerk of the Privy Council on July 1, 2009], and you know, the clerk was someone who had actual line departmental experience and not just central agency experience but actually worked at, you know, Fisheries and Oceans and different places and understood that there could be a positive relationship between a minister's team and a deputy's team, and that's how you got things done working collaboratively. I think things have worked quite well. I've come to realize that the way I thought things would work in Ottawa is how they do work, and it was just personalities.

Buffering, as a means of securing additional political control, was a principal reason for the advent of the formalized written political briefing note system used both at the PMO and ministerial levels. A spillover effect of this development was the greater isolation of the public service from more partisan aspects of policy advice. In short, partisan-political policy advice was at the time (formally) provided independently of the PCO, who in turn could provide their "professional" policy advice. The PCO advice remains sensitive to the political "tone" but could leave the partisan-political advisory aspects to others. Interviews with current senior PCO officials confirmed that there are ongoing interactions on a policy level and that the PCO was aware that the PMO was providing policy advice in parallel to the PCO. In fact, more than one official commented on the normative benefit of such a system. There was acknowledgment that political calculations were a recognized and an understood part of policy advice, and having partisan advisers served exactly the purpose of keeping the public service *out* of the partisan-political aspects of policy advice. A senior PCO official explained, "It's really important that theirs is a separate channel of political advice, and knowing that that's happening does make it easier" (PCO1). When asked to comment on the separate briefing system, the same senior PCO official explained,

We know that the PMO is doing, and they should be doing, and thank God they're doing the political advice. Because then there's no issue for us about how to in a nice way say, you know, there may be considerations in the context for governing to consider think about. No, someone needs to say, "This may be a complete firestorm with this stakeholder, with this MP, with this region, at a purely partisan level." That makes it easier for us to do our job, knowing he has his own separate channel of advice. And again if they're weighing in – and they don't, but in an extreme if they were weighing in without ever looking at the policy stuff or without regard to the substance of it – that would be a problem, but that's not a problem at all.

This type of response indicates that partisan advisers are not only recognized sources of policy advice, but are in fact providing policy advice that spans partisan-political and administrative-technical dimensions. This is an important point for those interested in the broader notions of policy work at the political-administrative nexus. Scholars have acknowledged for some time that appointed political staffs, and elected politicians, often must straddle both worlds, that policymaking and governance require evidentiary, technical, and political forms of knowledge and advisory work for policy to be legitimate and effective (Head 2008; Prasser 2006). Partisan advisers are unique in the sense that they are one of the few actors who can engage in "omnibus advisory functions" involving the connection of policy crafting and political manoeuvring (Rockman 2000), the "amphibians" that serve as policy professionals while retaining partisan links (Campbell 1988). Central agency officials interviewed readily acknowledged that partisan considerations were a reality in the policy advisory system. While partisan advisers could interact with officials or other actors on administrative-technical policy advisory terms, their partisan-political advisory activity was beneficially restricted to ministers' offices. However, as is detailed below, there were significant differences in how this was reported in the two subnational cases, further highlighting important distinctions in how policy advice, from various sources, was provided and used, and how the political arm engaged in advisory practices including but beyond the supply of partisan-political types of policy advice.

Buffering from the West Annex

First minister's office partisan advisers in British Columbia described considerable buffering. Premier's Office advisers interviewed from the Campbell governments (2001–11) characterized their role as primarily involving policy advice, policy development, and issues management. Respondents explained that the majority of their time was spent on policy-related activity linked to formal Cabinet and Cabinet committee activity, as well as informal and formal briefings to both the premier and the Cabinet. Buffering in BC involved a high degree of commentary on sources of policy advice within and outside of government. It was explained to consist of contestation of the scrutiny of public service advice. In this case, partisan advisers described their advisory role as a "public interest check" on proposed bureaucratic policy advice.

When one adviser was asked to describe her activities in the Premier's Office, she explained, "In our Premier's Office I saw my primary role as a strategic adviser to both the premier and the executive council on both issues and matters of public policy. And so I was the primary point person for political council on issues and policy" (P4). Another stated that the majority of her time was spent on policy and advisory-related activities. When asked to describe her role, she responded, "Fundamentally, it was policy advice, policy development, and policy coordination" (P3). It was explained that this was in large part a product of her ability to sit on more Cabinet committees than some ministers, providing a comprehensive view of government. As the adviser characterized it, "fundamentally, it was reading information, reading binders, interviewing and meeting with deputies, ADMs, and other senior civil servants. Analysing policies and developing policies: that was the fundamental task" (P3).

Buffering at the first minister's office in BC was, as with all cases, focused on ensuring that the first minister and Cabinet had the "complete" picture and were well informed. In the BC case, Premier's Office advisers reported engaging in a mix of formal and informal advisory activity. Formal policy advice in this case was not, as described above, produced via a parallel written political policy advisory briefing system. Rather, partisan advisers described their advisory and policy formulation as typically occurring in conjunction with institutionalized and routinized Cabinet activity. One senior Premier's Office adviser explained, "The policy side, which is in that case acting as the main liaison between the premier and the executive council and the public service ensuring that there was … that the ramifications of policy decisions were well thought through," adding, "So that was a big part of what I did on the policy side, was to gather that collective wisdom and make sure it was known to the executive council or the premier and played a role in ensuring that the right policy decisions were made" (P4). Here again we get a sense of the resource exchanges and advice circulating within the advisory system. The Premier's Office was a hub through which partisan advisers worked with central agency officials and ministers to ensure policy advice had been provided and challenged, and was available as needed. These are precisely the types of activities expected in a context now consisting of sharing truths with multiple actors of influence (Prince 2007; Craft 2014).

The same Premier's Office advisers interviewed in BC made it clear that they not only provided "content" themselves, but that they often commented upon the advice provided by others. They also made it quite evident that they were one of many sources of policy advice. They would provide their own advice in addition to the sources of advice communicated up the public service channels, and in concert with or in response to exogenous sources of policy advice. Another first minister's office partisan adviser described how advice giving was undertaken primarily through briefings and those would tend to be organized in conjunction with formal Cabinet committee work or a specific issue. Some of the briefings would be delivered only to the premier, and others would be shared with a wider group, which could include ministers as well as other first minister's partisan advisers. He explained that in terms of policy advice, "those would be prolonged sessions or meetings with him and/or with others present ... Cabinet ministers. Briefings on the budget, briefings on health, briefings on the Cabinet agenda, etc., which would be scheduled, those would be predictable, routine. That's mostly when I met with and gave advice to him. But in terms of proportion of the time, it was very dependent on the nature of what issues were breaking on a given week, what's before the Cabinet, how much time he needs in preparation" (P3).

The adviser further explained that there were also advisory functions tied to senior Cabinet committee obligations that the premier had, and those also required buffering on a range of issues or questions that may have emerged. Those interviewed from the first minister's office explained that while they rarely composed formal briefing notes on their own, they would often comment either in writing or orally on notes prepared by the public service. The written comments were, however, pithy comments in the margins, not detailed policy analysis and advice as reported in the federal case. The more political forms of policy advice were provided orally, after having gone through a briefing note prepared by the public service. Again, a key difference is that these public service notes were then revised by the public service to incorporate feedback received into a "master" note by public service officials. The policy advisory system in BC was thus more orthodox in the sense that the public service remained the steward of the formal policy advisory process, sensitive to the political context and tone and integrating feedback into "official" policy advice that would constitute the final advisory mechanism (i.e., decision notes, information notes, Cabinet submissions). This practice remained in place over the entirety of the Campbell administration, as opposed to the evolving practices that were detailed in the federal case. A long-serving partisan adviser from the Premier's Office detailed the process as follows:

But on more complex public policy questions, extensive briefing notes are already prepared by the public service, so we didn't replicate that process.

The lens that we applied to it was often to read the note. We might provide some input back to the deputy based on things we'd heard or on questions that were likely to come up, or to whoever was drafting the note. And then we'd often address those in the note. But that would become the one master public policy note that would be written. And then the advice would be provided in conjunction with the note, verbally. (P4)

Quantitatively, the amount of advice provided was by itself a clear instance of buffering. It provided a diversification of available policy advice to premier and Cabinet, provided by partisan advisers but based on public service research and recommendations. The first minister's office advisers' descriptions of their advisory activity were consistently presented as "administrative-technical." They were adamant that they did not provide "partisan" advice, but were rather a second opinion – again a public interest check – for elected political decision-makers. As will be detailed in chapter 5, minister's office partisans described their advisory activity in much more explicitly partisan-political terms. In the two other cases, within the first ministers' offices, a greater emphasis was placed on explicit application of a *political lens* to all policy advice (Head 2008; Prasser 2006). This speaks to important distinctions in content of policy advice, and how that is sought or marshalled not only across cases, but also within them at various institutional locations (Craft and Howlett 2012; Maley 2011).

Interviews with deputy ministers and central agency officials confirmed that the first minister's office in British Columbia was "policy heavy." When asked about the political arm of government during his time, Allan Seckel, then deputy minister to the premier, was frank in detailing that Campbell's chief of staff, Martyn Brown, was "extremely interested in policy," further explaining, "He's always wanting to know what the right policy was, as opposed to what … I mean he would put understanding policy first and partisan manoeuvring and strategy second – I think in terms of his priorities, in terms of how he would think about things." This type of response confirms that first minister's office partisan advisers in this case were engaged in buffering via active participation in policy advice. Seckel went further in distinguishing the two types of buffering, suggesting, "In fact you could argue, I think some would argue, that he had that balance the wrong way around, from a political perspective." As later chapters detail, this was quite the opposite for BC ministers' offices, where partisan advisers self-described, and were characterized by others, as engaged in partisan-political buffering. This suggests that attributions of influence linked to advisory activity deserve closer scrutiny than is often applied. Where it is occurring, its content and nature, and who is providing it and when, are all nuances that illuminate the political arm's core executive advisory activity. It also highlights tensions that flow from the increasing specialization of partisan advisers as direct sources of policy advice who may be blurring boundaries, or at least muddy expository accounts of the separate roles and activities at the seams of governance.

Buffering from the "Centre" in New Brunswick

Those interviewed from across the political and public service spectrum in New Brunswick identified Premier's Office partisan advisers as important sources of policy advice within that policy advisory system. Their buffering was found to span the administrative-technical and partisan-political dimensions and was described as occurring almost universally in a direct fashion with the premier, ministers, or senior officials. Many referenced the small size of the province as an important contributor to fostering close working relationships among political and administrative elites. This echoes published accounts that have long described this type of governance arrangements in the province (Hyson 2005; Bouchard 1999). Premier's Office partisan advisers were self-aware and candid in stating they were only one of many sources of policy advice; they recognized that others were also providing inputs into the system from a variety of vantage points.

In New Brunswick, partisan advisers at the centre characterized their buffering as principally geared towards major issues that were playing out on the political landscape, or dealing with any number of priority policy issues at play. They emphasized that they engaged in advisory activity on policy and governance issues that were not in development but rather were on the horizon, had emerged, or simply required their attention. Those interviewed described advising deputies and ministers in an ongoing fashion as well as the premier directly on a host of partisan-political and administrative-technical items. One first minister's office partisan adviser explained, much like those interviewed in the previous cases, that the buffering function involved contesting the provision of multiple types of policy advice on a number of fronts. On the one hand, it involved the scrutiny and contestation of

advice being proffered on its merit and logic. On the other, clear attention was paid to the partisan-political aspects of governance. At the
risk of stating the obvious, a partisan adviser explained that in many
respects it consisted of working backwards, that while a policy idea
may sound good or read well in a political manifesto, or departmental
memo, working it out in the real world was sometimes more challenging, and may not turn out as expected. The adviser went on to explain
that a Socratic method of sorts was used. Asking basic questions about
the logic, viability, or potential political issues, or implications in any
given circumstance was preferred. Consideration had to be given to
the technical merits but also the partisan-political considerations of
any given policy. As the adviser explained, "Premier trusts that what
I'm … if I say to him, 'Premier, I think you should really listen to this
because it's the right thing to do, it's a good thing to do, that I think
you're going to like it.' He would know that I'm telling him that not
only because I thought it was a good idea but that I thought it would
sell politically" (P1).

Interviews in New Brunswick made apparent that first minister's
office advisers' buffering was aimed predominantly at providing
advice to ministers and the premier, but significantly, also dialecti-
cally *with* officials. There was little doubt in this case that the Premier's
Office staff were "in tight" with senior officials. Advisers provided
content-based policy advice on existing policies and programs as well
as a host of issues beyond policy in development at any given time.
Their buffering was explained to involve pushing back or contesting
policy advice with officials or providing content-based clarifications
about expectations. Senior officials who interacted regularly with the
first ministers' offices corroborated this, as will be explored in the next
chapter. Partisan advisers at the centre explained that, at its core, their
function was one of ongoing exchanges with senior officials and ministers in attempts to blend or reconcile politics and administration.
One Premier's Office partisan adviser was quite clear in explaining
the reasons for this type of interaction with senior officials: "Where I
have to be, probably in contact with most of … with most of the deputy
ministers myself is when they seek some political direction on stuff.
When they seek advice, when they have important decisions to make
or recommendations, they would come through my office, through our
office to deal with that" (P2). Another echoed similar points but also
noted the importance of the advisory-based resource exchanges that

occurred, and the differences in the basic functions of each set of core executive actors:

> I would always listen to their [deputy ministers'] advice, that I would always seek their advice, and that they were free to give me more advice if they didn't think I had gotten it. But in the end, that me or the "royal we," with all the advice that they had given, might make another decision. And that that was no kind of inference that their advice wasn't good. It's just that that's just the way it was. I think most understood that, but I think that it was important that they understood that I understood that, that there was a difference between our functions, that I respected what they did. I respected that they work for the people ... that they had been here before we got here and they'd be here after we left. (P1)

Buffering in this case demonstrates similarities to the other cases in that it involved providing direct content-based policy advice that spanned partisan-political and administrative-technical dimensions of policy advisory activity. However, first minister's office partisan advisers in the New Brunswick case described more explicitly engaging in partisan-political policy advisory activity similar to their federal counterparts. A key difference, explored in greater detail throughout this study, was the greater frequency of deputy minister–first minister's office policy interactions reported in the New Brunswick case. This finding is not surprising, given that practice has long been a hallmark of the close political-administrative working relationship in the province. It is, however, significant when appraised through the lens of core executive resource exchanges. It suggests a direct pattern as opposed to one mediated or supplemented by ministerial partisan advisers, as in the other two cases.

First Ministers' Office Bridging Activities

Prime Minister's Office Bridging

Bridging at the PMO was described as frequent and intensive. Differences were again apparent in how such activity was undertaken by the PMO partisan advisers. For their part, chiefs of staff describe a more predominant integration of endogenous policy advice involving "administrative-technical" policymaking issues with the prime minister, senior PCO officials, as well as ministerial chiefs of staff. Both former

Harper PMO chiefs interviewed also described bridging involving their ministers' office counterparts consisting of both partisan-political and administrative-technical policy advisory integration, such as discussions about the policy options being developed by departments or on issues that had arisen in any given policy sector, or items flagged by key stakeholders. While both PMO chiefs emphasized that they could, and at times did, interact with line department senior officials, their administrative-technical bridging activity was almost exclusively with the PCO. For his part, former PMO chief of staff Guy Giorno reported, "[I] didn't spend much time speaking to line deputies. I didn't see a need for me to do that in doing my job. I spent most of my time with ministers or their chiefs of staff." Other senior PMO partisan advisers made clear their administrative-technical bridging was PCO-centric in that it was an easy way for them to leverage information located throughout the system. The PCO, as the public service counterpart to the PMO, provides a clearinghouse for public service policy advice and policy formulation. A former PMO director of policy indicated that three-quarters of all interactions with the public service would be with the PCO. As the adviser put it, "If I wanted to know something from Foreign Affairs, I could call up the deputy, and I did sometimes. But you'd also just talk to the PCO deputy, because all of the PCO assistant secretaries are really deputy's level" (P13). Former PMO chief of staff Ian Brodie reported similar patterns of interaction:

> I dealt with Kevin [PCO Clerk Kevin Lynch] and the [PCO] deputy secretaries frequently and then some of the deputy ministers. Over time I would get out, when the PM was on the road, to try to meet the deputy ministers and their department – what I would call my field trips. Time to leave the Langevin Block and go see actual people doing actual work in a real world environment. But for the most part, deputies would be in to see the PM on something for a briefing, and that's when I would meet them. But in PCO it would be Kevin, Angel who was his assistant, and the deputy secretaries.

Interviews with a range of junior PMO partisan advisers revealed similar patterns of PCO-centric administrative bridging. However, all PMO respondents emphasized that they also engaged in ongoing and iterative bridging with ministers' office's partisan advisers. The bridging described by these actors was replete with references to ensuring that everyone was singing from the same hymnbook, that policy advice of both administrative-technical and partisan-political varieties was being exchanged so that there were no information asymmetries and that policy advice was woven together for coherence (Parsons 2004; Di Francesco 2002). As one former director of policy stressed, the PMO policy team's role in bridging with ministers' offices was to provide help, direction, and assistance in resolving potential confusion. Directors of policy from the PMO emphasized two-way interaction with their partisan colleagues and with the PCO. It is important to emphasize the bilateral nature of the bridging reported. From the PMO perspective their central location facilitated awareness of a range of policy activities and issues that might not be on the radar of ministers, their staffs, or their departments. Thus on the one hand they were able to exchange PMO specific policy-based resources, but at the time they relied on ministerial office partisan advisers to provide intelligence, policy advice, and identification of strategic policy concerns that they may have come across. One PMO director of policy put it this way:

> There were two elements to that. One was dealing with caucus and Cabinet concerns. It's the role of the centre to ensure that things move smoothly, that people are aware of what the centre is thinking. So I would deal with chiefs of staff on a regular, regular basis, letting them know what our concerns were. But I would also deal with the Privy Council office. We worked very closely so that the flow of business through Cabinet and through the prime minister's suite went smoothly. So I would say you could probably divide it equally between Privy Council Office on the one side and other chiefs of staff and caucus on the other side. (P12)

It was explained that such bridging was useful as a tool for increased integration of sources of information and policy advice to and from ministers' offices and the PCO. PMO partisan advisers would use this in their interactions with the PCO to counterbalance policy advice that was coming from the central agencies with what their colleagues in ministers' offices were telling them. Contestation of policy advice is thus not strictly a partisan-political lens being applied, but rather seeking out policy advice from various sources, sifting and sorting it, and using it to optimize policy and governance outcomes. Bridging involved integrating the PMO's position on contentious policy, or conversely bridging back into the PMO information on the status of policy development or red flags from ministers' office partisan advisers. As a junior PMO policy adviser highlighted,

It was definitely both ways. More often I was reaching out to them [ministers' office partisan advisers] to ask them for information, to ask them about the status, you know: "How is your department doing? Are they getting the policy proposals together?" and so on. So, you know, the majority of the time, I'd say probably 75 per cent of the time I was going to them, 25 per cent of the time they were coming to me for information. And it was information about, you know, what does the prime minister think about this policy proposal? Does the prime minister support it or not? Or does PMO support it or not? So when they were coming for information, it was largely about that. (P15)

PMO partisan advisers also described bridging on the integration of exogenous sources of policy advice. Both former chiefs of staffs in the PMO reported limited stakeholder engagement on a policy level. In general, much like in the two provincial cases, the federal chief of staff in the first minister's office preferred, as a general rule of thumb, that stakeholder engagements be managed at the ministerial and departmental levels. Former PMO chief of staff Guy Giorno explained, "Most of the primary responsibility for stakeholder relations on a matter we would say rested with the minister and the department." However, Giorno did further explain that the PMO and prime ministerial stakeholder relations would be focused on groups or "community-specific" rather than topic-specific policy matters. Giorno explained that during his tenure he had in fact institutionalized the directors of stakeholder relations and directors of policy as the key avenues for stakeholder engagements. He stressed that while he took the role of external advice seriously and thought it essential, he was simultaneously very mindful of the ethical and media hazards around stakeholder/lobbying activities. Interviews with PCO officials confirmed that they also engaged little to no stakeholder consultations on policy.

Other interviews with PMO policy shop members generally confirmed these practices. From the PMO director of policy down to the junior policy advisers, those interviewed reported frequent interactions with stakeholders as part of their policy advisory activity. More than one former PMO director of policy remarked candidly about the value of meeting with stakeholders and of diversifying policy advice from sources outside of the public service. As the adviser explained, "Certainly it's valuable to have meetings from the outside, because it does provide a check on what the public service is telling you. It just means that you're not then completely at the … well at the mercy of your bureaucrats, of what they want to tell you" (P13). This type of response was also common with more junior PMO partisan advisers who frequently cited bridging exogenous sources of policy advice as a means to increase the availability of policy options for the PMO policy shop. However, it became clear that exogenous bridging in the federal case was heavily driven by activities at the ministerial office and departmental levels. Ministers' office partisan advisers served as feeder mechanisms to provide additional exogenous policy input into the advisory system. Thus, at the centre, partisan advisers were one of many sources of policy advice. They engaged in bridging that consisted of integration of central agency, ministers' office policy advice, and exogenous policy advice principally integrated from ministerial offices as well. This points to a complex and multifaceted type of resource exchange. In particular, reliance at the PMO on work made available from others: from PCO, who would serve as the aggregator of the collective public service advice; as well as from the PMO's ministerial office counterparts. For their part, when asked if they undertook bridging activities, a senior PCO official responded, "Not very much. There will be times where there'll be meetings with stakeholders more on the OP's [operations Cabinet committee] secretariat side of PCO who are following particular departments and, you know, interest groups will come in and see them on a particular file. But most of that happens in departments" (PCO2).

Exclusionary forms of bridging or so-called gatekeeping were also reported, but less frequently than at the ministerial office level. There was much less gatekeeping internally particularly with ministers or their chiefs of staff. PMO directors of policy and chiefs of staff reported having "open door policies." This was largely confirmed by ministers interviewed who saw the PMO as a "clearing house" in that it kept abreast of multiple concurrent issues and looped in with the other components of the political arm. It was clear from all that the predominant mode of interaction was at the staff level with escalation to direct ministerial or prime ministerial involvement as the exception rather than the rule. PMO policy staff interviewed described frequent and active attempts to monitor policy files and engage with their ministerial office counterparts. PMO chiefs also suggested they were not gatekeepers. In the case of Guy Giorno, he noted that as chief of staff he did not engage in gatekeeping. As he put it, "Some people have written that the chief of staff was a gatekeeper. I never saw that as my role. I never saw my role as to be the prime minister's top policy adviser. I certainly would give him advice on political matters. I didn't need to see him as … I didn't see myself as his only adviser. I saw myself as running a team, and that's what I did."

While some chiefs of staff may indeed be the top policy adviser, Giorno left policy advice, outside of his particular expertise in lobbying and other discreet areas, to others. When asked who Stephen Harper's top policy adviser was, Giorno laughed and responded, "Stephen Harper." For their part, ministers and chiefs explained that they tended to only go to the PMO for policy reasons if it was absolutely necessary. As one minister explained, "Typically the interactions are between staff who check those things out and then would just say, 'Here's how this is likely to roll out,' or whatever. But sometimes I would meet with or talk to staff that I needed to. There was nothing to prohibit that, but most of the time I would just leave it to my staff to check that part of it out. In general, they tried to deal with matters themselves" (M12). A former minister, Stockwell Day, explained that, when possible, it was always best to deal with policy matters without involving the PMO and particularly the prime minister. Day suggested this was a tacit understanding shared by most:

> There was an understanding, or ministers should have had an understanding through discussions with the prime minister what's expected generally or in some cases specifically on the file. If they were important enough, you'd talk to the prime minister. I, for one, wasn't one that liked to burden the prime minister with a lot of questions that maybe didn't have to be dealt with at his level. So, sometimes you deal directly with the prime minister, other times sometimes you deal with his chief of staff, or it could be a policy person or a communications person sometimes. A communication from the chief of staff to your chief of staff, you get the communication that way, so it's a mix.

This was the typical response from ministers. They had access to the prime minister or PMO staff if they needed it. The general practice was, however, to use their own ministerial partisan advisers to keep in touch with the PMO, and for bridging policy advice back and forth on particular files or emerging issues, or to alert counterparts to exogenous actors' policy advice. This further supports a greater allowance for potential influence of ministerial partisan advisers as core executive resource-exchange agents. The federal case therefore had clear discernible preferences for bridging. It suggests a core executive resource-exchange environment similar to that of the sharing of influence with multiple actors of influence (Prince 2007). That influence and core executive operation itself were also a product of spatially determined resources, such as those of the PMO and PCO as actors at the centre, but ministers' offices posed their own relevant policy-based resources and participated in resource exchanges. In addition, it reveals important differences in the *types* of resources that may be exchanged, particularly the potential utility and practices associated with the political arm's partisan-political policy resources (Craft, 2015a).

First Ministers' Office Bridging in British Columbia

Partisan advisers at the centre in BC characterized their bridging as involving the transmission of policy advice and information within the policy advisory system. A wide spectrum of those interviewed emphasized the synthesis and distillation of disparate sources of advice as a key advisory activity for first ministers' office partisan advisers. A premium was placed on their abilities, tied to their institutional location, to integrate sources' partisan-political and administrative-technical policy advice flowing within the advisory system. When asked about their patterns of interaction with other actors in the government, a first minister's office adviser explained that this type of synthesis and integration was fundamental:

> My job was primarily about taking large volumes of information and synthesizing them down to an understandable amount of information. Politicians and senior public servants are incredibly busy. The challenge with the advice is that there is so much of it, it's tough to digest or even read in the time that's available. So I think you need someone who can take a large amount of information because there's so much reading and the fact that you may not be able to read it all. You develop relationships with people and you can talk to them, get the input, synthesize down what the arguments for and against are, and relay that to a decision-maker and allow them to hopefully make a well-informed decision. (P4)

The internal bridging in British Columbia was marked by a clear structure and a strong division of labour within the Premier's Office that resulted in the chief of staff leading on almost all policy activity.

He was supported by a deputy chief of staff, who was a vital source of bridging and coordination, particularly related to "firefighting" or policy advisory needs tied to issues management. It became clear, however, that partisan advisers "at the centre" were engaged in policy advising that spanned administrative-technical and partisan-political dimensions. As one first minister's partisan adviser described bridging in work with senior officials, "They too, the smart ones that had a desire to reconcile the Cabinet or premier's policy direction, that was inherently something that they were pushing for, worked closely with us from early on, right through the Cabinet approval process. And they would be sensitive to their need to rely on us for political acumen and political support, including at the caucus level, because that's a body that the civil servants typically don't interact with at all." (P3).

Partisan-political bridging was explained to occur on an ad hoc and ongoing basis with senior Premier's Office staff playing key functions, relaying information gleaned from within the advisory system. The smaller size of the first minister's office meant that all partisan advisers at the centre dealt directly with the premier and Cabinet, as well as senior executives at both the central agency and departmental levels. Interviews were replete with references to ongoing bridging between first minister's office partisan advisers and ministers on a number of issues, departmental concerns, and operational considerations. Additional bridging was also reported to occur through a formal daily "morning meeting" that included all political staff. While similar meetings were held on occasion in the other two cases, BC was unique in the routinized occurrence of such meetings. When asked about these meetings, both central and minister's office advisers confirmed they were free flowing and involved the transmission of policy advice to and from the Premier's Office but were oriented primarily around the identification of policy issues, red flags, and reinforcement of short- to medium-term policy priorities.

Similar to the federal case, less gatekeeping was reported at the first minister's office level than at the ministers' office level. When reported, it was, as noted above, almost exclusively to prevent exogenous actors from doing "end-runs" around the responsible minister and department. Most ministers in BC noted having access to the premier if needed, but also referenced frequent interactions with partisan advisers at the centre. When asked to explain the purpose of these interactions, most responded that it was out of a need for coherence and coordination. As one minister put it, "Although it can be on a file that relates to the specific portfolio, it may be on a file that relates to ... that crosses multiple ministries, where there are different ministers that share responsibility for it. Or it may be a file that has nothing to do with your specific ministry but want to be engaged in the discussion" (M7). Most ministers provided similar responses, and some also noted that their interactions with the Premier's Office staff centred on "big" policy problems or Cabinet activity. In describing Cabinet-related policy work, one first minister's office partisan adviser made clear the policy work involved frequent bridging related to the exchange of information and its integration for Cabinet ministers. The adviser explained this bridging was ad hoc and informal and often conducted by phone with ministers. The adviser emphasized this was a fundamental component of the policy work undertaken, that it involved meetings that dealt with advice on a range of policy and political issues, or the context of governing: "That was a big part. It was probably the most significant piece of involvement with Cabinet, these sort of one-off meetings that happened regularly with various ministers" (P4).

Bridging exogenous sources of policy advice was also reported among first minister's office partisan advisers in BC. As in the federal case, interactions with stakeholders were described as much broader or group-based. Senior first minister's advisers rarely engaged in policy-specific stakeholder integration. Again, as in the federal case, a clear preference was articulated for "pushing out" policy-specific consultation and integration to ministers, their partisan advisers, and departmental officials. However, first minister's office advisers did report bridging to seek external sources of policy expertise or to test the validity of policy advice provided by the public service. When asked how frequently they went outside of government proper for advice, one partisan adviser at the centre stated, "It was frequent. You always have to be cognizant when you are seeking external advice that you are tipping the hand that you are thinking about change, so it would depend on the subject you are talking about" (CP3). Another senior partisan adviser in the first minister's office confirmed this view, explaining that very little time was spent dealing with stakeholders. The office did, however, frequently seek out expert advice on particular issues, or consulted with large associations in order to get a sense of broader policy issues or sectors. The adviser explained it was infrequent because ministries were the primary channel through which stakeholders interacted, further suggesting that those infrequent instances when the adviser did go outside of government to secure policy advice weren't with stakeholders but with "experts." When pushed to describe what was meant by "experts," the adviser explained that it was trade associations or other industry groups who had detailed knowledge about a whole sector. Long-serving former Campbell administration Chief of Staff Martyn Brown later detailed the Campbell administration attempts to improve its ability to integrate exogenous policy advisory inputs, primarily through more robust consultative policymaking in its second term. "The Campbell administration did far more to properly process contentious policy issues in its second term, which helped immensely. It took more time to lay out the nature of the issues it was aiming to address, and it did more to inform and engage the public in shaping those policies. Consultation efforts became more substantive and genuine. Policies were often adjusted to reflect public input and feedback, as opposed to being just more artfully imposed" (Brown 2012, chapter 2).

Speaking with officials, however, revealed a different picture. Most echoed the earlier point that ministries and the public service had longstanding relationships with stakeholders. They had frequent interactions with them on a range of matters regarding policy development on any particular file. Central agency staff interviewed confirmed the emphasis on departments leading such practices. Alan Seckel revealed that though some progress may have been made, the first minister's office had not been effective in this regard overall. When queried about the ability of the first minister's office to integrate exogenous inputs, Seckel was candid in his views: "My frank assessment would be that it didn't function particularly well. I think one of the criticisms I would have about the Premier's Office in British Columbia was that it did not have a consistent approach to dealing with stakeholders. Most of the stakeholder relations were pushed out to the ministries and ministers so they would be relatively more hit-or-miss."

It should be noted that the Premier's Office includes the deputy minister to the premier, who is a non-partisan public servant. The political and administrative arms are separate in practice but considered part of the same office. However, because they are political appointments, deputy ministers to the premier are selected, in part, for their ability to support and drive the current administration's agenda. They have close working relationships with the first minister and their staff and typically change when the government and/or first minister changes (Ruff 2009; Lindquist and Vaskil 2014). Determinations of how well integration was handled may be debatable, but there was general agreement by all parties that the bridging of exogenous policy advisory inputs was "pushed out" to departments and ministers' offices, the cascading effect being that first minister's partisan advisers bridged in exogenous sources of policy-specific advice that had been previously integrated into advisory systems by ministerial counterparts, or departments.

First Ministers' Office Bridging in New Brunswick

In New Brunswick, the bridging reported by partisan advisers at the centre was, like their buffering, predominantly with deputy ministers. The deputies interviewed explicitly noted that Premier's Office staff played important roles in the bilateral exchange of policy advice and information among political and administrative elites. Deputies in this case described interacting regularly with first minister's partisan advisers on formal policy work (e.g., Cabinet submissions) and informally on an advisory basis. The bilateral exchanges were reported to involve the provision and communication of policy advice as well as its solicitation. A great deal of bridging was described as involving first minister's partisan advisers providing policy advice to ministers, deputies, and the premier, or vice versa, on a range of current policy issues, actors, or policy sectors.

First ministers' office partisan advisers described engaging in administrative-technical bridging that flowed from interactions with deputy ministers. For example, it was reported that first minister's office partisan advisers were often used by public servants to reinforce or supplement previously delivered briefings or presentations provided to ministers, Cabinet, or the premier directly. This was explained to involve officials engaging in discussion with first minister's office partisan advisers to highlight the benefits of or validity of their policy advice or to clarify any confusion. One first minister's office partisan adviser explained such activity and also underscored the cacophony of voices that now echo throughout advisory systems: "Afterwards [after a briefing] too if there's something that premier has not, has missed or whatever. Something like the deputies can come back to me and say, 'I think he has got this and that and this, but can you talk to him again about this, because that's a really important piece and I don't want him to lose it.' And meanwhile he could have the deputy minister of finance in his other ear saying, 'I don't know, Premier. I don't know if we can'" (P1).

Another Premier's Office adviser explained that as an adviser, it was possible to play a crucial function of linking and spanning the political-administrative nexus. As the adviser explained, "I'm kind of the link there. As a matter of fact, on behalf of the premier, I'm the only one who interlinks both with the political and the non-political. You know, it's quite clear that there is no line of authority between a deputy minister and a minister in a department. Everyone kind of responds, answers to the premier. If there's a difference between the two, I'm in the middle" (P2). This type of response points to how partisan-political bridging can be important in the multilateral environment that now characterizes governance arrangements. However, in this case it was far more limited than as reported in the two other cases examined in this study. As will be seen in chapter 5, New Brunswick ministers' office partisan advisers universally pointed to their interactions with the first ministers' office as occurring through the premier's executive assistant, and for administrative or logistical items such as announcements or constituent requests. Partisan advisers at the centre confirmed this to be the case. When asked about policy advisory interactions with ministers' office staff, another first minister's office adviser made clear it was generally negligible. Again, in this case there was much less interaction among Premier's Office partisan advisers and their ministerial counterparts. Most matters were not policy related but rather logistical or constituency in nature and as a rule of thumb were dealt with between the ministers and Premier's Office executive assistants. The only exceptions would be for highly sensitive political matters. As a Premier's Office adviser put it, "The rare exception some EAs will call me, and I will return their calls. For most of them it's for the right reason" (P2).

All ministers interviewed in this case reported dealing with the premier's senior partisan advisers directly, if not the premier himself. This was a modus operandi quite different from that of the federal case reviewed above, which saw far more active partisan-political bridging among ministers' offices and the PMO. In the BC case, such interactions were typically related to vetting policy options with Premier's Office staff, or to provide advance notice of policy issues or advice on specific departmental items that the first minister's office might be seeking. In New Brunswick, ministers interviewed suggested universally that Premier's Office staff were influential, but did not report that they felt they were gatekeeping them or their ministerial staff. All ministers interviewed reported the ability to access the premier, if needed. However, most also made clear they went through senior Premier's Office staff as a preliminary step, to avoid unnecessarily going directly to the premier. One minister explained that, given his portfolio, he dealt more with the Premier's Office chief of staff as opposed to the principal secretary who oversaw other policy files. In describing his interactions, the minister made clear that the chief of staff would often engage in bridging to provide a heads up on contentious or complicated policy issues, and to relay the premier's policy position:

> And if there's something like he [chief of staff] thinks that I should be doing, he'll be the one to hit me with it first. I kind of have a chance to think about it and get ready for premier, because I know that's next, that's coming next, which is good. It's great. Because you have a chance to think about it. I'm not always ready and I have a tendency to lean towards [one policy solution] and premier against, which is great. He brings up his arguments and I bring up mine, and we then we kind of work it out together, which is good. (M3)

Ministers again frequently referenced the small size of the province as producing a close, collegial, and direct relationship with the premier. They also made it clear that this created a climate where senior partisan advisers could play pivotal bridging functions on the transmission of policy advice to or from the premier. The bilateral resource exchanges were notably very direct, as compared to the federal case reviewed above. Responses from the full range of deputies interviewed were well in keeping with traditional accounts that portray them as the most influential policy players in the day-to-day policy work of departments, and with direct lines of accountability to the premier and their chief of staff (Hyson 2005; Savoie 1989; Bouchard 1999, 2014). Deputies frankly discussed engaging in bridging practices to alert the first minister and his partisan advisers about potential policy issues that may emerge, and provide advice on the performance of their ministers. As one deputy explained, "Sometimes there is an issue. I've had ministers who the premier has said, 'Be careful if these issues come up in the files that you keep the ministers away from them,' because they have maybe some business connections indirectly, and if they get involved, this could become, you know, a political sort of issue. If there is a sensitivity with something the minister is doing and I'm really not sure, I would give the Premier's Office through [chief of staff] a heads up" (DM3).

New Brunswick Premier's Office advisers, like their counterparts in the other cases, made explicit a preference for ministers and departments to deal with stakeholders. However, they noted that they did engage in both formal and informal bridging with external stakeholders and experts on policy matters. This was described in the context of the diversification of policy advice and policy ideas. Senior partisan advisers explained that external actors were a key source of the "questions" they would then bridge in to officials to contest the comprehensiveness and validity of the policy options being considered. One adviser explained that it was at times difficult to consult sufficiently with stakeholders, given the obligations and competing pressures of governing, but it was nonetheless something that the adviser *tried* to do. As the adviser put it, this type of policy work was undertaken "enough at least so that they will still send me things and keep me in their loop. But then I would ask for verification from the departments, and they're very good about that. They send you the facts, right? They send you briefing material on whatever. And then, you know, if you don't believe them or don't like their slant, you can always check it out yourself or challenge it" (P1). This sentiment lays bare the fact that the advisory system is a complex and interactive ecosystem. Partisan advisers, particularly those in senior roles, receive and contest policy advice from a variety of sources and often use the streams or supplies of policy advice to ensure they have a comprehensive account of an issue or policy options. Advisers' participation in such systems increases policy responsiveness and shores up contestation of public service advice, through their own scrutiny and analysis or leveraging that of others, and further supports their function as buffers and bridges. There were, of course, clear limitations in advisers' ability to undertake that role, given the competing demands for their time and attention.

In addition, those interviewed made clear that partisan advisers could precipitate issues being addressed that otherwise might not garner the attention of the public service as part of that ongoing policy work. Stakeholders were seen as a valuable source of new policy ideas in terms of their ability to point the government towards issues requiring resolution. A senior Premier's Office adviser explained that part of policy work involved the bridging in policy advice that alerted the public service to items that may not be on their policy radar. While partisan advisers at the centre were most concerned with implementation of their platform and policy agenda, their bridging could be used to diversify the public service's views on policies or flag policy opportunities.

In a telling exchange, one adviser explained at length that it was being in the Premier's Office that allowed the adviser to have influence, through that locational position, to move policy through the policy process and broader system of government. Given the many competing policy items at play at any given time, he explained that this type of policy work consisted of drawing focus to secure a resolution for individual or stakeholder policy issues if the "system" had not done so. As the adviser put it, "They wouldn't get solved if there was no interest from the political arm, because it's just not big enough, or because it just doesn't fit well enough, or for whatever reason it's not on their radar" (P1).

Lastly, a higher number of respondents cited negative bridging or gatekeeping of policy advice occurring with first minister's partisan advisers compared to their ministerial counterparts. Both of the first minister's partisan advisers interviewed referenced gatekeeping of exogenous sources of policy advice and stakeholders. Partisan advisers in the first minister's office also underscored the point that accessibility was part of the New Brunswick governance style. Again, the smaller and more direct political-administrative style means that the premier himself serves as the final arbiter of potential conflict between ministers, or between a minister and his deputy. Thus, in the New Brunswick case, partisan advisers stressed their role in mitigating resolutions that required the first minister's intervention. Gatekeeping in this case involved control of political and administrative access to "the centre," physically and for policy advisory reasons. As one adviser stated, "As I said, I'm kind of the centre of the hub. If MLAs [members of the legislative assembly] aren't happy, it's ending up on my desk. Or worried about something, or want to meet with the premier, I'm always in the middle" (P2).

From a policy perspective, partisan advisers at the centre agreed that while accessibility was important, they acted as gatekeepers to "push out" stakeholders to ministers and departmental officials. Asked how policy-related requests from stakeholders are managed, one adviser explained that the Premier's Office had formalized mechanisms for dealing with some regularized stakeholders, notably organized labour. In all, the adviser explained that significant portions of the stakeholder requests are deflected to ministers and departments first. The adviser noted a gatekeeping role to prevent stakeholder groups from trying to perform end runs around departments and ministers: "So we're saying no as much as often as we're saying yes. I'm trying to control the traffic sometimes, I'm saying, 'No, the premier won't meet with that guy or that group, but send him to the minister'" (P2).

Conclusion

First ministers' office partisan advisers have policy-based influence. In the three cases examined, this was partly a result of their ability to engage in policy advisory systems. As buffers and bridges, advisers broadened the available quantity and qualitative content of advice within their respective advisory systems. They were clear participants in the direct provision of content-based policy advice and engaged in ample integration of *other* sources of policy advice as well. There was little doubt that they contested, challenged, and circulated various types and supplies of policy advice. The findings detailed above support the importance of locational factors as a determinant of advisory systems activity and influence. Respondents explicitly referenced the institutional location of first ministers' office partisan advisers as providing them with unique opportunities and resources for buffering and bridging. Yet as underscored in this chapter, important differences emerged in the nature of this policy work, with whom it was undertaken, and how. This suggests caution in attributing policy advisory influence to such actors *solely* on the basis of their locational proximity to the first minister, and that there is a range of ways in which they can exert influence and affect the operation of advisory systems.

The cases shared some basic similarities in that partisan advisers' buffering and bridging were described in essentially similar terms. Respondents from across the cases reported first ministers' office partisan advisers were clear sources of content-based policy advice, contesting policy advice from various sources, on partisan-political and/ or administrative-technical grounds. Bridging was also described similarly across the cases. Partisan advisers were described as integrating and synthesizing policy advice flowing throughout the advisory system. The endogenous nature of their bridging in all three cases reveals that this set of partisan advisers explicitly prefer to "push out" external bridging to departments, ministers, and their partisan advisers. This is an important finding, as it sheds new light on advisory system brokerage practices and confirms an important function for Canadian ministerial offices in this regard (Craft 2013; Maley 2011).

Some important differences were also readily apparent. The federal case involved much more intensive and frequent buffering and bridging, along both partisan-political and administrative-technical dimensions. This was a consequence of the larger contingent of PMO partisan advisers, their explicit and undivided focus on policy work, and a parallel written partisan-political advisory system. The federal case benefited from its multiple layers of partisan advisers who could leverage resources at the ministers' office level to supplement direct interactions with senior officials or ministers. The case stood out in terms of the institutionalized nature and intensity of partisan-political advisory activity. The two subnational cases were found to have much less capacity at the first ministers' office level to dispatch partisan advisers to contest policy advice on partisan-political grounds, or to challenge, scrutinize, or offer policy advice as an overlay within their respective advisory systems. These activities occurred but were restricted to the most senior first ministers' office partisan advisers. When it did occur, partisan-political buffering and bridging were directly undertaken with ministers and deputy ministers. Finally, the PMO and BC first ministers' offices reported low levels of gatekeeping. The most frequently reported instances were in New Brunswick, likely the result of dedicated stakeholder relations staff in both of the former cases and most certainly because there was a longstanding expectation of substantial accessibility to the New Brunswick Premier's Office (Hyson 2005; Bouchard 2014).

These differences raise four implications for core executive resource exchanges within advisory systems. First, the orientation of partisan advisers' policy advisory-based resource exchange is susceptible to variation. Federal administrative-technical bridging was PMO-PCO heavy, supplemented by additional partisan-political bridging within PMO and with ministerial counterparts. The policy advisory-based resource exchanges were more frequent and varied, and they involved more actors in the advisory system. In contrast, the New Brunswick advisory system was characterized by "direct" administrative-technical bridging, with deputies and partisan-political bridging occurring directly with ministers. Resource exchanges were not mediated or supplemented to the degree they were in the federal case. Second, resource exchange orientation can have endogenous and exogenous orientations and patterns. This was most discernible in the shared preference for "pushing out" stakeholder-related advisory activity among ministers, their staff, and departments. Third, the instruments used for policy-based resource exchange can differ, with important consequences for how buffering and bridging is undertaken and the advisory system operates. This was most vividly demonstrated by the unique presence of a written partisan-political advisory system in the federal case. It provided additional formal channels for buffering that supplemented the oral advisory practices used in all three cases. Finally, while institutional location was important, it was limited in explaining differences among the cases. The "layered" or hierarchical configuration of multiple partisan advisers in the federal case greatly enhances the PMO's buffering and bridging capacity. However, despite a similar number of Premier's Office partisan advisers in subnational cases, the divisions of labour and the buffering and bridging practices differed. Thus, configuration and location reveal only part of the story.

These resource exchanges and policy advisory activities are linked directly to policy responsiveness and attempts to secure political control. PMO partisan advisers were able to increase political control to a much greater extent than their provincial counterparts through more robust partisan-political bridging activity, in large part as a result of their greater numbers and the layered PMO configuration. Resource exchanges were systematic, and in all instances policy advice was contested and scrutinized by partisan advisers. However, the PCO retained its ability to provide its non-partisan policy advice directly to the prime minister. Premier's Office partisan advisers in the two subnational cases, though differing in intensity and instrumentation, increased political control and diversified the quantity and/or qualitative content of policy advice. The shared practice of "pushing out" stakeholder advisory inputs suggests that less political control, in these three cases, was secured by integration of exogenous policy advice directly *by first ministers' offices*. Lastly, partisan-political buffering and bridging, as described above, also created boundaries to prevent partisan-political exposure for the public service – particularly in the federal case. Senior officials were aware that such advisory activities occurred but that the separate partisan-political policy advisory system insulated them from those aspects of policy advice. The subnational cases also included officials reporting that they were insulated from potential politicization, but in both cases they still had to integrate feedback and seek political context when framing their official policy advice. This chapter leaves little doubt that first ministers' offices are important advisory system actors. The evidence detailed above adds specificity and new findings on the content and processed-based nature of their influence and participation in advisory systems. Chapter 4 now turns to an examination of if and how these actors engaged in policy formulation.

Movers and Shapers at the "Centre"

Introduction

One principal argument advanced in this book is that partisan advisers' influence as policy workers extends beyond advice giving to a range of non-advisory policy work. This chapter examines first ministers' office partisan advisers' substantive content-based "shaping" and process-based "moving" in policy formulation. This is particularly germane for investigations of first ministers' office partisan advisers, given that they are widely characterized as *the* most influential of partisan advisers (Aucoin 2010, 2012; Savoie 1999a, 2011; Doern 1971). Understanding if, and particularly how and when, these actors engage in formulation offers considerable opportunity to better model, analyse, and understand policy formulation itself – not to mention how the political arm contributes to core executive operation. A growing body of Canadian and international research points to these types of substantive and procedural forms of policy work extending to other "stages" or parts of the policy process (Craft 2015a). Activities like agenda-setting, decision-making, and implementation are not the focus of this study. This is in part to keep the scope of the study manageable, but also partisan advisers are one of a small set of privileged participants in what is widely considered to be a narrow and restricted policy formulation process (Sidney 2007; Howlett, Perl, and Ramesh 2009). Formulation is one of the least well-studied aspects of public policy, given that access to elites and other difficulties plague comprehensive analysis. As such, careful and focused examination of partisan advisers' formulation activity offers tremendous opportunities to better understand that aspect of policymaking, but also the partisan-political facets of formulation. This is the second chapter to focus exclusively on first ministers' office partisan advisers. Along with the previous chapter, it provides for a more robust comparison of this group of partisan advisers policy work across the three cases, and facilitates comparisons with their ministers' office counterparts in subsequent chapters.

First ministers' office partisan advisers were in all three cases acknowledged to be active movers and shapers across many of the formulation dimensions set out in chapter 1. Universally, all categories of actors interviewed emphasized that first ministers' office advisers were pivotal to "front-end" formulation actors, such as in appraisal and dialogue sub-phases, along both partisan-political and administrative-technical dimensions that involved translating platforms into actionable government policy items, planning and sequencing, process management, coordination, and alignment of policy priorities with partisan-political commitments. All three cases also made clear that moving and shaping extended beyond the discreet initial front-end activity to ongoing and iterative formulation, often undertaken with a spate of actors during formulation sub-phases. In both front-end, or direction-setting, and iterative policy work, all three cases involved partisan advisers at the centre participating in policy formulation through official public service policy instruments, often tied to Cabinet activity.

This chapter also examines the horizontal or interdepartmental and vertical or intra-departmental aspects of their moving and shaping. As actors who can and often must engage in system-wide policy work, many respondents described first ministers' office policy formulation involving "across government" or "whole of government" policy work. In each case, horizontal administrative-technical formulation was often described as particularly pronounced in appraisal, dialogue, and formulation sub-phases. For example, substantive shaping involving the establishment of initial parameters of policy direction, or ongoing shaping in concert with senior officials as policy was formalized, or dialogue and consultations with officials as policy was being developed. In the subnational cases, this administrative-technical horizontality involved greater department-level deputy minister interactions, whereas in the federal case it was consistently described as occurring between the PMO and PCO actors. First ministers' office partisan advisers across the cases also noted some horizontal partisan-political formulation. It was typically reported as involving dialogue, formulation, and consolidation sub-phase activity associated with Cabinet and Cabinet committee activity. In the two subnational cases, this type of moving and shaping involved more direct first minister's office to minister interactions. As this chapter details, the federal case involved a much greater frequency and intensity of vertical moving and shaping along all dimensions and sub-phases. The comparatively more muscular PMO policy shop and the layered configuration of partisan advisers were drivers of additional vertical activity in a fashion similar to their advisory system participation. The findings in this chapter add precision to how, as core executive actors, partisan advisers may engage in different kinds and intensities of policy-based resource exchanges, and at various formulation sub-phases.

Procedural Formulation in First Ministers' Offices

PMO Policy Movers

PMO partisan advisers reported a range of moving that was distinct to them as PMO partisan advisers – specifically, horizontal moving along both partisan-political and administrative-technical dimensions tied to overall policy coordination and oversight activity. Moving was often described as involving policy coordination and monitoring of memoranda to Cabinet development occurring at the department level, as well as process management for Cabinet and Cabinet committee business. Additional vertical intra-PMO moving was also commonly reported. Comparatively, this case was marked by the greatest degree of vertical moving. Again, this was a product of greater number, and the layered configuration, of partisan advisers in the PMO, and the participation of all PMO policy staff in *formal* public service policymaking mechanisms (e.g. Cabinet memorandums, Cabinet/committee work). PMO partisan advisers reported moving along both partisan-political and administrative-technical dimensions. While pronounced at several sub-phases, it was highlighted at dialogue and formulation sub-phases. However, interviews also revealed that PMO policy team members engaged in more moving at appraisal and consolidation sub-phases, compared to their minister's office counterparts. This involved coordinating policy-specific information and providing feedback in the appraisal sub-phase, setting the framework or parameters of policy development, or coordination for Cabinet-related policy work involving brokering support for items, and monitoring formal policy development.

Former PMO chiefs of staff interviewed described their policy work in process-heavy terms, consisting of significant strategic planning, consultation, process management, coordination, and sequencing through long-term exercises to design and implement the government's strategic policy agenda. This was achieved in part through the establishment of the key Cabinet items that were required, and planning and sequencing activities flowing from those activities. It was also reported to involve considerable day-to-day process management to deal with emerging policy items and coordinate and adjust as required. When directly questioned on whether they spent more time on the substantive or procedural aspects of policy formulation, former PMO chief of staff Ian Brodie was quick to reply, "Process for sure, but process rules." Former Harper PMO chiefs explained at length the importance of procedural aspects of formulation, including monitoring, coordination, sequencing, and consultation. Both are worth quoting at length on the matter:

> I spent an enormous amount of time on process. Process is how things get thought through and brought to conclusion. And if the clerk of the Privy Council and the prime minister's chief of staff are not out there reminding people that this has to come to a conclusion because we need to get this to Cabinet agenda by next Tuesday, or January sixteenth, or whatever. I go back to our annual priority-setting exercise in the spring and into the early summer. That's where the influence on the Cabinet process and Cabinet agenda for the chief of staff, at least in my time, was clearest. Because you'd have an idea at the end of that of when there would be a Cabinet discussion needed to make a decision. That process was what basically set the major subjects for Cabinet or P&P to discuss that year. And then after that, the combination of the bureaucracy and the PMO policy staff sort of takes over and manages things from there, so I'd say I had very little to do with that. (Former PMO chief of staff Ian Brodie)

> I think that you would've described all of those as process-related, right? Ensuring that caucus was consulted. Ensuring that there was proper attention paid to what the commitments of the party were. Ensuring that there was balanced consultation with stakeholders. Ensuring that regional differences or interests were taken into account. Considering how this would be communicated and marketed. Ensuring there was a sound plan to explain the policy to the public. That should be the bulk the vast majority of a political staff member's interaction, intersection, with the policy process. (Former PMO chief of staff Guy Giorno)

Vertical moving was a significant part of the chief of staff's reported activities by sheer virtue of the role as head of the PMO. Both chiefs interviewed reported a high degree of delegation to their staffs to manage detailed aspects of policy formulation, but both noted important functions for themselves in the most salient policy development milestones of government; for example, in the articulation of the government's policy agenda through the Speech from the Throne, budgets, and mandate letters. Mandate letters are centrally (PMO/PCO) created documents given to new or reassigned ministers and deputy ministers. They outline the general ministerial (and departmental) parameters, priorities, key deliverables, and budgets, and they identify other departments/ministers they will need to work with (Zussman 2013). Their vertical moving tended to be linked closely with the prime minister and then back down into the PMO staff. This was achieved partly through the continued use of regular morning meetings similar to those of PMOs past, which involved partisan adviser–only sessions but also commonly featured PMO/PCO joint meetings where officials from both offices met with the prime minister. An additional avenue of vertical partisan-political moving was the well-explored transmission of partisan-political policy advice up the chain through the PMO briefing system. In formulation, the key difference is that such policy briefings were aimed explicitly at policy items *in development* rather than general counsel or policy advice that could span any number of current or expected issues, topics, or concerns.

Directors of policy described typically holding a morning meeting to review any pressing policy-related issues. PMO advisers reported vertical partisan-political moving and universally emphasized the PMO policy shop's hierarchical structure and processes as a key cause of vertical moving. As one adviser put it, in the PMO, "I interacted most often, obviously, with my boss, who coordinated overall policy. So, we were a team of, I think, we were five policy advisers. I interacted most often with my boss in PMO" (P15). When asked to describe what function he, and the PMO more generally, played in policy development, a PMO policy adviser explained, "Our role was to guide policy and do signal-checks with the prime minister and staff [partisan advisers at the PMO and ministers' offices] to make sure that policy was going in the direction that you wanted it to go in." "Signal-checking" was commonly cited by a variety of respondents in the federal case, a common dialogue sub-stage to ensure that policy formulation items were progressing appropriately and identify any potential roadblocks or risks. The adviser went on to explain how he perceived the PMO policy shop's role in Cabinet committees in very procedural terms akin to a police officer managing traffic:

> The one part of the traffic cop is just to rewind a little bit. Is what's coming up from the department and the ministers in line with what the prime minister wants? You give it a green, a red, or a yellow, light? Back to that minister's office and say, 'Well this isn't exactly what the prime minister is asking for, for you to put in your documents to Cabinet.' Or, you say, 'You know, these documents in a sense these that are going to [particular Cabinet] committee, that's not what the prime minister wanted, so you should probably want to pull that off the agenda. Or the prime minister will talk to the ministers around the table and tell them it's not what he wanted and it will be voted down and that's not good for you.' (P18)

PMO partisan advisers also reported frequent horizontal moving on both partisan-political and administrative-technical dimensions. This is in keeping with findings from other systems that have detailed such horizontality (Maley 2000, 2011; OECD 2011, 2007). This was explained to be a product of their institutional location at the "centre" of government and involved moving at all sub-phases with counterparts in ministerial offices. Moreover, PMO partisan advisers in the policy shop all noted they had significant responsibility for, and involvement with, the process-based management of Cabinet and Cabinet committee policy development. In addition, their moving was often described as "strategic" or "government-wide." It involved considerable coordination of policy formulation occurring within the PMO itself and between the PMO and PCO, and was often linked to formal Cabinet activity. Junior partisan advisers, for example, tasked with their ministries and policy areas, reported a dual coordination function of ministers' offices and PCO-centric moving. PMO partisan advisers explained working horizontally on administrative-technical and partisan-political dimensions as a means to expedite policy development or to remove identified roadblocks. This is also precisely the type of core executive resource exchange that facilitates executive governance. Core executives are not only the organizations and process that coordinate policy, but they also "act as final arbiters between different parts of the government machine" (Dunleavy and Rhodes 1990, 4; Rhodes 1995). Moving was often described by partisan advisers as procedural policy work aimed at advancing policy measures or better coordinating them as they went through formal policymaking processes – with public service and partisan-political actors – but also resolving conflicts throughout the core executive. Another PMO partisan adviser described precisely such activities in detailing the policy process and PMO's functions in it: "Before we got to Cabinet there were times when, you know, a particular policy piece was really difficult to move forward, either because the public service wasn't supportive of the direction we were taking or because maybe the Cabinet ministers themselves had different perspectives and different views as to what the policy should be" (P15).

Partisan advisers at the centre more commonly reported such consolidation sub-phase moving along both horizontal partisan-political and administrative-technical dimensions than their ministerial office counterparts. PMO partisan advisers could facilitate moving policy on a partisan-political dimension in light of their proximity to the prime minister and Cabinet. That is, they could engage in coordination or sequencing with counterparts knowing (roughly) future Cabinet/committee agendas or timelines, what had been said at Cabinet committees, or how the PCO/PMO would likely react to departmental policy work. As such, first minister's office partisan advisers are particularly privileged by their central location. This supports previous research that has detailed the nodal influence of central offices (Savoie 1999a; Aucoin 1990; Hamburger, Stevens, and Weller 2011). Indeed, several of the PMO policy shop advisers also described using PCO staff to lubricate policy formulation at the departmental level. A PMO director of policy emphasized that the PMO reminded ministers' policy teams and chiefs of staff that they were there to help.

PMO partisan advisers almost universally articulated more frequent horizontal administrative-technical moving with PCO staff than with departmental deputy ministers. This horizontal administrative-technical moving was described as occurring throughout formulation sub-phases. Junior staff reported mixed patterns of interaction that included significant PCO-oriented moving but also considerable moving in concert with ministerial partisan advisers in their policy areas. Procedurally, this was often explained as part of ongoing bilateral signal-checking to ensure that policy development was unfolding as expected. As one adviser explained, interactions with public service officials were bidirectional: "So there's a big element of face-saving and signal-checking throughout the system because no one wants to be on the wrong side of the ultimate decision, right? And so it really would depend, right? I'd say it was, I don't know, again maybe 60:40 but it could have been 50:50, but it again really depended on what was happening at the time" (P18).

When asked why the adviser interacted with PCO officials, it was explained that it was predominantly for memoranda to Cabinet or specific files. As the adviser put it, "Usually around specific pieces of policy or legislation, or you know regulation or something like that. You know, it was very much that was the nuts and bolts side of it." Horizontally, administrative-technical moving was reported to be particularly salient at dialogue, formulation, and consolidation sub-phases. In short, there was significant policy moving at both the "front end" and "back end" of formulation. At the front end, moving involved appraisal and dialogue sub-phase activity consisting of coordination of policy direction and process management in formulation. At the back end, signal-checking, sequencing, and coordination were commonly reported activities as policy items approached formal Cabinet disposition. This is well summarized by the description provided by a junior PMO policy adviser in response to a question aimed at assessing her general policy functions. "I'd say my primary role, the primary role of the policy shop as a whole was to ensure that the government's policy agenda moved forward according to the government's timelines." When pushed to explain how that occurs, she elaborated at length:

> Breaking that down, what that meant was we would go from throne speech to ministerial mandate letters to sort of priorities within priorities. So our job was really, a lot of our job was just to ensure ministers' offices and their departments moved forward on the policy priorities given to them in a timely way. And then what that looked like in terms of specifics was as the various departments and ministers' offices developed policy proposals and, you know, the memoranda to Cabinet. We from the Prime Minister's Office would review every memorandum to Cabinet, or MC's as well called them, just to make sure that the were consistent with the government's goals. (P15)

Indeed, Cabinet committees were a focal point for many moving-related activities along all four dimensions. At the junior level, PMO advisers were managing the process around their Cabinet committees that involved horizontal moving with ministers' offices and PCO counterparts. When asked to describe if they were engaged in the substantive or procedural aspects of policy formulation, multiple former PMO directors of policy responded, "Both." Procedurally, this entailed early engagement in the appraisal sub-phase followed by intense oversight and coordination at the formulation and consolidation sub-phases. The sequence of policy formulations is important and when partisan advisers engaged reveals important insights into conjunctures of policy formulation that were emphasized. Moreover, it highlights that there continues to be a division of labour among political and public service actors. Two former PMO policy directors explained their formulation activity and underscored a procedural emphasis and temporal considerations:

> Sometimes we were involved in the idea generation, but I would say that most of the ministers' agenda is already determined. And so our role would be on the *process, making sure that things were properly shepherded through the system* and that there was political input and, you know, sort of political oversight at all of those stages. Well, we would redraft some things and make sure that, you know, the minister's office they would be looking at it politically, but in case they hadn't, you know, we would be able to ask them questions and make sure there was proper oversight. (P13, emphasis added)

> At the front end, there wasn't as much work. The department would go away and churn some drafts up, and churn some stuff up, and so you wouldn't pay a lot of attention to that, other than making sure that the [minister's] chief knew what the key elements that you wanted to see in that were. So a fair amount of work would be, once you saw that first draft, giving feedback to the department, coordinating that feedback with the bureaucrats. So there was a fair amount of work there. Then, it would go back to them. Then, the majority of the time I would spend would be working it through the Cabinet process, making sure that ministers understood what the prime minister's view were on this and what we were looking for from them. (P12)

Partisan advisers interviewed below the chief of staff level spoke about their functions in coordinating policy work that had to be dealt with by Cabinet and Cabinet committees. This involved significant horizontal administrative-technical moving, with senior PCO officials dealing with the sequencing of policy through the Cabinet process.

When asked to describe their role in Cabinet / Cabinet committees, a PMO director of policy made clear that moving extended to partisan-political and administrative-technical dimensions:

> We had extensive involvement in the Cabinet committee system. We were consulted on the constitution of the Cabinets. You know, we sat in on every ... we consulted regularly every week with the Privy Council Office over Cabinet agendas: which items go forward, which items don't, which items need more work. We would provide advice to the prime minister in the Cabinet meeting itself. You know, it would be not at all uncommon for the prime minister who had read all the briefing notes to look up and say [PMO director of policy], you know, "This note says this, is there anything more that you need to say on this?" So you're on the spot there. Typically as [partisan adviser] it would be either I would be there, the policy person would be there, depending on the Cabinet committee. Typically, it would be either the policy director or the policy person whose area that was. (P13)

Partisan advisers from the PMO policy shop also reported significant moving in relation to Cabinet. They explained that when Cabinet was sitting, it would increase the need for them to interact with both ministerial office partisan advisers and senior PCO counterparts. This was particularly tied to the process-heavy nature of the Cabinet decision-making system. Each memorandum to Cabinet had to be sent to the Cabinet papers division of the PCO by a certain time, thus requiring coordination by the PMO and PCO to ensure that items on the Cabinet committee agenda were in hand. Interviews with senior PMO and PCO officials confirmed that the committee system played a dominant role in the Harper administration's Cabinet system more generally. One long-serving former senior PCO official, with experience over several recent administrations, described differences in approaches to the organization and operation of Cabinet:

> [Full] Cabinet hardly ever meets in this current government. Maybe once a month. Cabinet is a very diminished institution. Everything is done in committees and largely two committees that run the show: OPs [operations committee] that is chaired by the putative deputy prime minister, and Priorities and Planning, which is chaired by the prime minister. My sense is, my recollection is that for Harper, Cabinet doesn't exist. Already the clerk's role is somewhat changed. But the clerk absolutely attended

the Priorities and Planning meeting with the prime minister, and so did the [PMO] chief of staff. I don't recall anyone else. Similar, someone from PCO, often the clerk and somebody from PMO, often the chief of staff went to OPs. That was similar for the Chrétien Cabinet. With Martin there was more PMO participation, more [political] staff participation in everything. (PCO3)

A priority role for Cabinet committees was also confirmed in interviews with two then senior PCO officials and by published insider accounts from former PMO staff (Carson 2014). Their accounts of the activities of senior partisan advisers included pronounced activity at the "front end" in appraisal and dialogue sub-phases. This type of activity was horizontal and administrative-technical in the sense that it consisted of the larger strategic coordination involving planning and sequencing of policy work, as well as partisan-political as it involved the provision/confirmation of general political direction to the PCO. PMO partisan advisers reported most commonly undertaking what could be termed "transactional" types of interaction over "nuts and bolts" aspects of policy formulation. This too was along horizontal administrative-technical dimensions and was explained to involve iterative exchanges between the PMO and PCO officials (at low to mid levels) in the dialogue and formulation sub-phases. A senior PCO staff interviewed described that it as an ongoing and iterative exchange: "We have a virtually daily and multi-daily interaction. So for my job, it's [PCO Cabinet secretariat] and strategic advice to the government and it's me and [senior PCO official] or [PCO official] talking to [PMO director of policy] or one of the policy people on a specific policy file, and that's daily, virtually. Economic advice the prime minister has a senior economic adviser that's part of [PMO policy] team that we deal with daily, well and right now, multi-daily and on weekends" (PCO2).

The greater overall reliance by Harper on Cabinet committees for the triage and "heavy lifting" versus full Cabinet created more potential points of access and increased the opportunity for PMO policy staff to insert themselves in and manage formal policy formulation. PCO officials interviewed categorically confirmed regular interactions with PMO partisan advisers on this front. It is also supported by published accounts from observers and insiders who have documented Harper's policymaking approach (Carson 2014; Wells 2013; Martin 2010). Ministers interviewed readily acknowledged that the PMO has crucial procedural functions in the development of policy, as was evident in the comments of one minister who, when asked if he engaged with PMO staff on a policy level, stated,

> There's people there that can thwart your agenda. But that expression or that attitude that if you know the right person in the PMO, it will all come clicking into place, I think is a far less prevalent now than it was twenty years ago. That's not to say that PMO is not powerful, because it is. Because there's a bunch of things that matter to stakeholders and others. It may not be, they may not have the ability to, you know, run around the minister, do an end run, and do a piece of legislation that they want. But it can be as simple as when it gets tabled in the House of Commons. You know, it can either be soon or it can be a year from now, because the PMO obviously controls the sequencing of a lot of the government activity. They just say we just can't ... we can't roll that out at this time, we can't afford it, or we can't do two big controversial things at the same time, or there is a bunch of reasons behind it. And an individual minister can't know all that stuff, because they're just hunkered down in their own business. (M12)

This again emphasizes the influence the PMO can wield in managing the processes around policy formulation. Senior central agency officials in the PMO and PCO coordinate and control. Part of their role involves adjudication of the readiness of MCs and other Cabinet business prior to them getting on the formal agenda. This has obvious implications for policymaking. Respondents, like the minister above, also underscored that the PMO coordinates and integrates policy formulation as it moves towards formal Cabinet decision-making. Former ministers speaking on the record confirmed that PMO partisan advisers were consequential procedural actors. As former minister David Emerson put it of his time in the Harper Cabinet, "Generally the system was lubricated by the chiefs of staff, who would communicate back and forth or constantly about what the minister was or was not doing and make sure that there was no cross-threading that was going to be destructive to the government." Stockwell Day, another long-serving Harper minister, also emphasized appraisal and dialogue sub-stage activity with PMO counterparts:

> Sometimes you wanted clarification on something, or it may be something that hadn't been discussed in previous meetings with the prime minister.

It may be a new approach you're thinking of bringing forward, but in general terms you want some sense of it from the PM. You don't want to bring something forward that doesn't have any hope of getting Cabinet or caucus support. So it could be something you initiate or something initiated by the prime minister himself or from his office. I always found this prime minister, Prime Minister Harper, if you needed to see him, he would always make sure there was ample opportunity to do that. Especially if he knew you were going to be concise, get to the point, and that the item was important. So for me, I never had a problem with getting a hold of the prime minister, and certainly obviously he never had a problem getting a hold of me.

These responses again point to the important "signal-checking" and other moving that the PMO undertakes for policy-based coordination and resource exchange with multiple actors, throughout formulation. It is important to recognize that the accounts and explanations provided by all categories of actors emphasized the concurrent and often overlapping nature of resource exchanges among partisan-political and public service elites. The PCO managed the Cabinet processes but did so in part based on input from the PMO. The PMO derived much of its procedural moving influence, particularly along the administrative-technical dimension, from its ability to marshal, leverage, and focus PCO energies on specific government policy priorities. The PMO also leverages its ministers' offices partisan advisers as instruments for improved systemic process management and coordination. The federal case thus demonstrates the important and iterative nature of moving in that policy-based resource exchanges were essential and ongoing aspects of core executive policy development.

Moving at (and around) the Centre in British Columbia

First minister's office partisan advisers in this case explicitly described formal policy formulation as a key part of their day-to-day duties. They described moving that spanned partisan-political and administrative-technical dimensions. Similar to their federal counterparts, advisers in this case emphasized its occurrence in the context of formal policy formulation, particularly Cabinet and its committees. One first minister's office partisan adviser unpacked overall functions and apportioned about 10 per cent for human resources involving ministerial assistants and the remaining majority for policy. As she put it, "Probably 70 per cent of the time attending committees, so policy development, policy participation, policy enhancement. And the other 20 per cent of the time was divided by advice to the premier directly and other meetings" (P3). Her self-perceived primary function as a core executive actor involved policy development. This characterization also supports the utility of the framework developed in chapter 2 that understands policy formulation and advisory work as separate buckets or types of policy work.

Moving at the BC first minister's office level was described in much more horizontal and administrative-technical terms, with less emphasis on verticality or partisan-political types of moving. The smaller first minister's office resulted in reduced vertical partisan-political and administrative-technical moving within the Premier's Office. As such, most of their moving involved horizontal activities with ministers, central agencies, and deputies. On both fronts their horizontal moving was associated with Cabinet and Cabinet committee work. In contrast to Ottawa, horizontal partisan-political moving in BC was cast as more frequently and intensively occurring directly with ministers and to a lesser degree with ministerial partisan advisers. Their moving was particularly pronounced at the appraisal, dialogue, and formulation subphases. Respondents described horizontal administrative-technical moving as involving "front-end" appraisal and dialogue sub-stage activity. As one first minister's office partisan adviser put it,

> They want leadership, they want direction, and they want clarity. Their expertise is in executing. Where they excel is in reconciling the general direction and vision you want to embrace with how you practically do that and giving feedback, saying, "You can't," or saying, "This is how you have to modify your vision or idea." This is where I worked really well with them, saying, "This is what we want to do or where we want to go and how do we get there." And then you set to the hard task of saying, "This is what it means to get there," and then you weigh the options, the pros and cons, the impacts, and you decide whether you are going to do that in some shape or form. That's what the civil service does is it looks to the elected leaders for direction and vision, not partisanship. (P3)

Another senior first minister's office partisan adviser described at great length how her participation in formulation was fundamentally a matter or coordination of formulation actors and options. That is, she engaged in horizontal administrative-technical *and* horizontal partisan-political moving with Cabinet ministers on Cabinet and Cabinet committee business, as well as with deputies or other policy experts outside of government. This was explained as a means to ensure that formulation and consolidation sub-phase activity would be as informed as possible, with decision-makers given a full spectrum of policy options or a "complete picture." Emphasis was placed on the dialogic consultation management required to ensure formulation was well executed.

A marked difference to emerge in interviews in the BC case was the involvement of senior first minister's office partisan advisers in almost every facet of process-related activity involving Cabinet and Cabinet committees. While federally, junior partisan advisers could be dispatched to monitor and coordinate with the PCO on any given initiative or Cabinet committee, such activity was the ambit of senior first ministers' partisan advisers in BC. Interviews also revealed that their moving extended beyond participation in the partisan-political priority policy initiatives to also include day-to-day moving as policy was developed. That is, references were again made to first minister's office partisan advisers spending time on formal priority policy items and "housekeeping" or operational items that would inevitably emerge and populate the policy agenda of government. Another partisan adviser emphasized moving in policy development. Describing policy as usually occurring in waves, the adviser used language very much akin to Savoie's (1999a) notions of an ongoing housekeeping track and a second track for the government's key policy priorities:

> There's the day-to-day decision-making that doesn't require legislation. It may not even require regulation, but it needs to be rooted in some sort of policy decision. So, that is ongoing, and that would consume probably 10 to 15 per cent of my day. And most of that is very informal, people calling and saying, "I'm confronted by this situation and what do you think I should do?" and a discussion ensues and a decision is made. When the House is sitting or in the lead up to a legislative session through committee meetings, like legislative review committee, the amount of time I would spend on policy would ramp up, because you're actively making significant policy decisions if you're drafting legislation and writing it. It could increase to, you know, 30 to 40 per cent of my day. And then when the House is actively sitting, Cabinet met daily, and part of my job was to brief the Cabinet on the issues of the day and what we were doing about them. When the House was sitting, I would say that policy was more like 70 per cent of my day. (P4)

Several partisan advisers confirmed that limited horizontal moving involving first ministers' and ministerial partisan advisers occurred via formalized "daily meeting" with all political staff. It was explained that the daily meeting was a forum for the Premier's Office to advise or coordinate with ministerial staff on pressing policy issues and to hear from them on any items they thought ought to be flagged. As one first minister's office partisan adviser explained, "There'd be some dialogue about what the priorities were that day, and from there if issues emerged throughout the day, they might contact me, or if I heard about something coming down the pipe I might contact them" (P4). Additional horizontal partisan-political and administrative-technical moving was reported tied to "firefighting" or "issues management." While the federal PMO had a separate "shop" to tend to such items, the BC partisan advisers at the centre also tended to firefighting linked to immediate and unexpected concerns that emerged through the public service or in response to media on programs or policies. The BC case thus also displayed ongoing moving that spanned the four key dimensions set out in this study. As core executive actors, their policy-based resource exchanges were, in a procedural sense, closely tied to Cabinet and Cabinet committees. There was, however, much less intra–first ministerial moving, given the much smaller number of partisan advisers. Also, greater moving was reported with central agencies but also deputies, ministers, and to a lesser degree ministerial partisan advisers.

Moving at the Centre in New Brunswick

Partisan advisers in the first minister's office in New Brunswick reported administrative-technical and partisan-political moving as an integral part of their formulation activities, particularly at dialogue and formulation sub-phases. Premier's Office staff have for some time now been recognized as an important procedural player on policy grounds in New Brunswick, with one observer finding that "traditionally when seeking policy direction, deputies turn to the chief of staff, who represents the ideal route for accessing the premier and who is authorized to speak for premier" and from whom "they receive their mandates and requests for policy development" (Bouchard 2014, 111). The New Brunswick case shared the BC predilection for horizontal moving along both administrative-technical and partisan-political dimensions. This was again the product of the considerably smaller first minister's office. However, the New Brunswick case was unique in that there was an explicit agreement between the chief of staff and principal secretary on their division of labour. Both agreed that the chief of staff would focus on all things "political," while the principal secretary dealt with items that were "more policy than politics." This division was reported as largely successful, with some issues and priorities necessarily overlapping. It was described as a 40:40:20 proportion, with 40 per cent the ambit of the chief of staff, 40 per cent for the principal secretary, and the remaining 20 per cent shared between the two. Such a division of labour necessitated administrative-technical and partisan-political moving, as the two most senior partisan advisers coordinated strategies and priorities, managed processes related to their respective bailiwicks, and ensured that everyone was "on side." These activities were by their nature spread throughout formulation sub-phases. The responses from the full range of interviewees, however, confirmed that by far the largest proportion of their moving was horizontal and usually associated with Cabinet policy processes, particularly with the Priorities and Planning and Management Board committees of Cabinet. While senior partisan advisers from the first minister's office noted considerable interaction with central administrative agencies, specifically the Executive Council Office (ECO), interviews revealed much greater interactions between the Premier's Office partisan advisers level deputy ministers than in either of the two previous cases.

Horizontal administrative-technical moving linked to Cabinet business was reported as occurring at all formulation sub-phases and involving interactions with officials and ministers as policy was formalized. In contrast to the two other cases, horizontal partisan-political moving was consistently described as much more direct between first minister's office partisan advisers and ministers. Virtually no references were made to any such activity involving ministerial office partisan advisers. Horizontal administrative-technical moving was most frequently reported in the context of participation and oversight activities linked to Cabinet processes. When asked about their interactions with Cabinet ministers and senior public servants, a first minister's office partisan adviser described playing a pivotal role in assisting policy initiatives through cabinet processes:

> They use me, if you will, for whatever it is they would like to push forward. I don't generally go to Cabinet or [Cabinet committee]. I attend [Cabinet committee] every week. But, if need be, if things aren't going the way I want them to, I attend those other meetings, and they know that. So when I show up somewhere, at all the places they know this is serious,

you know, and I'm not going to let it go. Or that the premier has said, you know, "Will you keep an eye on this for me?" He'll send me notes sometimes, on a letter, or whatever, and he'll say, you know, "Keep an eye on this for me." And they know that's what I'm doing, because the premier can't. There are so many balls in the air all the time that he needs to pass some of that over to people like [senior partisan adviser] and I to keep an eye for him. (P1)

This statement is indicative of first minister's office partisan advisers' horizontal moving at the formulation and consolidation sub-phases linked to Cabinet processes. It further points to important monitoring and coordination as well. These procedural types of formulation were a mainstay of senior partisan advisers in New Brunswick. Throughout interviews with first minister's office staff, it became clear that there was also considerable moving along both horizontal administrative-technical and partisan-political dimensions at dialogue and consolidation sub-phases related to assisting items clear hurdles to be successful in Cabinet committees. As a first minister's office partisan adviser described at length,

If they think that they are going to get a rough ride in some way, through Cabinet, through board of management, they often ask for my help in getting through board of management, simply because sometimes you get a great idea and not all the signs, or people don't always see that it's a wonderful idea or that there is a payback involved, or whatever. So it depends. If it's big or long-term, I will usually see a one-pager or they will have a meeting with me, they will ask for a meeting with me at the early stage of what they are developing. So anything in their mandate letters which was most of our Charter for Change [party platform] I don't usually have to worry too much about, unless, like I say, it's the smaller issues that they feel maybe are less important and they can shove off to the side because they don't have time, or they're told to tighten their belt and they don't know where to do it. And so, unless I pick those things up and drive them, they would be lost. (P1)

This statement underscores the important function that moving can serve. It can be instrumental for the successful development of policy that, as the adviser put it, might otherwise be "lost." This case saw intense activity reported between the first minister's office and central agencies but more frequent interactions described as occurring with deputy ministers. Again, the small size of government overall, and particularly the executive, was a frequently cited reason for close relationships between deputies' and first ministers' offices partisan advisers. Respondents often described administrative-technical moving as involving appraisal and dialogue sub-phase activity. One senior partisan adviser explained it as consisting of providing direction and setting the parameters with senior officials: "Most of the discussions that we have with both ministers and deputy ministers are more about moving forward with some stuff. And so we're talking very often because [deputy] is keeping me informed and at the same time we're giving [the deputy] general direction of where the government would like to go with that in that sense and [the deputy] is going to put that together" (P2).

Horizontal partisan-political moving was explained to be primarily partisan adviser to minister but included greater emphasis on consolidation sub-phase activity. That is, multiple respondents noted that the first minister's office partisan advisers were key actors able to settle policy disputes that entailed horizontal or government-wide considerations. Further, first ministers' office partisan-political moving was frequently reported as involving management activities related to dialogic activities of consulting with caucus or ministers, such as in "firefighting" and resolution of particular contentious files, as well as brokerage with "off side" ministers. As one first minister's office adviser put it, "If they come as a group of MLAs like the [city] crew, or the [town] crew, or whatever, that has a political issue, and they would come to [senior partisan adviser] to help with it. Or some large policy issues that crosscut departments, and I look after [the file] too, so they tend to talk to me about things like that as well" (P2).

Echoing the other two cases, senior Premier's Office advisers in New Brunswick reported a difference between ongoing policy work that the public service has been developing (that may have predated the government), and policy priorities of the current government. Partisan moving was also raised in conjunction with the latter, that monitoring and steering to ensure successful completion of the political agenda were fundamental for first minister's office advisers. The first minister's office staff interviewed pointed to their ability to keep the partisan-political policy priorities moving through the government, which was full of policy already in development. One first minister's office partisan adviser explained, "But if that's important to me, or if it's important to one of the people that ran in the election, if it's important to [senior partisan adviser], we can keep that moving, or otherwise it would be lost" (P2). When further explaining the moving function, the adviser was quite conscious that both pre-established policy items desired by the public service co-existed with partisan-political commitments. The adviser saw his policy function in large part as a matter of ensuring that partisan-political policy objectives and commitments were translated into public policy:

> As a group of civil servants tries to develop a program, say, that would answer or be the answer to a political promise. It can get quite lost in translation. It could in fact be something that they had been working on before, and they try to put a square peg in a round hole even, and they say, "Oh well, we wanted to do this and so we'll make this fit." We'll just dress it up with their political ends sort of wording around it and, well, just make it fit and continue on. And in a lot of ways the government continues to function with or without politicians, and good thing, you know. And probably most of what they do has very little to do with anything we would be all that concerned about, you know. And I don't say that in a bad or nasty way at all. It's keeping the wheels greased, like keeping the thing moving along. The train is big, and there's a lot of statutory things that have to get done, no matter who's here. A lot of those things are going to happen. You tend to concentrate on the things that wouldn't happen if you weren't here. (P1)

Interviews with all categories of participants, across the political and administrative spheres, revealed that first minister's partisan advisers were seen as able to improve the coordination of formal policy activities. Like the other cases, first minister's partisan advisers' moving spanned the formulation sub-phases and were significantly tied to Cabinet-related work. They shared the same tendency of the other provincial case towards reduced vertical activity, but as opposed to their BC counterparts reported considerably more explicit partisan-political activity, particularly in coordination among agents related to platform implementation, formal policy development, and budgeting.

First Ministers' Office "Shaping"

PMO Shapers

PMO partisan-political content-based formulation was most often described in relation to the appraisal, dialogue, and formulation, and to a more limited extent consolidation sub-phase activity. Shaping included formal "front-end" policy development involving PMO partisan advisers providing input into the creation of mandate letters, throne speeches, and one-off departmental policy initiatives. It was also described by PMO partisan advisers to occur continuously and was again frequently referenced in conjunction with Cabinet-related activity. PMO partisan advisers' shaping was reported as ample, at all sub-phases, and spanning both partisan and "administrative-technical" dimensions. One PMO chief of staff interviewed explained that the government's policy agenda was orchestrated and planned well in advance. The partisan adviser described policy development at the elite level as involving weaving – combining the partisan-political policy priorities of the government-of-the-day with policy work that had been percolating in the public service. As former PMO chief Ian Brodie explained,

> We went through an annual priority-setting exercise, which the PM was very disciplined about. Driven by the drafting of the throne speech, what was going to go into the government, and a few other pieces the PM's international travel and was involved in would drive some international travel. This is an effort that started in April or May of each year and was codified in an internal priorities document, or a series of documents, we didn't have a single fixed document for it. But each year we did it a little bit differently but priority-setting exercise in PMO, priority-setting exercise in the PCO, and then the PM making a final decision about, you know, stitching the two together. Usually the two sets of documents were quite similar.

This overarching planning and prioritizing exercise described by the former PMO chief speaks directly to the role senior PMO partisan advisers play in shaping the content of key government policy initiatives. These high-level meetings were early in the mandate of the government and charted the course of how partisan electoral policy positions were to be fleshed out through the machinery of government. They were explained to involve intensive and in-depth appraisal and dialogue sub-phase activity among senior PMO-PCO officials. The PMO chief went on to explain that the prioritizing and planning shaped other policy development milestones. Interviews also confirmed that mandate letters remain a fundamental lever by which the Prime Minister and his office provide policy direction to ministers and senior public servants, and shape government-wide policy formulation (Savoie

1999a). As Brodie further explained, "The mandate letter process was then a sort of a distillation or a slicing of the priority-setting exercise in the PMO but parcelled out by portfolio." Senior partisan advisers, however, took great care in noting that mandate letters are not simple or crass partisan-political marching orders. Rather, these documents are an explicit vehicle through which substantive shaping is possible and involve an intricate knitting together of public service policy or operational imperatives with the priorities of the government. As former PMO chief of staff Guy Giorno described it, "It's hard for something these days to get oxygen or time if it's not grounded in a mandate letter. But a mandate letter isn't based entirely on political agenda. It's based on housekeeping things or operational things or requirements of good government that the public service has identified and initiated. So I would still say most by them (drafted by the public service). Except for the fact that the government sets the overall agenda." This "stitching together" of the government's key policy priorities and the imperatives that the public service identified is precisely the type of resource exchange that fuels core executive operation (Craft 2015a; Eichbaum and Shaw 2011). The chiefs' description points to their important function in articulating the political arm's policy priorities and giving them life through their integration into the broader policy work, but also highlights their ability to engage in unique facets of the politics of policy work.

A range of senior PMO partisan advisers revealed that there was some evolution in how mandate letters are produced as well as the role of PMO partisan advisers in their crafting. Multiple respondents confirmed that the PMO's role in mandate letter preparation and writing became increasingly "hands on" as time went on in the Harper administration. The first series of mandate letters were driven by the PCO as the government found their footing. Accounts suggest that traditionally PCO Machinery of Government secretariat, with some input from others during the drafting, almost exclusively drafted mandate letters (Savoie 1999a). Those interviewed from the PCO and PMO for this study confirmed that important changes occurred with mandate letter-writing. The Priorities and Planning section of the PCO has increasingly become involved, and, as one PCO official put it, the process has become more "open and collective." Another key change reported is that the PMO sought to exercise a more "hands on" approach, seeking greater and earlier involvement in the document drafting. From the perspective of PMO advisers, this was described to have become a more comprehensive process in that it would involve a back-and-forth exchange of drafts with deputy secretary PCO-level officials. In keeping with available studies, these letters are pivotal for the establishment and communication of policy priorities and an essential vehicle by which the government of the day gives shape to its policy priorities. Two senior PMO partisan advisers made this clear in explaining the importance and evolution of the PMO approach to mandate letter writing:

> Because these mandate letters became a much more powerful exercise in *shaping* the government's agenda. As we went along, they sort of became more specific in the sense of "you should take the lead on climate change issue, but here are three ministers you must consult during the process, and here's when we want to discuss this on the Cabinet agenda, so work back from there, but it has to get into the Cabinet decision-making process." Or, "This is an issue that's going to come up in the budget, so you must have your submission in to the finance minister and the Finance Department by such-and-such a date, or whatever. Here's money you should expect to be able spend on this, or we don't expect to spend additional new money on this, or manage within existing resources. This is a policy issue that will require legislation, so keep in touch with [senior partisan adviser]." (Former PMO chief of staff Ian Brodie, emphasis added)

> When this government came in, basically the Privy Council Office handled the whole job. We seized a significant part of that function back into the Prime Minister's Office and particularly the policy office. So by the time the Privy Council Office got the letters, the drafts of the letters, you know, they were pretty well finalized. There might be a few things that, you know, the prime minister would look at and meet with the clerk and say, "Oh, you know, I forgot this, or this isn't quite right." But typically you would have a staffer [partisan adviser] in the room that would help finalize it. But most of the drafting was done in conjunction with the prime minister, in the policy department, and then would go up to PCO. (P12)

This type of shaping is thus a clear example of attempts to secure political control over the policy agenda through substantive policy-based core executive resource exchanges. At the highest order, partisan-political and public service policy priorities had to be integrated to produce a coherent policy agenda for government. In keeping with existing practices, the letters were sent to ministers and their deputies. Shaping or substance-based policy formulation was not limited to throne speeches and mandate letters. PMO partisan advisers described ongoing shaping as an iterative activity occurring through content-based contributions to formal policy development. For example, many reported contributions to, and scrutiny of, departmental memoranda to Cabinet and other policy development underway within departments as well as central agencies. While he was not interviewed for this study, the appointment of Nigel Wright as PMO chief of staff was widely seen as a positive recruitment of an experienced hand, not only for his political experience and instincts as a former Mulroney PMO policy adviser and speechwriter, but for his substantive experience in the private sector, and financial sector bona fides. Assessments suggest that he was no mere political "hack" but perceived as a thoughtful and legitimate policy player, one account being that Wright was often engaged in moving and shaping, that he was "actively managing dozens of files. Wright contributed to important public policy – on foreign ownership rules, competition in the telecom sector and especially CETA, the free trade deal with Europe" (Pullen 2014). When asked how an adviser engaged in formulation at the "front" or "back end" of the policy formulation stage, a junior PMO partisan adviser described it as follows: "Did we do some policy creation? Yes. But it wasn't, you know, for the most part we weren't going out and researching things by ourselves and developing the memoranda to Cabinet. I want to say we were more editors of the policy proposals that were submitted to us, but editors from a political process. So we would edit, we would question, we would push back on the proposals that came forward" (P15).

Shaping was described as involving the adjudication of content-based policy materials to ensure consistency or alignment of formal policy outputs with previously articulated and democratically mandated policy positions. The adviser above and another respondent understood that their content-based contributions largely involved adjudicating public service policy development work for its consistency or "fit" with articulated partisan-political policy direction or positions. Interviews revealed that ongoing shaping was clearly linked to attempts to secure political control and policy responsiveness. As two PMO advisers explained,

We would just have to constantly reinforce what we wanted out of the bureaucracy. You know, constantly reinforcing, "Look, this government got elected to do X. We're going to do, you know, to the degree it's not

completely unconstitutional, we're going to do X." Again it was quite iterative. It was always initial briefings from the bureaucracy, "Is this is even
possible, OK, what are the options?" Then we would get policy papers, so
draft memoranda to Cabinet. And our job in PMO was to scrutinize those
policy documents as they were being drafted as well as briefing notes to
the prime minister, but our job was to scrutinize them and to make sure
that the policy proposals that actually came forward were not being wate-
red down so much that they no longer reflected the political commitment.
I say we were editors. We weren't looking for grammar and stuff like that.
What we were looking for as we were editing the proposals that came
forward, we were looking at the proposal and assessing the proposal to
see if it was true to the political commitments that were made. (P15)

The other side of it is like when you are talking about here, you get some
something from staff, from the bureaucrats, from PCO, or whatever.
And you write your own note on top of it. Sometimes you write that
note to the PM, or sometimes you write that to the chief of staff and say,
you know, "This is what they're advising, and the prime minister has
stated he wants this, or our platform has said this, or, you know, our
government mandate is to do this, and I believe that this, you know ...
this isn't consistent with such-and-such, and therefore my advice would
be to alter it this way or speak to so-and-so. The risks are here. So, you
know, we should probably do this, this, and this to assess the risks before
we move forward." (P18)

If policy proposals, in various draft stages or finalized iterations, were
found to be inconsistent with previously articulated policy position or
direction, they would be returned to the department and minister for
reworking. Often it would be accompanied with precise suggestions on
what was expected or suggestions to improve the content. Many PMO
partisan advisers explained this was common, as departments and ministers' offices worked through the development of Cabinet submission.
PMO partisan advisers explained their involvement in formulation
occurred at the department level, as active engagement throughout formulation. Again, emphasis was on early horizontal shaping along both
administrative-technical and partisan-political dimensions at the dialogue
and formulation sub-phases. Partisan advisers at the first minister's
office would leverage their ministerial counterparts' partisan-political
advice and knowledge of departmental policy advice for their first

minister's office shaping. Again, it is important to distinguish shaping from buffering, in that it was directly and explicitly undertaken with formal policy *in development*. That is, PMO partisan advisers would review and scrutinize a memorandum to Cabinet that had been developed by ministers with their departments to ensure consistency and alignment with the partisan-political policy intent and existing commitments. As one partisan adviser explained, this involved considerable substantive policy-based resource exchanges with partisan-political and public service core executive actors. As another adviser recounted, policy-based resource exchanges were multi-layered, multi-actor, multi-type, and iterative as policy was being developed:

> The Conservative Party makes a commitment, they get into government, they decide, "OK, were going to push ahead with this priority." We would then say to officials, "OK, tell us how to make it happen, give us some options." So what would happen on any given policy file is that the bureaucracy would come to us with some initial ideas. We got briefed in the Prime Minister's Office, we got briefed by the Privy Council office on the officials' side. From a political staff perspective, I worked regularly with the minister's office and so the minister's staff would be telling me what they were thinking and the briefings they were getting from their officials. (P15)

Additional horizontal administrative-technical shaping also occurred via interactions between senior partisan advisers and PCO officials. Interviews with both sets of policy actors confirmed that PCO officials dealt primarily with PMO policy directors for briefing material headed to the prime minister. "Clerk's notes," as they are called, were described as the principal instrument by which the PCO, via the clerk, could raise items for prime ministerial attention. Directors of policy would have input, often informally in the dialogue or formulation subphase prior to formal drafting of these notes. Many described opportunities to informally exchange policy-based resources in the run-up to the development of formal policy instruments like such notes. One adviser gave an example of what that looked like: "Just off the record what do you think the, you know, what would the view of the political staff be? And I would say, 'Off the record, I think it will be this.' And they say, 'Well that's helpful. Thanks. We're not that different.' And then we could save our ammunition for the things that we really disagreed on" (P12). Several former senior Chrétien and Martin PMO partisan advisers consulted for this study described this type of informal consultative exchange as their established practice. It was informal and conversational, with the PCO then integrating senior PMO partisan advisory input in the formal and written policy briefs and documents prepared by the PCO and sent to the prime minister (Goldenberg 2006; Jeffrey 2010; Savoie 2008).[37] One PCO official commented on this signal-checking and also noted that it was useful for the PCO to know whether the political policy analysis had been completed: "We certainly can talk to them about, you know, "'Have you done the homework? Is the political analysis all cooked? Are you sure how you're going to interact with this? Have you reached out to the various ministers' offices and gotten their regional input or all of that?' We can certainly give advice on how it will, systems, should work. But it's really important that theirs [partisan advisers'] is a separate channel of political advice, and knowing that that's happening does make it easier" (PCO2).

In the Harper PMO this was additional to the formal written and informal oral advisory practices that the PMO were providing as outlined above. Another Harper PMO director of policy, when asked in which "stage" of policymaking he engaged the most, clearly pointed to policy formulation rather than agenda setting. This was a consistent finding from interviews. Mandate letters, Speeches from the Throne, budgets, and MCs all offered PMO partisan advisers opportunities to shape policy through front-end substantive, content-based policy calibration. However, all first ministers' office partisan advisers were quite clear that they engaged in ongoing and iterative shaping as policy was developed. Both types of shaping involved considerable resource exchanges that were similar to those of advisory systems in that they involved public servants and partisan advisers. Together with the moving above, it suggests exchanges that span formulation sub-phases and considerable PMO and PCO exchanges that provide shape and form to the content of policy.

First Ministers' Office Shaping in British Columbia

Premier's Office partisan advisers in BC described significant horizontality in their shaping at formulation sub-phases. Some involved "front-end" shaping during appraisal through Speeches from the Throne, but unlike their federal counterparts, considerably less participation was reported in mandate letter–writing (known as letters for departmental service plans, in British Columbia). However, shaping during the appraisal sub-phase was described along partisan-political dimensions related to electoral platform development and the Speech from the Throne. First minister's office partisan advisers reported translating key electoral and partisan-political priorities into actionable policy. Additional intensive and ongoing administrative-technical horizontal shaping was also noted on formal policy-development mechanisms linked to Cabinet and the budget. There was significantly less vertical shaping in this case, much like moving, which is attributable to the smaller number of partisan advisers in the first minister's and ministers' offices. The limited shaping of this kind involved appraisal and dialogue sub-stage activity centred on translating platform items into initial policy parameters and direction.

Partisan advisers described their roles in departmental service plans as supportive and peripheral, and consisting primarily of formulation sub-phase activity. As one adviser put it, "No, I didn't participate in those. I would see them and read them beforehand, but fundamentally those were set and written by the deputy minister to the premier" (P3). Another explained in greater detail that they changed over time, explaining,

> I think initially they were subject to much more sort of political scrutiny in terms of ensuring that they met the objectives of the premier and the government. I think that over time it became a much more public service function, the public service would base the content of those letters. Basically try to make them reflect the throne speech, the platform. It tended to be … the letters would be drafted by them and they'd come to our office and we'd review them in conjunction with the premier and ensure they aligned with our thinking, and then they would go out the door. (P4)

Similar to the New Brunswick case as detailed below, in the BC case partisan advisers at the centre reported marked involvement in drafting the party platform, which would subsequently shape the policy agenda of government. This was described in relation to questions about their policy work in general. One partisan adviser explained that political staffs were important to the development of these documents and that they were developed while government was in office. The adviser elaborated, "Often while liaising with people around government and getting advice, it's not like we just invented them, but we played a big role in coming up with those ideas" (P4). It was explained that while in government, partisan advisers would begin to give thought to the future policy agenda of government, which would be expressed first via a platform in the next election. They described engaging in shaping whereby they would consult with any number of actors inside or outside of government to generate potential ideas or look for ways to refine of calibrate existing policies. Their shaping was characterized as appraisal sub-phase-heavy in that it was intended to provide the broad framework and policy direction that, subsequent to an election, could be used to underpin key policy documents.

This type of horizontal partisan-political shaping would then form the basis of a guiding document to which first minister's office staff would then engage in administrative-technical shaping, to convert the mandated policy positions into concrete policy. However, in this case, first minister's office partisan advisers reported that once the initial direction had been formulated, they tended to disengage and allow the deputy minister to the premier, the premier, and the Cabinet office staff to take the lead on the letters sent out to inform departmental service plans. Additional front-end appraisal sub-phase activity was reported on the Speech from the Throne. While the service plan letters were seemingly less crucial, partisan advisers at the centre cited the throne speech as a key partisan-political instrument. One first minister's office partisan adviser explained that it was a subsequent step to platform development: "The second phase, the second place related to that is the throne speech, the most significant public policy statement from the government each year that's driven primarily by the political staff in the Premier's Office and the premier himself or herself in terms of what the content of that is, with input from other people, but it is a politically concocted document. So those are I think the big policy points that are done from the sort of the conceptualization idea" (P4).

Partisan-political shaping, as in the two other cases, was described as involving the application of a partisan-political lens to formal policymaking (Head 2008). This was not described as intended to politicize the public service. Rather, it was described as centred on the policy itself and quintessentially involved the adjudication of consistency or alignment of policy work with electoral platforms and the publicly articulated policy positions or commitments of ministers and the government. In the BC case, the first minister's office partisan advisers were involved in predominantly horizontal partisan-political shaping through "front-end" policy instruments such as the platform develop-ment and throne speech exercises as detailed above. However, advis-ers were also active in ongoing partisan-political shaping fuelled by their participation in Cabinet and Cabinet committee involvement. Partisan advisers at the centre were described as key actors who were able to adjudicate if changes were required to ensure government policy matched the previously articulated policy positions. Ministers interviewed were aware of this policy work, as one minister explained there were instances where the Premier's Office would have views on the expected legislation or new program design. As the minister put it, "Sometimes I, and sometimes my ministry, thought that those didn't necessarily add value from a ministerial perspective, although you could potentially see the value from the political perspective." When asked if, how, and when the politics of policy work was reconciled with public service formulation, a first minister's office partisan adviser made it clear:

> There's sort of a political check done to make sure that whatever they come up with actually does align with what the party meant. Or if what the party meant turns out to be stupid, to figure out how to change it. So the-re's that second phase of input there when they [partisan advisers] come forward. And then there are two separate areas of public policy on top of that, where political staff has a large amount of input. The first is on issues. Occasionally an issue will come up that shows a public policy gap and it will require a quick response. So that could be, you know, perhaps ... I don't know ... a disabled child is not eligible for whatever reason for some type of government service and it may not make sense. It just doe-sn't, from a political staff perspective. Even though the way the policy is written, they're excluded, it may not make sense on a practical level. In that case, political staff in conjunction with their ministers may play a significant role in how to change the policy and seeing it right through to delivery and execution. (P4)

In the BC case, horizontal administrative-technical formulation by first minister's office partisan advisers was described to more fre-quently involve central agency officials (notably the deputy premier's office) and to a lesser degree senior departmental officials, particularly in shaping multi-departmental policy items. Shaping was a key part of what partisan advisers at the centre reported doing. One adviser put it succinctly when asked about his policy work: "Fundamentally, it was reading information, reading [Cabinet] binders, interviewing and meeting with deputies, ADMs, and other senior civil servants. Analysing policies and developing policies, that was the fundamental task" (P3). Deputies confirmed that they had occasional dealings with Premier's Office partisan advisers, but that they were more regularly with ministerial advisers. Most were quick to point out that the deputy minister to the premier and his office handled the bulk of the "corporate" government-wide policy work with Premier's Office advisers. This was confirmed in interviews with senior Cabinet officials who noted that deputies were often immersed in their own departmental policy issues and administration. Two responses were indicative of others from a range of political and public service actors who emphasized the direction-setting function of the Cabinet and Premier's Office:

> There's no doubt that there are options that have come forward from the public service that have been reshaped in order to find a compromise or to find a solution that deals with both the objectives of the programs and the sensitivities of politics. (BCO1)

> The Cabinet really does set clear priorities and directions. It's almost like they're the head of the freighter or a flotilla and all the ministries are like little ships, and they line up their course to achieve … to implement those goals and be aligned with them. So they're continually realigning their business and their work and providing advice on how to achieve their priorities. (BCO2)

Like their federal counterparts, first minister's office partisan advisers indicated that they worked at the strategic level. Similar language was used to describe "ongoing" formulation within government and the need for Premier's Office partisan advisers to engage in strategic direction-setting and appraisal sub-stage activity. When asked where policy ideas came from, and if that had evolved, one first minister's office adviser simply responded overwhelmingly, "From the Premier's Office," explaining, "But the system was wholly incapable on its own proposing, propounding system change. It much resists that, and most ministers don't spend their time consumed with that. They spend their time executing against government direction, which is normally initiated, in our case at least, from the Premier's Office, whether it's from the premier or [Premier's Office partisan advisers], or the deputy minister to the premier and/or other senior bodies like agenda and priorities [Cabinet committee]" (P3).

In addition, partisan advisers often described shaping tied to Cabinet and committee work. This would involve directly providing content for specific policy in development, involving ad hoc activity with individual ministers, as well as more routine and formal content-based formulation with policy development occurring at full Cabinet, or in Cabinet committees. As one first minister's office partisan adviser explained, subsequent to the public service going through its formal policy development processes, the adviser would then engage in shaping. She explained that she would essentially read all available briefing material on a policy issue and then return to Cabinet committee, on behalf of the premier, with input on where the government should go. Responses detailed that in BC, Premier's Office partisan advisers were active in substantive policy development throughout all formulation sub-phases. When asked to detail how she participated in policy work at various policy cycle "stages," the adviser provided a detailed description tied explicitly to Cabinet. The response is representative of other senior first minister's advisers interviewed, who described engaging in moving and shaping, and it is worth quoting at length:

> Agendas and priorities [Cabinet committee] would be fundamentally at the front end, initiating. And a small portion of that would be, relatively speaking, would be decision-making at the back end, because that is where it comes through Cabinet. Treasury Board, which took an awful lot of my time. That's very cyclical budget preparation, but it's not just the annual budget cycle, which is basically budget's coming to Treasury Board by ministry and being deliberated on by ministry or by government agency, but also ongoing monitoring of all ministries for their fiscal performance. But it would be debt planning, capital planning, and the like. So it would be equally at the front end and the back end. And legislative review committee, that's mostly at the latter stages, at the back end. You get requests for legislation, initiated by Cabinet or by the ministries directly. By the time it would come to the legislative review committee, you would be analysing a draft bill, so well into the policy process. Or finalizing a draft bill before it would be approved by Cabinet. Many other committees like economic development, or all of the government caucus committees, or we had reconciliation and recognition committee of Cabinet, First Nations issues that those would be early-stage issues generally, or late stage. Or largely entertaining submissions before they would make it to Cabinet. So it would be across the board. (P3)

Partisan advisers reported significant involvement in ongoing horizontal shaping activities apart from "front-end" policy formulation mechanisms, such as service plans and throne speeches. These were clear opportunities for partisan advisers at the centre to engage in content-based shaping. This was explained to involve shaping at multiple sub-phases, notably appraisal, dialogue, and formulation. As one Premier's Office partisan adviser put it, "There would then be, of course, refining, editing, *shaping* the submissions as they would come in to all the Cabinet and Cabinet sub-committees" (emphasis added). Another described intensive shaping at the formulation sub-phase that, in the adviser's words, involved adjudicating how closely the given policy aligned with its intended goal. Such accounts were very similar to the other cases. As one first minister's office partisan adviser explained it, "Is this what ... does this policy proposal achieve what we said we wanted it to achieve, and is this what we want it to do?" The adviser went on to explain, "It's when it's near completion, so that's when it's about to go into legislative review committee, or when it's about to go into committee processes, or even into Cabinet" (P4).

Again, the shaping described above differs from buffering. Partisan advisers were not providing policy advice as one of many actors within the policy advisory system related any number of potential policy items, issues, or events. Rather, they were part of the privileged group of authoritative policy actors who directly contributed content or designed and developed specific policies being formalized within government. It was apparent that the core executive policy-based resource exchanges in the BC case were again heavily oriented to Cabinet processes, and also very central-agency focused. While first minister's office partisan advisers referenced engaging with deputies, considerably more interactions were reported from advisers and public service elites as central agency focused. The deputy minister to the premier quarterbacked those exchanges.

First Ministers' Office Shaping in New Brunswick

New Brunswick first minister's office partisan advisers reported shaping at the appraisal, dialogue, and formulation sub-phases along both administrative-technical and partisan-political dimensions. Formal partisan-political shaping was evident in descriptions of appraisal sub-phase activity in the creation of mandate letters and budget development. Similar to the other cases, it was described as ongoing and occurring through formal Cabinet-related mechanisms such as memoranda to Cabinet and informally through interactions with other actors in government. The New Brunswick case stood out, however, as horizontal administrative-technical shaping was again more frequently cited as a product of regular policy-related interaction between first minister's office advisers and deputies. This was commonly described as involving discussions with deputies about the content-based design and translation functions flowing from the electoral platform, ongoing policies being developed in departments, or policy items that deputies thought may be difficult to get through Cabinet.

Much like the other cases, first minister's office staff reported partisan-political shaping as consisting of the application of a political lens to public service policy development at the appraisal and formulation sub-phases (Head 2008). Their shaping consisted of suggesting changes or requesting amendments to particular policies during their development. At the outset of formulation, for example, during the appraisal sub-phase, they described providing direction flowing from the first minister, or setting parameters of what the expected policy would look like in finalized form. Moreover, shaping was repeatedly described as involving dialogue and formulation sub-stage activity during policy development to ensure that policy reflected the stated priorities and government commitments as articulated through electoral platforms. First minister's office advisers repeatedly stressed the importance of translating partisan-political objectives and commitments into policy. One adviser's general approach to policy formulation was described as follows:

> This sort of sounds like a broken record, you know, but we ran on a platform and we've tried to be true to that platform. So, I guess the first filter is, does it seem to fit? Or is it just the right thing to do, regardless and … but does it seem to fit? So if it seems to fit, then you know, if it's a policy I wouldn't necessarily clear it with anybody else, if I just thought, like, that dog won't hunt. It wouldn't ever get any further than me as far as that goes, if it was coming up through this way, trying to get support, for instance. If it's something that gets all the way through into sort of the larger advisory group, then it would be not only does it fit, but does the equation work. You know, they say in French, "Ça vaut la peine." It's worth it, it's worth the trouble. There is some of that. Why are you doing

it? Does it fit with your agenda? You know, who is going to be affected either positively or negatively? (P1)

The platform then informed the further appraisal sub-phase shaping involving development of mandate letters, which, as the first minister's office advised, were part of what was called a "translation" function of converting or integrating partisan platform commitments and policy initiatives into concrete policy measure through the public service. Mandate letters were cited as a primary vehicle through which this was accomplished. When queried about mandate letters, those interviewed explained that they had done mandate letters, and the process was basic, in that it was a division of the platform by ministry and involved clear instructions to ministers and deputies. Those interviewed explained that the transition team consisted of the premier's principal secretary, executive council office, an external academic, as well as former elected politicians who all assisted with the drafting. This indicates the diversity of external actors that can be mobilized by partisan advisers for advisory system or formulation activity. Ministers and deputies also referenced the importance of the first minister's office partisan advisers in policy formulation, particularly in their formulation sub-phase activity, on a partisan-political dimension. A minister explained, when describing his perspective on policymaking in general, that all files went to Cabinet's priority and planning committee to review the pros and cons of the proposal before it went to the executive council. As the minister explained, "Everything is vetted through the Premier's Office, whether it goes to them before it goes to public policy committee, or whether it goes to them after the committee has reviewed it, but it is always vetted by the Premier's Office" (M2).

Deputies interviewed all described first minister's office staff as being influential in policy formulation and reported positive relations with the first minister's office on policy work. Senior public servants often described their interactions in the context of horizontal policy initiatives that could be facilitated by partisan advisers at the centre. One deputy explained, in addition to process facilitation, Premier's Office advisers would bring in content-based policy ideas and options for consideration on specific policy objectives. Their shaping was in part a product of early appraisal and dialogue sub-stage activity with actors inside the system, and was driven by stakeholders as well. As the deputy put it, "Second reason is that [the principal secretary] might have had ideas: 'I've met some people and have an idea I'd like to talk to you about it, but bring a couple of staff.' They say, 'Well, that's a bit farfetched but here's something we could do'" (DM2). Deputies were quick to point to the role first minister's office staff played in adjudicating the readiness of proposals before they went to Cabinet committees. Shaping in this sense involved alignment and calibration to ensure that policy dovetailed with partisan-political objectives or commitments. The same deputy elaborated on the nature of policy interactions with first minister's office advisers with a typical scenario:

> I'm working on something and we're about to bring something to Cabinet, but I'm not too sure, you know. We might get a rough ride, or maybe it's not something they want to do, or it's a tough decision. I might call [the first minister's office partisan adviser] and say, 'Look, can we get together? I want to bring a staff and explain something we're working on and see if you think it's got a chance of going through. I don't want to go waste Cabinet's time on something if you tell me, "My God, [deputy], don't even darken the door with that thing," right? Or, "It's pretty good, but I want more information," or whatever.'" (DM2)

Ongoing horizontal partisan-political shaping was reported to generally involve activities at either appraisal or formulation sub-phases. At the front end, this was salient in the provision of political direction at the outset of policy development. In describing policy formulation, another first minister's office adviser explained interaction with public service actors very much in core executive resource-exchange terms. As the adviser put it, "We have a relatively small government. We have twenty-two, twenty-four deputy ministers, and so very usual for them. And this is another 20 per cent of my job, I would say, is to meet and discuss or exchange or negotiate with deputy ministers in terms of what they want to do and what we want them to do" (P2). This involved bilateral negotiations about ongoing policy work that the department or broader public service may have on the go, and the important policy direction to which the government wants responsiveness. The characterization from a range of actors across the political and administrative spheres was that departments and individual senior public servants, along with ministers and the Premier's Office, all had pet policy projects. Partisan advisers, for their part, had clear objectives about ensuring that mandate letters and other priorities received enough oxygen in the system. Horizontal partisan-political shaping was also emphasized to involve iterative "translation" similar to that of the mandate letters

but occurring more consistently in conjunction with the operationalization of the platform through formal policymaking. When asked
why the adviser would typically intervene with deputy ministers, the
adviser responded, "Just to make sure that the policy direction is on
line with our political direction in the most noble sense of politics" (P2).
When pushed to expand on what that meant, the partisan adviser went
on, "If we feel like the deputy minister is not providing the minister
direction, or he is providing some direction that we don't think it should
be like that, we would … I would call the deputy minister, say, 'Look,
according to our policy or direction we would, our minister is telling us
this is where you want to go, and this is not what we want to do.'" In
responding to a question about how he approached policymaking and
what functions were undertaken, another senior partisan adviser made
explicit the connection between contestation and partisan-political formulation. The adviser's "translation" and alignment functions were
undertaken to ensure substantive policy and programs reflected new
or previously stated partisan-political policy commitments: "I guess
my job is twofold, really. One is to make sure that their interpretation is
what we would agree with. Because you get a line in a political document and it could mean anything to anybody really. So one of my major
jobs is interpretation. And not only in the front end, but all the way
along. As a group of civil servants tries to develop a program, say, that
would answer, be the answer to a political promise, it can get quite lost
in translation" (P1).

This type of response points to shaping throughout the formulation
sub-phases. Partisan advisers would establish and/or confirm the first
minister's priorities and direction at the appraisal sub-phase, monitor
and signal-check with officials during development of formal policy
options, and then re-engage in the formulation sub-phase with direct
emphasis on consistency with stated political direction. In this case,
horizontal partisan-political shaping was less frequently cited in relation to ministerial partisan advisers, procedurally and substantively.
The first minister's office in New Brunswick reported much more horizontal partisan-political shaping directly with ministers. Senior partisan advisers explained that while they were informed of each other's
work, they had previously established that if items were more policy
than politics, they fell under the purview of the principal secretary. If
they were more political than policy, the chief would deal with them.
There were obvious areas and times where such matters would overlap, and those cases would call for collaboration, and first minister's

office partisan advisers were happy with that division of labour. Such a sharp distinction along political-policy lines in a first minister's office was unique to this case. It reveals important organizational differences that are salient to the type and nature of core executive policy resource exchanges.

Conclusion

First ministers' office partisan advisers in these three cases were engaged in a broad spectrum of policy formulation, including but extending well beyond determinations of partisan-political feasibility. The chapter brings to light important ways by which their participation in *formal* policy development hinged upon resource exchanges with other policy actors, particularly core executive actors. Partisan advisers at the centre were singled out for their ability to engage in moving and shaping explicitly at "front end" policy formulation. In all three cases they were involved in appraisal and dialogue sub-stage activity to establish initial policy parameters. This involved conveying the government's policy direction and charting policy paths through mandate letters, budgets, and Speeches from the Throne. This is in keeping with studies that have long noted their policy influence as being particularly wedded to these types of policy direction-setting instruments (Savoie, 1999a, 2003; White 2001). However, the findings presented above further detail how partisan advisers engage in policy work at different times in the formulation of policy, confirming, for example, that first minister's office advisers have unique access to policy-based core executive resource exchanges at this earlier conjuncture of formulation. Clear differences were apparent in the types of instrumentation and with which actors these exchanges occurred, mandate letters clearly being a crucial instrument for the political arm in the Ottawa and to a lesser degree in New Brunswick, with little to no reference to the equivalent in British Columbia. In that case, while departmental service plans were clearly used to set and monitor policy priorities, they were primarily of concern to public servants. PMO advisers' increasingly "hands on" approach to *drafting* mandate letters signals another way by which political control and policy responsiveness were sought and exercised in that case. Focusing on the actual policy work that advisers undertake in formulation also illuminates distinctions tied to their use of policy instruments or preferences for certain forms of policy work over others (Jordan and Turnpenny 2015).

Importantly, moving and shaping in all three cases was clearly not restricted to systemic instruments used to set policy direction. Rather, advisers were quite active in moving and shaping in ongoing and iterative fashions at many sub-phases. Fundamentally, this policy work was often characterized as "translating" and "knitting together" priorities with the ongoing policy work bubbling up in government. It consisted of specification, elaboration, signal-checking, and coordination to operationalize the policy priorities of elected officials into concrete policy measures. In addition, these actors often framed their moving and shaping in horizontal or interdepartmental terms. That is, their formulation on both partisan-political and administrative-technical grounds was often reported to occur in concert with a number of core executive actors.

The two subnational cases were marked by drastically less vertical or intra–first ministerial office formulation. The smaller first ministers' offices clearly limited the amount of intra–first ministerial office formulation occurring. This is well contrasted with the comprehensive intra-ministerial PMO moving that characterized core executive operation in Ottawa: the layered configuration of partisan advisers and a "stand-alone" PMO policy shop facilitated much greater capacity for and participation in intra–first ministerial process management and coordination. Core executive formulation-based resource exchanges were evidently more frequent and sophisticated. PMO partisan advisers could bring to bear knowledge gained from ongoing monitoring of departments and policy files as well as interactions with PCO counterparts, or related to Cabinet committees they shadowed. Similarly, PMO policy directors were able to leverage the additional capacity of their small policy team for improved policy coordination and process management. Horizontal partisan-political moving was also reported in all three cases at all formulation sub-phases. Partisan advisers were continuously engaged in partisan-political process management and coordination throughout formulation. Differences again emerged among the federal and subnational cases regarding with whom partisan-political moving was undertaken. The two subnational cases shared a more direct form of such activity, whereby first ministers' offices dealt with ministers, whereas the federal case included direct interactions but also extensive PMO–ministerial office interactions spanning formulation sub-phases. In addition, it included substantial horizontal partisan-political policy coordination and process management linked to Cabinet activity and formal departmental policy work.

Shaping was also clearly occurring at formulation sub-phases and along partisan-political and administrative-technical dimensions. It included explicit references to working continuously with officials during the development of Cabinet submissions. A range of activities were documented, including commenting on and suggesting revisions to policy options, leveraging policy knowledge about other files or from other actors to contribute to the refinement or contestation of policy at formulation sub-phases, or working with ministers and/or their staff to ensure partisan-political aspects of policy development were addressed. Throughout the cases, partisan-political shaping was characterized as ensuring consistency and alignment with previously articulated partisan-political policy goals and commitments. Partisan advisers at the centre were key actors in shaping to minimize "slippage" or drift of policy content in initial policy intent and expectations. In all three cases, such horizontal partisan-political shaping was described at all formulation sub-phases.

These differentiated types and patterns of moving and shaping raise implications for how core executive resource exchanges relate to attempts to secure political control and policy responsiveness. For one, they suggest distinct types of resource exchange patterns may prevail amongst different sets of actors within the core executive, or preferences for the exchange of particular types of resources (Craft 2015b; Elgie 2011; Eichbaum and Shaw 2011). This was most clearly illustrated by the greater vertical moving and shaping along both dimensions, and all formulation sub-phases, documented in the federal case. These formulation activities provided tangible mechanisms by which, through intra-PMO formulation activity, partisan advisers at the centre could seek to increase political control. Procedurally, greater signal-checking and intra-PMO process management and coordination facilitated PMO oversight of policy in various stages of development at various locations in government. As detailed above, vertical PMO shaping resulted in greater formulation capacity to scrutinize, calibrate, and align content-based formulation on partisan-political and administrative-technical dimensions. In one exchange with a former PMO policy director, the need for this type of policy work was made clear. The adviser described being well aware of the difficulties of getting policy done at all. That is, the systematic and public service pushback that could at times sideline the government's policy agenda. The adviser explained candidly that partisan advisers' policy work was essential sometimes, "knowing that half of them they'd [the public service], you know, find ways to shoot down, and half of them they would find ways to sideline, or a quarter of them, and a quarter of them would get through" (P12). This speaks not only to the function of moving that ensured forward motion of policy, but also the content-based policy alignment involving the coupling of partisan-political policy priorities and commitments with the imperatives the public service may identify, or policy already working its way through the government (Gains and Stoker 2011; Maley 2000; LSE GV314 Group 2012).

Partisan advisers in all three first ministers' offices explicitly described their formulation as produced primarily through their ability to leverage other policy actors' resources. That is, they characterized their formulation as the product of a "two-way street" relationship based on mutual influence between political and administrative actors (Krause 1996, 1999). In the BC case, first minister's office partisan advisers detailed their moving and shaping as a product of interactions with ministers, their staff, and a combination of central agency and deputy minister–based interactions. In New Brunswick, moving and shaping at the first minister's office level were described as heavily oriented towards interactions with deputies and ministers. Lastly, the federal case was replete with PMO references to moving and shaping empowered by interactions with ministers' office partisan advisers and PCO officials. This is an important distinction that adds further support to a principal argument of this study that a more accurate depiction and understanding of partisan advisers as policy workers is gained through coupling locational and activity-based considerations. It also further supports notions of asymmetrical core executive power dependence and resource exchange (Marsh et al. 2003). It was clear that first ministers' offices had ample and unique policy-based resources and influence of their own. Nevertheless, they clearly also depended on other actors in their core executive to be able to take full advantage of their policy levers and resources, and access others. As such, the findings support the asymmetrical approach to core executive power dependence and point to distinct patterns of resource exchange and dependence, in how advisers seek to undertake their policy work (Craft 2015b; Elgie 2011; Eichbaum and Shaw 2011).

Chapter 5

He Said / She Said: Ministers' Office Buffers and Bridges

Introduction

A key contention of this study is that partisan advisers, as part of the political arm of government, can be consequential at different institutional locations within the core executive. Despite the attention that the "centre" has rightfully attracted, it is crucial not to overlook ministerial office partisan advisers. They too may be exchanging policy-based resources within their respective core executives. Using the buffering and bridging concepts, this chapter examines if, how, and with what consequence these advisers in Ottawa, British Columbia, and New Brunswick participated in advisory systems. The focus is on their substantive direct provision of policy advice (buffering) and their potential integration of *other* sources of policy advice within their respective advisory systems (bridging). The evidence from these Canadian cases complements that of Westminster studies, which have found that ministers' office advisers are often direct suppliers of policy advice, and strong participants in the circulation of *various* sources of policy advice for decision-makers (Gains and Stoker 2011; Maley 2011; Eichbaum and Shaw 2010; LSE Group GV314 2012).

As participants in advisory systems, partisan advisers in only two of the three cases were found to be buffering. Where reported, it was characterized as spanning the partisan-political and administrative-technical dimensions. It was universally described very much as an overlay advisory activity provided as a supplement to in-depth, detailed, and often very technical policy advice from other sources. Across the cases, ministerial partisan advisers engaged in partisan-political policy and administrative-technical forms bridging. In each case, partisan advisers were reported by political and administrative elites as increasing access to, and exchange of, policy advice between political and administrative spheres. As foreshadowed in previous chapters, ministerial partisan advisers were not only engaged in bridging within the core executive, but in two of three cases also undertook frequent and intensive exogenous bridging. They were key interfaces for the integration of stakeholder policy advisory inputs into the advisory system for ministers *and* departmental officials. This chapter details differences across the cases in how and with whom ministers' office partisan advisers engaged in advisory system activity and also in comparison to their first ministers' office counterparts. Buffering and bridging are not only important vehicles for the quantitative and qualitative diversification of policy advice for the political arm, but are consequential to the operation of advisory systems and the types and nature of core executive policy-based resource exchanges.

Ministerial Office Buffering

Buffering at the Federal Ministers' Office Level

There was little doubt that federal ministerial partisan advisers engaged in buffering. All categories of actors confirmed such activities were core to partisan advisers' day-to-day policy work. It was described as providing policy advice that contested departmental policy advice or inputs received from stakeholders, caucus, or even the first minister's office. In Ottawa, the policy advice of partisan advisers physically buffered public service advice. That is, as detailed in chapter 3, a written partisan-political policy advisory system was in place at the ministerial office level that produced *separate* written briefing notes. These were provided as an overlay to *all* forms of policy advice proffered to ministers from either the public service or external actors. Ministerial partisan advisers engaged in policy advising in four principal ways: (1) working with officials during the development of their policy advice in an iterative and ongoing fashion; (2) providing formal written partisan-political policy advice as an overlay to formal departmental policy advice or that of stakeholders; (3) engaging with stakeholders during the development of policy advice related to its partisan-political and administrative-technical aspects; and (4) providing oral advice to the minister on any or all of the above. A key difference at the ministers' office level from PMO-PCO practices was that respondents detailed a system that involved ministerial office policy advice and the formal departmental policy advice being combined into a single package and provided to the minister *at the same time*. Comparatively, partisan-political policy advisory activity at the federal level was much more systematic, formalized, and comprehensive than reported in either subnational case. Federal ministers and deputies confirmed that partisan advisers engaged in written and oral policy advice that spanned the partisan-political and administrative-technical dimensions and was undertaken with a broad range of policy actors.

The formal written partisan-political policy advice provided was described as concise, typically a one- or two-page document – providing a general partisan-political policy overlay, not in-depth policy analysis. Those interviewed explained that this partisan-political policy advice ensured: (1) appropriate political context was provided; (2) salient and contentious items were highlighted; (3) consistency with stated partisan-political policy objectives was adjudicated; and (4) a recommendation and rationale was provided for the minister(s). For example, as one minister's office director of policy described his policy advisory role, "I provide advice both from what can crassly be called the political to sometimes I provided policy advice in situations where the minister, for whatever reason, prefers my advice to the department, or wants a counter-position to the department, or simply for whatever reason doesn't want to consult the department" (P22). Another adviser had a similar characterization and described partisan-political buffering performed by ministers' office partisan advisers as a Socratic exercise. As the adviser described it, "How did it mesh with the party's platform? How did it mesh with the mandate letter? What other things were at play that would make this successful or not? What kind of political considerations would we have to consider? What other ministers might we have to dialogue with or other members of Parliament?" (P26). Partisan advisers thus engaged in considerable contestation through ongoing and direct contribution of content-based policy advice.

The hierarchical configuration of the PMO was also in place in ministers' offices, with a chief of staff having overall responsibility for policy, but often relying heavily on the director of policy and a team of junior partisan advisers. At the most senior levels, chiefs and directors of policy provided their own direct policy advice and/ or supplemented that of their junior partisan advisers or departmental officials. All categories of ministerial partisan advisers described themselves as primary sources of partisan-political policy counsel to their ministers. Chiefs of staff interviewed reported that their advice was often provided verbally, as opposed to being written briefs that they had themselves composed. They may write a short note or comment upon officials' policy advice or their own policy shop's partisan-political policy briefs, but most often they provided oral policy advice directly to their ministers, fellow partisan advisers, or officials. As chiefs explained, this was primarily a consequence of their management obligations, including oversight of all other "exempt" staff and operational requirements of a minister's activities. Thus, the policy advisory role of chiefs of staff was a strategic one emphasizing the partisan-political buffering that was seen as crucial to policy work. As one chief of staff suggested, "The policy role of the chief of staff is to ensure that not one of those dockets [departmental policy files] gets to the minister's desk by itself unaccompanied by a political memo from either the staff or from the chief of staff. Explaining what the political implications of that are, you know, how they fit with the party's platform, how they fit within the particular geographic area, and, you know, basically what the partisan politics of this is, so that the minister is not uninformed of the implications of this" (P27).

From this perspective, there were crucial resource exchanges in a minister's office, with partisan advisers exchanging their substantive policy advice on their particular files. It was also a resource exchange that involved contesting, challenging, or "pushing back" on public service policy advice. This was characterized as largely a matter of ensuring that it was consistent with overarching partisan-political policy objectives of the minister and government. Most described their advisory functions as being a matter of ensuring their ministers received comprehensive policy advice, with all options appropriately canvassed. A number of advisers, of various levels of seniority, made clear they understood their function in the context of being *one source of advice among many* that ministers consulted. In keeping with other published accounts, departmental officials, Cabinet colleagues, caucus, PMO partisan advisers, and external sources formed the constellation of advisory sources that ministers may consult (Esselment, Lees-Marshment, and Marland 2014; Bakvis 1997; Benoit 2006). However, ministerial partisan advisers were unique in that their policy advice could and often did span partisan-political and administrative-technical dimensions. They sought to combine both in some respects, ensuring that policy advice was "complete," that their minister had all the required information but that a political lens was applied to it as well. This reflects well the advisory system concept that understands an array of advisory supplies, differences in demand, and distinctions based on the content of policy advice and its purpose (Craft and Howlett 2012; Prince 2007). Two responses from partisan advisers about their advisory activity versus that of the public service are revealing on the matter:

> The quality [of public service policy advice] is top notch. I mean, they spend a lot of time, and they work very hard, and the quality is there. But simply because it's a high-quality product doesn't mean it meets your objectives. Often it was a very solid policy recommendation, but it was a policy recommendation contrary to our political stripes, and in that case, even though it was a high-quality recommendation and a non-partisan recommendation, it was not one that we could accept as a political office. The quality is always there. It's a matter of whether or not the recommendation that the department makes is in line with the government's policy bent or direction. (P26)

> We're not there to add an additional layer of red tape and have a specific opinion on everything. But sometimes there's something coming through where you read advice from the public service that comes from one perspective. Then you remember having talked to stakeholders, and having had discussions with members of Parliament, having read interesting research, and you find that there are maybe other perspectives to be considered than the one from the public service. And then you just bring that forward to the minister, or you suggest him to speak to additional people who have a different perspective. It's more about making sure that the file is complete and the minister has all the facts before making a decision. (P21)

Ministers and deputy ministers confirmed that partisan advisers were active participants in the policy advisory system. Interviews revealed that ministers often received departmental policy advice as well as that of their partisan advisers at the same time. However, this pattern may vary, based on the particular preferences of ministers and the nature of the policy area they are responsible for. Of note, federal ministers all reported that they expected their partisan advisers to work with departmental officials long before they, as ministers, would become involved in the advisory process. As one minister explained, "The mechanics of it are that prior to receiving a PowerPoint presentation, or 'deck,' or a policy paper, prior to that, almost always my chief of staff and senior public servants will have already worked with the [lower-level] bureaucrats to take off any rough edges that they found obvious" (M12). Policy briefs, information notes, and so on that required a minister's attention would be provided along with their partisan advisers' policy advice. As former minister Stockwell Day explained,

> If I had any questions, political staff would usually look at the items and work on it with officials and then usually in the form of a memo would give me their thoughts or advice on the particular issue. I would then, if then I had more questions, I would either give them a call or meet with them or just fire something back, saying, "I need more information on this or more information on that." The chief of staff is supposed to tie it all together, and it's a person certainly among the political staff will have the most influence on the minister, because he or she would have talked with political staff on the item, talked with the officials, and is ultimately there to give the final advice to the minister. So chief of staff position is absolutely critical.

These responses illustrate the complex web of policy advice within which partisan advisers operate. Ministers interviewed clearly articulated an expectation for their partisan advisers to work in lock step with departmental officials and stakeholders outside of government, to inform and reinforce the political policy agenda and weed out options that were known to be politically unfeasible. Ministers also made clear that their partisan advisers reacted to the policy work of the department but also proactively kept close watch on the advice being generated to ensure it met the needs of the minister and government. In short, partisan advisers pushed for greater responsiveness from officials but served important functions in generating content-based policy advice apart from that of the public service. Reflecting on his time as a Liberal and Conservative Cabinet minister, David Emerson explained, "The political staff is much more reactive and interactive with public servants. They see their role as much more, you know, the stewards of the politics of advice." Emerson went on to detail how in his experience the two sources of advice were provided: "Predominantly, the core, boilerplate advice comes out of the public service, and then it is reacted to by the political staff in the minister's office. So you'll get two separate – or even combined, depending on the minister's approach – briefings from public servants and political staff on any given issue." Another minister echoed this experience and summed up cogently how these two supplies of policy advice are combined. These practices are striking to the extent to which they reveal that buffering provides policy advisory contestability and involves the exchange of partisan-political policy advisory resources within the core executive:

> I would make sure that when I got the briefing book to read, so did my senior [partisan] policy adviser. And if he or she had advice or concerns or whatever, then they always gave me a cover sheet that came with it. I got the policy advice, the political policy oversight, at the same time I got the bureaucratic advice. I would receive both documents at the same time. I would get, for instance, a deck, a PowerPoint presentation. Attached to it would be my political policy adviser's overview of that presentation. It came stapled together. It was a one two punch. It was the same moment. I got the advice and the critique at the same time. (M12)

Deputies interviewed tended to emphasize that public service officials provided the "professional" and "technical" policy advice, and partisan advisers typically provided partisan-political policy advice. It was apparent that all deputies were quite pleased to leave the latter to ministers' offices. Deputy ministers explained that the minister benefited from a difference in the perspectives provided on policy issues and that the partisan adviser performed different advisory functions. These were most often presented as complementary rather than adversarial. Normatively, deputy ministers interviewed did not perceive ministerial partisan advisers as encroaching on their advisory roles. Deputies were quick to dispel the myth that they alone were the sole sources of advice, readily acknowledging that partisan advisers were one of many sources of advice ministers consulted. This sentiment was well captured by one deputy minister who summed up what many described: "We're probably a very important, maybe the most important source of policy advice, but everybody's giving advice to ministers on policy issues. We're probably the only people who are providing advice consistently day in and day out to ministers and commenting on advice that ministers are getting from other people. So, you know, policymaking is not just the domain of the public service" (DM11). Another deputy echoed these sentiments and saw the advisory functions of partisan advisers as separate and distinct and captured well the cut and thrust of trying to advise a minister: "Here in the department we'll do a briefing note, and then political staff will do a one-page, you know, their view on the thing, and I think they take ... obviously their job is to take a political view on the thing. Sometimes they will disagree, sometimes they will agree with us actually, and we find ourselves in alliance on some issues with the political staff on issues. You know, we perform two different functions" (DMO8).

However, deputies all noted they provided non-partisan policy advice and could not provide the more partisan-political forms of policy advice. Again, they were happy that ministers had partisan advisers to provide that dimension and content of policy advice. Deputies noted that they had frequent policy-related interactions with ministerial staff. Most often it was with the chief and policy director. Overall, these exchanges were described as positive. When asked what, if any, function partisan advisers should play related to policy advice and how best to achieve a healthy political-administrative policy advice equilibrium, another deputy responded, "I understand when there's sometimes that the chief of staff will talk to the minister about issues and it's not appropriate for me to be there" (DMO8). The deputy went on to describe at length the policy advisory role of partisan advisers and its relationship to other sources of policy advice:

> I think they always should [provide policy advice to the minister], but they have to remember their role. First of all, their role is to understand the policy advice. Maybe *policy* is not the right word here, the public service advice, right? Then, to add the political dimension to this that nobody else can. And so, you know, I think that when the system is working well the minister is getting my advice, signed off by me on behalf of the department, and then he's got a political note on top of that that says, "Minister, there are these political issues, and they can be managed in this way." Or, "This is a real problem for us and I don't know how we're going to manage this kind of thing." He should get both of that. They should be involved in the policy process but not on the technical side on the political side. (DMO8)

This telling response makes plain something that is often overlooked in academic treatments of policy advice, which at times suggest that activity is the sole ambit of the public service. In a sense, the deputy is acknowledging that the advice provided is biased in the sense that it is the public service's. Others engage in policy advice but there are distinct suppliers who provide distinct types of policy advice. Several partisan advisers confirmed they understood and appreciated the non-partisan status of the public service. They explained that they were cautious about activities that might be construed as politicizing the public service, particularly when dealing with officials below the deputy and assistant deputy minister levels. This extended to their direct dealings with public service officials in the development of policy advice, as well as when they interacted with exogenous stakeholders. As to the former, as one chief of staff explained, they saw their policy advisory function as in part involving "educating officials" about why they were proceeding along a certain policy direction or had particular policy goals in mind. In doing so, the chief explained, "Obviously we always had to be mindful that officials were there to do non-partisan work, and so we had to avoid, you know, pushing them too far in the direction of the political, but we needed them to understand it so we could accomplish our goals" (P28). With respect to the latter, many partisan advisers emphasized that they engaged in continuous informal stakeholder consultation, which was described as at times explicitly political. Such partisan-political policy advisory interactions with stakeholders were managed carefully to avoid undue politicization of the public service. As another chief of staff put it, "You didn't want to put public servants in an embarrassing situation either, so you would tend to conduct the meetings, you know. I mean, there's a policy component for every meeting and everyone can be part of that, but there may be other aspects that public servants should not be part of and they would recognize that" (P27). However, as has been made clear, this is not to suggest that partisan advisers do not challenge and push back on public service or other supplies of policy advice. In part their institutionalization and specialization, particularly as partisan-political policy workers, underscores the tensions embedded in political-administrative relations in the Westminster tradition.

Elite political and administrative actors were therefore quite aware of the distinctions in the types of policy work they engaged in. To be effective, ministers required both. However, what often goes unacknowledged is the degree to which these two are provided, if they are provided separately, when they are combined, and when they are provided to ministers. The federal case demonstrated a considerably greater contestation occurring through buffering by ministerial partisan advisers. Importantly, it also suggests that deputies recognize a "political" form of policy advice as legitimate, and that both sets of actors appreciate the requirement for non-partisanship in public service actors and functions. It, however, was not an easy relationship or equilibrium to navigate.

Ministerial Partisan Advisers' Buffering in BC

BC partisan advisers were found to share greater similarities to their federal counterparts than those in New Brunswick. All three sets of actors interviewed in BC (ministers, deputies, and partisan advisers) described partisan advisers as active contributors of policy advice. When asked to describe their role in general, partisan advisers often stated that first and foremost it was to provide advice to their ministers. They frequently described challenging departmental policy advice from a partisan-political perspective. If they thought public service policy advice on a matter was not politically viable, they would contest it and offer their options for amendment, revision, or all out rejection. Like the federal case, most explicitly stated that it was, however, the minister who was the decision-maker. One minister, when queried about experiences working with officials and their provision of policy advice characterized the situation in rather extreme terms, acknowledging it was an exaggeration for the sake of emphasis:

> Typically, the recommendations on briefing notes or decision notes tend to be, you know if you choose option A all will be well with the world, everyone will love you, and it will be a wonderful day. Option B results in the immediate death of all three of your children, your pet will be mutilated, and your house will be burnt down. You tend to get options that tend to be the really good option and the really, really bad option, and not much in between those two places. And that isn't always comforting, because clearly there is a wider variety of options, but that has never created an environment where I haven't personally pushed back and said, "That's not good enough. I want more work done and I want more options available." (M7)

Advisers were seen as a means to ensure options for the minister were robust and multiple sources of policy advice were available. When asked specifically about their provision of policy advice to ministers, several partisan advisers explained that they provided a mix of policy advice. One adviser responded, "I'm not shy about sharing my advice with the minister, the deputy minister, and the ADMs [assistant deputy ministers]. Whether it be policy or legislation and that advice centres on many things. Whether it be public perceptions, or political ramifications, or is it actually good policy. I like to think I'm able to contribute in all of those areas and through the process" (P10). From their perspectives, their advisory activity included administrative-technical policy advice on the department's policy work, and a secondary component that was much more explicitly partisan-political. On this front, the adviser added, "Generally the advice that I would give, I'm with a few exceptions, I'm happy to give it to the minister and the deputy minister when they're both sitting in the same room" (P10). There was clear recognition that some partisan-political advisory activities needed to occur away from public service officials. Many also were clear that they were expected to add value to advisory activity by engaging in partisan-political buffering. Minister's office advisers more readily and explicitly acknowledged this type of buffering compared to those interviewed from the BC first minister's office. The latter seemed reticent to be characterized as partisan at all. When asked directly about partisan-political buffering, to unpack what that means, a minister's office partisan adviser responded:

> So you're thinking about the politics of the situation. So you'll have, in many situations you'll have a deputy minister providing advice from a certain perspective, but then an MA [partisan adviser] provides advice from a different perspective. It doesn't mean that the advice is really that different. In most cases it's the same. But sometimes there can be considerations that need to be brought up and that you wouldn't expect a deputy minister to bring them up. So it could be that this particular problem is affecting a certain geographic area of the province and guess what you've got five caucus members, caucus colleagues, who are going to be affected by this, so we need to think about that. (P20)

Partisan advisers in British Columbia reported greater concern than their New Brunswick counterparts over the range and comprehensiveness of policy advice available to their ministers. Respondents in several instances referenced occasions when they felt that departmental officials were not providing enough options, or that the context and/or consequences of policy advice had not been sufficiently detailed, or did not take into account the political reality of the day. Moreover, advisers often noted their participation in the development of policy advice, in concert with officials, before the minister was involved. This mirrors the activity reported in the federal case but without the written partisan-political briefing system. Without exception, BC partisan advisers reported that their buffering was oral and informal. The policy advisory system involved partisan advisers providing their views to departmental officials and ministers during the development of policy advice, but with the public service remaining the final source of "official" policy advice provided to ministers in written form. Partisan advisers provided an additional verbal partisan-political overlay and ensured that their ministers were informed on departmental policy, or offered alternative forms of policy advice, all the while ensuring context and potential political opportunities and pitfalls were identified. It was also clear that advisers recognized that they engaged in different kinds of policy work based on their location within the core executive. They were quite aware of spatial implications associated with the nature of policy work that first minister's versus ministers' office advisers undertook. The distinction was also clear for the first minister's office advisers, with one adviser characterizing his minister's office counterparts' policy work in the following terms:

> Ministerial assistants were much more focused on their ministries' policy development. All of the materials for house preparations, estimates for budget, bills, Question Period, issues management, and you'd be hoping and expecting and relying on them to be very knowledgeable about their ministry, about the issues of the day, the policies that were in the works, and able to offer to them some advice to them [the minister] in similar fashion to myself and others who were offering to the premier – a bit of a foil or political lens, if nothing else, of the advice coming from the civil service, especially in the early days. So you would be hoping, or expecting, that the ministerial assistants were offering political advice that would be very much aimed at ensuring the ministers were well informed and the information they needed to make reasonable decisions, recommendations to Cabinet, or to the public, and most importantly didn't step in the "goo." (P3)

This again reflects locational distinctions in that ministerial partisan advisers were expected to be detail-oriented with their own departmental files and policy dynamics. They were seen to be sources upon which ministers could depend for partisan-political policy advice but also important to the circulation and advisory-based resource exchanges within the core executive. Ministers and deputies confirmed that partisan advisers were active advisory system participants. One minister explained, "The Victoria political staff are the ones that both provide assistance, they provide advice, they provide some communications skills. There is a much more personal relationship. I use them also as a sounding board" (M4). Other ministers explained that they saw their partisan advisers as colleagues and not as subordinates. They were expected to be "on top" of the departmental policy files and active contributors to the overall policy advice process. Ministers reported that they expected their partisan staff to raise red flags on departmental policy options and more generally to challenge or contest, not only with the departmental officials, but with the minister as well. A minister explained, "My expectation is, whether we're going through regulatory changes or legislation, that they've read it and that they challenge the thought. Otherwise what are they doing there?" (M6) When pushed to provide greater detail on what that means, the minister explained,

> My expectation is that [the partisan adviser] will be on top of the files with me and that we will discuss them as peers, frankly. And we will challenge each other on different things and, of course, when you … somebody who you strongly believe in, you think they're very talented, and you have a lot of confidence in, it's pretty easy to have a relationship where you can challenge each other. [The partisan adviser will] also stay on top of the relationship with the deputy and the assistant deputies, because [partisan adviser] does that level of communication with them as well. So [partisan adviser] has a very good working relationship with the bureaucracy. That's my expectation. (M6)

This leaves little doubt about the relevance and utility of partisan advisers for ministers and the policy advisory system. Partisan advisers were expected by their ministers to perform a policy advisory function that spanned both the administrative-technical and partisan-political dimensions of advisory work. This is important, as it signifies distinct content-based propensities to engage in resource exchanges with various actors. The adviser would ideally comment on the specific technical or non-partisan merits of policy advice flowing from the department but was also clearly counted on to apply a political lens to all policy advice. In all instances advisers were clearly a principal source of partisan-political policy advice for the minister. Again, this reflects the reality that in BC, advisers are now part of multilateral political administrative nexus. They engage with public servants, ministers and caucus members, other partisan advisers, and external stakeholders and policy communities. The nature of their advisory work is linked to their interactions with these policy actors, and involves different types of policy advisory-based resource exchanges.

Deputy ministers in this case shared their federal counter-parts' normative stance of seeing partisan advisers as accepted and required components of the advisory system. As will be explored in the next chapter, deputies acknowledged that partisan advisers had, to some extent, developed expertise that enabled them to proffer administrative-technical policy advice. However, most cast the bulk of partisan advisers' policy advisory work as partisan-political. This was described as an important component of policy advice and one that they as non-partisan public servants were unable to provide. As such, deputies in this case frequently acknowledged the utility of partisan advisers' ability to "cover off" the partisan-political needs of minis-ters. A deputy explained that from her perspective advisory activity involved the public service providing its "best advice," engaging in "free and frank" policy-advisory practices with ministers. She also can-didly acknowledged a political dimension to policy advice, eexplain-ing that the partisan-political aspects of policy work were outside the departmental purview and this was where ministers' partisan advisers were crucial. As she put it, "I can tell you what the best thing to do is. But you have got a bunch of political forces you have to weigh. I don't even have a clue which one should win out in this case. So ministers also need to look to their political staff, and that's why they're there to give them advice on that front as well" (DM5). Another deputy minister explained at length how the streams or different forms of advice would be coupled, pointing to the importance of advisory resource exchanges. It was partly a logistical or access issue, because getting things done required many hands, but it also reflected a current of change high-lighted in the introductory chapter. That advisory context, and policy work more generally, is not the product of bilateral "speaking truth to power" but rather better characterized as "sharing many truths with multiple actors of influence," "weaving," and "making sense together" (Prince 2007; Parsons 2004; Hoppe 1999). As the deputy put it,

> Where they [partisan advisers] don't have any sort of involvement, and that's a problem for a number of reasons, whether it's just because you can't be taking things directly to the minister all the time and because by and large the role of deputies and of the public service is to try and provide that balanced, independent, non-political advice to them, and it's really their political staff that are there to help provide them with the political considerations and analysis. So that when you have the program options and consideration in mind, that balanced with the political considerations

you always tend to arrive at, in my experience, at a more reasoned and balanced sound decision than you do by not paying any attention to the political or program considerations. (DM6)

These responses from BC deputies acknowledge the advisory function of partisan advisers as serving, in part, to insulate public service officials from partisan-political aspects of policy work. That is, partisan advisers provided the political context and analysis via partisan-political policy advice that deputies could not and should not provide. Several partisan advisers explained that they provided such forms of policy advice in private to avoid politicizing their public service counterparts. The emphasis was again placed on providing ministers with frank analysis of the partisan-political implications of policy advice, or drawing attention to potential political or administrative-technical consequences of adopting the recommended public service advice, or that of stakeholders. Several deputies corroborated such explanations with descriptions of partisan advisers engaging with stakeholders on partisan-political or administrative-technical dimensions related to issues stakeholders may have. Across the board, deputies underscored that they saw policymaking and governing as involving a partisan-political dimension. While acknowledging these as legitimate components of the policy process, they appreciated that they could be left to ministers and their staffs. This confirms the important policy-based resource exchanges that partisan advisers engage in, and that these consist in part of different types of policy advice that address a partisan-political and/or administrative-technical advisory practices common in core executives (Craft 2015a; Head 2008; Esselment, Lees-Marshment, and Marland 2014).

Ministers' Office Buffering in New Brunswick

In New Brunswick ministerial offices, partisan advisers engaged in negligible buffering. Partisan advisers themselves reported low levels of direct policy advisory content-based activity. Instead, ministerial partisan advisers almost universally described their functions as pertaining to constituency issues. Summing up the role of partisan advisers in New Brunswick, one partisan adviser explained, "I guess that's the point of being an EA is to try and keep that stuff [ministerial constituency problems], to try and deflect it away from the minister so they don't have to worry about it" (P9). When asked to describe the typical nature of the policy-specific work undertaken, a long-serving ministerial office partisan adviser responded, "Some was to look at the departmental work in the sense I'm not the minister but there are things that he has to keep his eye on, that he wants direction followed. Others, of course, is everything from the constituency office in handling local issues to helping him with the planning and the day-to-day work on the more provincial issues" (P8).

Ministers and deputies reported much more direct interactions with each other than were reported in either of the other two cases. They were frank in detailing that all significant policy matters related to the department or Cabinet were dealt with bilaterally among themselves, with little to no involvement of partisan advisers. Partisan advisers were seen by all respondents as constituency focused and used by ministers for local political needs. As one senior New Brunswick public service official put it, "In the situation I'm in, it's [partisan advisers' policy work] more bringing case-specific issues not as much in policy." Ministers reported using their partisan advisers for political tasks versus involvement in the policy advisory or formulation process writ large. Two ministers provided contrasting views on what their advisers did, but again suggest that it was much more "big P" political and organizational work as opposed to "pure" policy advisory activity. As they put it,

Some ministers would deal with their deputy ministers through their political staff. I dealt with the deputy minister directly, and rarely would the political staff deal with the deputy. It depends on the personality of the minister. I was considered to be a strong type of character so I didn't need the political staff buffering stuff or doing my bidding for me. (M8)

Everything goes through him [the partisan adviser], like politically. Especially if there are nominations to be made, he controls all that. I don't even want to see that. You know, as long … I keep that with the staff. If they come to me and say, "What do you think about this guy running this section?" "Well, you know, get it through my EA [partisan adviser]. What he decides goes with me." So, I leave it up to him, because if you try to play too many things, you'll get boggled. That's, you know, usually … that's the way … that's what he does. He'll work with the staff to make sure that politically I do the right thing. We have communication officers which also give us good advice, what I should be saying to the media, and all this type of thing. But he controls what I do, he controls my agenda, and you know, and then he tries to balance it out so I don't get overtired, and things like that. (M3)

The above makes clear that there are, of course, personal preferences for how ministers use their staff – something long recognized in the academic literature (Aucoin 2010; Doern 1971; Lenoski 1977). Yet it also underscores that in some instances gatekeeping or control of access to the minister is benevolent – that is, that ministerial staff can serve a positive function in helping to ensure that policy work, among the other competing ministerial interests, is manageable for the minister in question. Deputies interviewed in New Brunswick expected partisan advisers to provide ministers with partisan-political policy advice; this, along with the bulk of their work being the constituency-related "firefighting," was reported to be their main tasks. The direct deputy minister–minister relationship meant partisan advisers played a less significant insulating or exclusionary role. Nevertheless, deputies described healthy and positive relationships with partisan advisers at the minister's office level in New Brunswick. One deputy did, however, note where clarifications on roles and protocol for dealing with officials was required:

I typically insist that my bureaucracy have very open relationships with the political staff. Typically, you can get yourself in trouble if – and I've had them – some of the [partisan advisers] think they have more powers than they do, and they tend to maybe disrespect the bureaucracy. You need to haul that in pretty fast. You need to bring them into your office and give them a little talk: "You know that these people are doing the best they can. If you have got issue with people, come to me. I run this department, you don't. OK?" (DM2)

This statement captures a broader sentiment that deputies expressed in all cases. They made it quite clear that they, as deputies, would resolve any confusion over appropriate roles and responsibilities and were quite capable of addressing partisan advisers who may be seeking to overstep their boundaries through inappropriate attempts at providing direction to officials. Again, it is important to emphasize that deputy ministers were aware of the tensions between neutrality and responsiveness, and recognized that partisan advisers were there to ensure that government achieved its electoral and partisan-political policy goals. However, officials seemed intent on ensuring that the public service remained non-partisan and professional in advisory and policy development activity.[38] The takeaway here is that in New Brunswick the distinction was clearest that ministerial partisan advisers were much less likely to be active in buffering. This supports studies that suggest distinct propensities for partisan advisers to undertake policy work (White 2005, 2001), as well as more nuanced and differentiated patterns of central agency and departmental interaction (Bernier, Brownsey, and Howlett 2005; Savoie 1999a).

Ministers' Office Bridging

Federal Ministers' Office Partisan Advisory Bridging

Advisory system activity involves not only the direct supply of policy advice but procedural activities tied to the circulation and use of *other* sources of policy advice. In the federal case, ministerial partisan advisers were heavily engaged in such bridging. It was often described as occurring with a range of actors and it further signals the frequent and intensive advisory-based resource exchanges at hand in that case. It involved bridging among partisan advisers themselves, with departmental officials, as well as with actors outside of government. As was the case with their first minister's office counterparts, the greater number of partisan advisers in ministerial offices provided additional channels through which interactions on policy advisory grounds could take place, as compared to the subnational cases. When asked why an adviser interacted with other partisan advisers in other ministries, a director of policy responded,

> It was either to signal-check what we were being told by the public service it was within the sort of views of our colleagues because sometimes messages get, I wouldn't say intentionally changed, but misinterpreted. So when one of our officials would tell me that the minister of [department] doesn't like this. I actually want to hear it from the minister's office. "Have you seen this, have you heard about this, is it true the Minister doesn't like it? If so, why and how can we work on it?" Occasionally it would come true that, or be discovered that really the minister's office had never really seen it, that maybe that someone in [department] in the bureaucracy

didn't like it or maybe spoke too generously on behalf of the minister, and so it would come back that way. (P25)

This type of "signal-checking" was also reported when partisan advisers described their patterns of interaction with the first minister's office. This echoes the findings for first minister's partisan advisers who repeatedly emphasized bridging with their ministerial level counterparts, such as in signal-checking on how policy items were progressing or in exchanges to seek out policy direction or partisan-political policy advice. Minister's office partisan advisers reported seeking out PMO input as they developed policy advice for their minister, or to assist him in dealing with problematic files. Bridging was often but not always tied to formal Cabinet business and stakeholder consultations. Of note, it was only in the federal case where ministers' office partisan advisers reported engaging in formal Cabinet-related policy advisory work. This spanned the "administrative-technical" and partisan-political dimensions. For example, partisan advisers described working with the officials as they prepared policy documents for ministers (e.g., briefing notes, information notes, etc.), and ongoing bridging with PMO partisan advisers on their ongoing dialogue with stakeholders on policy files. Within ministerial offices themselves there was a range of bridging activities taking place. The other internal dimension of bridging was between political and administrative spheres. Bilateral exchanges with officials were widely agreed to be a principal function of partisan advisers, and one of their main uses for improved policymaking and governance. One adviser explained, "Because of the way we operated and functioned as an office, the minister's policy advisers worked very closely with the associate deputy minister and the directors general to ensure that the policy advice that came up was not completely out of left field" (P26). Bridging between partisan advisers and public servants was seen as a pivotal means to secure responsiveness and could avoid pitfalls and information asymmetries.

Interviews with deputies revealed that such "front-end" iterative policy advisory work was not seen as a form of politicization of the advice that would be prepared. Deputies made clear that they continued to deliver their "frank and fearless" advice, but that it was useful to consult with partisan advisers to ensure they understood ministers' expectations and context. In addition, they knew very well that it was important for the ministers' advisers to understand the key issues on any given policy file. Deputies suggested that bidirectional advisory-based resource exchanges were important, not only for them to get a sense of the ministers' thoughts, but also for the utility it provided for advisers to provide input back to the minister. As one deputy put it, "If they don't understand [what] the policy is, they can't give political advice, and if we have to stop until they catch up, then everything's gummed up. So we're trying to keep them constantly up to speed, remembering that there are thirty of them and [thousands] of us. And they can't go in-depth on any file unless it's kind of mission critical for the minister. If they do, they're neglecting a huge number of files" (DM8). This again supports the idea that partisan advisers are often focused on strategic, specific, priority areas. They may be pulled into others but often rely on the public service to brief them, so they can engage in the policy issue themselves. The point is that any speculation that partisan advisers at any location have usurped the public service advisory role, or are able to cover all the required policy ground was simply not the case. As one adviser put it, the job often feels like one is drinking from a fire hose.

Recent surveys of senior Canadian public servants have found that in some cases officials interact more frequently with ministerial staff than with ministers (Bourgault and Dunn 2012, 2014). Therefore, the importance of efficient and effective policy-based resource exchange and coordination is crucial to well-performing core executives. The presence of ministerial advisers can again be understood not only as potential gatekeepers, but as conduits who facilitate bilateral exchange among the political and administrative spheres. They may facilitate overcoming information asymmetries or the avoidance of policy failures tied to process, policy, or even politics (McConnell 2010b; Howlett 2012; Craft 2013). Many senior public servants interviewed explained that senior officials interacted and met with ministers' office staff on policy matters frequently, in light of the fact that advisers had more day-to-day access and interactions with their minister. In many instances this would have clear implications for policymaking in that, as one senior official put it, "You could also use the minister's staff to test ideas or to convey messages to the minister, because they would also have day-to-day contact with [the minister] because it's [the minister's] immediate staff. Or to give the minister heads up" (ADM2). In addition, officials noted that partisan advisers' bridging was a very useful means for departmental officials to better understand the minister's motivations and policy positions. As one deputy put it,

> Typically, within ministers' offices one or two people are very strong on the policy side. They usually play an exceedingly important role, because they can help explain to the [departmental] policy analysts in ways that they'll understand from a policy perspective, why it is the minister wants to go one direction or another, based on the political context. And so the short answer is yeah, there's usually is some strong policy people within the minister's office, and thank God. (DM9)

These responses clearly indicate significant bilateral advisory-based resource exchanges between officials and partisan advisers. The bridging reported by officials in the federal case, as well as both subnational cases, clearly occurred with officials at various levels of authority, despite official PCO and TBS guidelines indicating that "normally" and "to the extent practicable," partisan adviser interactions should occur through the deputy's office (Treasury Board Secretariat 2011, 3; Privy Council Office 2011, 46). This was reported by all categories of respondents as not practical or representative of actual practice. Deputies insisted that ministers' offices' interactions were generally with senior officials and that they would always keep the deputy's office abreast of interactions. However, public service and partisan advisers were quite candid in detailing that in practice it is impossible to seek restricted and deputy-minister-exclusive contact. Running a department, and ministers' obligations and functions, required greater fluidity and flexibility. Most acknowledged that while there were protocols for appropriate behaviour, in many instances there was flexibility to ensure that the hectic pace of policy-making and governance could be effectively tackled. As one deputy explained, there were formal and more informal day-to-day practices:

> It is true, however, that there is a lot of relationship between ministerial staff and other levels of the department – you know, the assistant deputy ministers and the general directors and that. Just … it's too complicated. You know, you can't have a choke point in the system. You have to have a kind of a little bit of a distributive relationship between the minister's office and the department. So not everything funnels through me or my office. That would be just impossible. And in particular, formal requests will come down and, as I say, there's a process for that. But there's

day-to-day contact. You know, the minister's office will have, you know, a staffer assigned to each branch of our department. (DM11)

This also reflects the specialization of partisan advisers in that as they expanded in number and became institutionalized features of the political executive, their functions were aligned to specific policy files or sectors. This was, as noted earlier, longstanding practice in PMO policy shops and ministers' offices that attempted to "cover off" the minister's policy files. Partisan advisers seldom had the same degree of issue- or domain-specific expertise, but their task was to provide additional advisory and management capacity for ministers' offices on particular policy issues and files. The development of a challenge function for policy in the political arm of government is a significant and evolving trend in the Westminster family of systems (Eichbaum and Shaw 2010; Rhodes, Wanna, and Weller 2010)

A second key bridging function of partisan advisers was to deal with advisory inputs from actors outside of government. Partisan advisers reported frequently meeting with stakeholders and detailed how they used such interactions for due diligence in departmental policy advice. They reported such external sources of policy advice were useful to supplement available policy advice and a key policy resource by which they could further contest and validate departmental policy advice. This is in keeping with Canadian (Bourgault and Dunn 2012), and international findings (OECD 2011, 2007; Eichbaum and Shaw 2010; Malley 2011). Interviews with a range of partisan advisers yielded similar explanations for how and why such bridging was undertaken. Key questions to be asked included, How might stakeholders react? Did subject-matter experts outside of government agree with public service advice? One adviser explained that, with some stakeholders, interactions were almost daily, while with others they would be more irregular, and at times they were just to seek some outside thinking or use stakeholders as sounding boards. In other instances, it was in reference to particular policy initiatives that were working their way through the system. As a director of policy put it, "Sometimes in the crunch of, you know, doing a specific regulation or project or something. Some you hear when there's an issue every six months or they send you their report and it might be interesting. So no, stakeholders are crucial" (P21). A chief of staff juxtaposed well the fluid and often overlapping natures of stakeholder bridging that spanned political and policy dimensions along with its pertinence to policy work:

> Typically what you would do is, you wouldn't, you know, go to stakeholder X and say, "I want you to write this policy for me." What you would do is say, "We've got three really important areas we're working on. Who are the stakeholder groups we need to get input from?" Then go out or have them come in and talk to them, hold roundtables and that sort of thing. That was an ongoing thing. So getting policy advice from outside was just a regular, regular thing, and the departments were doing that too. Sometimes we'd meet independently with those guys, other times we'd meet together, but it was ongoing, every day, every week. (P27)

For their part, officials reported being aware that ministerial partisan advisers were engaging in ongoing policy-based interactions with stakeholders. Deputies saw this as appropriate and even advantageous for improving the overall quality and quantity of policy advice within the advisory system. In describing the policy advisory role that partisan advisers played, one senior deputy minister specifically referenced the ability of partisan advisers to integrate stakeholder advice and feedback:

> There are a few on the political side, policy advisers who really are technical experts as well and know the subject matter really well. But for the most part, if they do get into our side of the house, they're amateurs. And it's not their strength, right? Just like we should not try to tell you how the stakeholders in this particular constituency, you know and I don't just mean electoral constituency. I mean, you know, the folks in our minister's office are meeting with stakeholders all the time all the time right. And they're taking their calls and that. So they should really have the pulse of that, and that's what they can bring to bear that nobody else can. (DMO8)

As set out in chapter 1, bridging may also take on the form of an exclusionary or "gatekeeping" type of practice (Craft 2013; Tiernan 2007). That is, partisan advisers can limit or prevent sources of policy advice from reaching decision-makers. Respondents across the board noted that partisan advisers play a role in gatekeeping sources of policy advice from the minister. This was not typically described to involve inappropriate "funnelling" as understood by Walter (2006) and Eichbaum and Shaw (2007a). Rather, it was described as triaging whereby partisan advisers would "sift and sort" priorities items for the minister. It was less about filtering what they perceived to be unwelcome or politically unfeasible policy advice and consisted more in emphasizing items and policy advice that dealt with established "priority" policy items. Ministerial chiefs, and, to a lesser extent, directors of policy, reported that they exercised such control to protect or shield ministers from overexposure or overwhelming them with departmental officials and external stakeholders. One chief of staff explained, "A big part of my job was controlling sort of access to my minister – access to the minister from the department and access to the department from the outside world, the stakeholder world. So there I just ... I needed to make extra certain we were using [the minister's] time in the best and most productive way" (P28). Of course benevolent or inappropriate gatekeeping is easier to describe and define in theory and more slippery in practice. Governance is a human endeavour, and optimal bridging is to a great extent a product of those involved in the trilateral political-administrative nexus – a product of the discretion of partisan advisers in their approach to that function, the appropriate use of advisers by the minister and the deputy minister, and the effort by all three actors to ensure healthy relations prevail through abiding by their respective roles and functions. Suboptimal political-administrative relations at the seams of governance are in part, then, the result of a breakdown of one or more actors involved. From a core executive perspective, actors are expected to exchange resources, given their mutual dependence, but there are clear instances where breakdowns can occur.

Multiple ministers corroborated the type of response provided by the adviser above, that demands on their time far outstripped the available hours in the day. Ministerial partisan advisers did double bridging duty, serving as gatekeepers and as integrators of those sources of policy advice from the policy actors that ministers were unable (or unwilling) to meet with. Chiefs were often the partisan advisers in ministers' offices who triaged meeting requests. A minister explained that his chief would take a lot of meetings, "usually the ones [stakeholders] he had to tell no to. He met with them or the senior policy person met with them, and they just had to do their best to faithfully represent to me how that meeting went, because I couldn't meet with everybody" (M12). David Emerson was more explicit in discussing the functional nature of minister's office partisan advisers' activities. Emerson's description of a chief of staff was replete with notions of bridging:

The chief is always the person who is the gatekeeper, filtering the advice you're getting. But I would say a good chief is not the person who sits there scratching their head, basically coming up with advice to give the minister. The chief is the person who is much more a conductor, so making sure the different points of view from the political advisers are sifted and sorted and weighted appropriately, and so on, and making sure that we're not getting cross-threaded with the public service, and so on. I see the chief of staff role as obviously a wise political counsel, but also as somebody who is very much managerial in the performance of their role.

Such bridging confirms that the policy advisory activity of partisan advisers consists not only of buffering – or providing their own content-based policy advice – but extends to important integration, management, and prioritization of sources of policy advice within advisory systems. It was striking how much more apparent the frequency and intensity of exogenous stakeholder policy-based resource exchanges were at the ministerial office level in the federal case. It was quite apparent that ministers, their offices, and departments were all key channels for stakeholder policy inputs. Some undoubtedly occurred with PMO partisan advisers, but by PMO's own admission it was ministerial partisan advisers who were expected to tend to such bridging. This again points to the importance of careful attention to distinctions in how advisory-based policy resource exchanges are undertaken and by and with whom (Craft 2013, 2015b; Maley 2011; OECD 2011).

BC Ministers' Office Partisan Advisers' Bridging

BC partisan advisers reported that their close proximity to ministers made them an effective hub for multilateral policy advisory exchanges with advisory system actors. Partisan advisers described their bridging as involving the integration of variously located sources of policy advice to inform their ministers' decision-making on strategic policy priorities and on an ad hoc issue-driven basis. Several partisan advisers interviewed highlighted their ability to provide access to the minister for decisions, and expressed an ability to help advance items through the system both from a partisan-political and public service perspective. One partisan adviser with experience in several portfolios explained, "I was respectful of them as professional public servants and I also helped them have access to the minister, which they needed to get to achieve their goals" (P11). Another senior partisan adviser stressed that a significant amount of her role in policy development entailed the coordination and integration of information from political and administrative sources. The adviser's description of her policy advisory functions abounds with bridging:

> So oftentimes I'll be actioning [the minister's] will with the bureaucracy or with other politicians or with the Premier's Office. And vice versa, the Premier's Office uses me, uses my office to communicate their direction to the bureaucracy and to the minister. It's just one of the pathways of information and directions that flow. I see myself as also as just sort of, almost like a hub, like the centre of a wheel. There's just a lot of information that is constantly coming in and coming out of this office, from the civil servants themselves, the ministry, the policy people, the communications staff, which is the public affairs bureau in BC, and the Premier's Office. And then my job is to make sure that the minister, of all the information that I'm receiving, [the minister] is receiving what he needs to have and that [the minister's] direction is being received back to all of those bodies. (P5)

Such responses were common, and they emphasized how partisan advisers integrate an array of policy advisory supplies. Ministers confirmed that, overall, partisan advisers were not only sources of policy advice, but also important bridges with departmental officials and a host of other actors. One minister characterized partisan advisers' typical policy advisory activity as tending to partisan-political and administrative-technical aspects of advice. Essentially it was about advisers being well positioned to identify potential policy or political challenges and opportunities that the minister should be aware of, and this was fuelled primarily through bridging activity. As the minister put it, "Silence would be the typical response to something that made sense and worked both bureaucratically and politically. The ministerial assistant would only pop up to, you know, get involved if (a) they had a concern, and (b) they would run it by the minister and the minister shared the concern, and (c) didn't want to raise the issue himself or herself directly to the bureaucracy" (M9). Deputy ministers also confirmed that partisan advisers engaged in bridging. They universally confirmed frequent policy advisory–related interactions with partisan advisers that often did not include the minister. One DM explained, "Often you are working through the political staff or subject to the political staff being able to pass on and interpret any particular issue or direction or matters that you bring to their attention" (DM6). Another stated, "So, I interact with the political staff as much as I do the minister. And often that is an easy way, an easy conduit to the minister" (DM5).

Partisan advisers were seen as bridges to ministers but were also often cited as key sources of policy advice from exogenous stakeholders. As one senior official explained, "They are active with the minister with a bunch of stakeholder engagements, so sometimes feedback that they want to provide … sometimes they act as a conduit to the minister on certain lower-level issues where I don't need to speak to them [the minister] directly" (DM4). One senior first minister's office partisan adviser explained at length the important role ministerial partisan advisers could play in bridging, which involved considerable opportunity to facilitate policy-based resource exchanges. Notably, such bridging was tied to the institutional location of partisan advisers, with proximity being a key advantage in that advisers knew what the minister needed and how they approached their role (Aucoin 2010). The first minister's office description of their ministerial counterparts clearly suggests a prominent role in facilitating policy-based resource exchanges. As the adviser put it, "The political staff needs the public service way more than the public service needs the political staff. But where the political staff can add value for the public service is around helping facilitate the flow of information around the minister and helping the public service get decisions in a timely manner" (P4).

Another aspect of bridging was the interactions among partisan advisers themselves. Those at the minister's office reported frequent dealings with their counterparts but a more uneven pattern of interaction with the first minister's office. Comparatively, there was nowhere near the PMO-ministers' office interactions in the federal case. Advisers reported two principal reasons for their direct interactions with their ministerial counterparts. Several noted that overlaps and spillovers between ministries was key reasons for their dealing with counterparts. One ministerial partisan adviser explained, "You would interact, because especially on the environment side and agriculture as well, and IGR [Intergovernmental Relations Department] all the time, because your issues overlap" (P11). In addition, several advisers reported that they passed on information that was related to policy development in their ministry or stakeholder information that they thought would be salient to their counterparts. As one ministerial partisan adviser explained, "Letting them know, 'OK our staff in the bureaucracy came to us with this decision note – how's that impacting your stakeholders and such?' And so, 'OK, staff was saying they were talking to your staff. Does your minister know about this?' Or, 'Hey, you know, we're hearing some word out of some large stakeholders on this issue [and how] it could affect you. Can you ask your bureaucrats to look into it for us?'" (P11). Ministers confirmed such activity. As one minister put it, "Often as a minister I might deal with them [other ministers' partisan advisers] directly, but more typically it would be the ministerial assistant that would be that bridge" (M5). Such responses highlight how the political arm seeks to coordinate policy and governance. Again, the linkages with core executive resource dependence and exchange are clear, as is the horizontality of the policy work that advisers undertook. Policy coordination and coherence are significant challenges for contemporary governance and core executive operation (Di Francesco 2000; Rhodes 1995; White 2005). The types of responses above,.and the comparative differences charted across these three cases, suggest important ways by which partisan advisers can iron out wrinkles as policy and advice circulate throughout government generally (Craft 2015b; Dahlström, Peters, and Pierre 2011; OECD 2011).

Partisan advisers also reported frequent bridging with external stakeholders and subject-matter experts in BC. Those interviewed commented on the significant importance of knowing how stakeholders might react, and using such groups effectively to diversify and broaden available sources of policy advice. One partisan adviser explained it as a big part of the job: "I seek their advice sometimes, depending on the stakeholder group. And mostly, just making sure the door is open" (P5). Several ministers confirmed this view of partisan advisers as key interfaces – internally on political and administrative fronts as well as externally to stakeholders. Bridging extended to partisan-political and administrative-technical dimensions. It included efforts to secure support from key electoral constituencies, but was also frequently cited as a means to contest or validate policy options or to seek out policy advice. When asked to explain the primary function of partisan advisers, a senior minister pointed to the extent and importance of bridging in relation to both officials and exogenous actors within the advisory system:

The ministerial assistant is really the interface between the minister's office and the ministry. That, you know, obviously there is an almost constant interaction between the minister and deputy ministers. But I think that where the ministerial assistant is invaluable is working a lot with the deputy minister, but with other staff in the ministry as well. You know, things where the ministry needs the attention of the minister, it's often through the ministerial assistant in terms of what the issue is, what the priority is, and it's often the ministerial assistant who in turn will do some of that outreach to other stakeholder groups to bounce ideas off, or to try and gauge what reaction there might be to various government policy initiatives. (M5)

Deputies also confirmed that partisan advisers were heavily engaged in discussions and consultations with departmental stakeholders. Advisers' ongoing interactions with stakeholders on policy matters was an additional channel to communicate potentially salient information that, it was explained, stakeholders sometimes preferred to provide only to the minister's office. Partisan advisers may have more informal relationships with stakeholders or receive information about stakeholders' attempts to deal with public service officials that could be beneficial. Partisan advisers could scrutinize suggestions or raise red flags and integrate suggested policy advice into the political or administrative spheres. Moreover, stakeholders could provide political context to ministerial partisan advisers more openly than they could to senior public servants. One deputy minister lauded the role partisan advisers had played in championing legislative reform on a particular issue: "It was the political staff that were really reaching out to some of the constituents and stakeholders, who were really, I think, trying to influence, you know, if we do this particular course of action, this is the result that will happen. Here's how the stakeholder group will respond and what they will say. Again, I think they provide a strong role in providing ongoing advice to the minister" (DM6).

Bridging in the BC case was also commonly reported to involve gatekeeping. Gatekeeping was not simply an exercise in limiting access, although that formed part of the activities reported. More often it was described as sorting policy advice for the minister, to ensure that key policy items were prioritized. It should be emphasized that some variance was observed on this front. Some ministers reported that they expected their staff to engage in such gatekeeping, while others reported it was kept to a minimum. How frequently partisan advisers played a gatekeeping role and to what degree it was related to policy was contingent upon the minister's preference. For example, one BC partisan adviser explicitly drew out the gatekeeping function that some attach to ministerial adviser policy work, explaining, "I would say the best Coles Notes version of the way I see myself is letting the minister know what he needs to know when he needs to know it. So it's a very much ... well, one part, one aspect of it is a sort of a gatekeeper role. It's keeping him aware of the things he needs to know and not bothering him with things he doesn't need to know things that I can make decisions on" (P5). Ministers were fully aware that partisan advisers' influence, in advisory systems, was in part a product of their ability to provide or limit access. One minister detailed how partisan advisers could exert influence through control of access, prioritization, and control over the sequencing of policy advisory inputs:

> They take on direct responsibility for the establishment of priorities. In terms of ... so they know that you know your schedule is relatively limited, your availability is relatively limited, and the desire for people to meet with you probably exceeds the hours and days that are available for you to connect with people. So, a lot of times they are able to shape your views and opinions by who it is that they deem to be most important for you to connect with and talk to. (M7)

In this sense, the gatekeeping role and activities of partisan advisers in the BC case was much more explicitly tied to patterns of interaction among departmental officials, the minister, and stakeholders. Partisan advisers were thus able to facilitate or impede the integration of sources of policy advice within the advisory system. It was clear that bridging was less endogenous among partisan advisers themselves than in the federal case, but it was quite prominent between partisan advisers and officials, as well as with external stakeholders. These differences further support a key argument of this study that policy-based influence, and core executive operation, hinges on more than simply whether partisan advisers are present. The types of advisory resources they exchange and with whom, along with when and how, all help to provide a better handle on core executive dynamics and the policy work of partisan advisers (Craft 2015b; Shaw and Eichbaum 2014).

Ministers' Office Bridging in New Brunswick

Partisan advisers in New Brunswick were more active in bridging than buffering. They themselves reported engaging in bridging to increase the exchange of policy advice between departmental officials and their ministers. Interviews with ministers confirmed that they frequently relied on their partisan staff for such purposes. When asked whether the minister's political staff had a policy function more generally, one minister explained that the partisan adviser's "daily function is to meet the needs of me as a minister, to get me the information, so I don't have to go around and ask individual staff all the time." The minister went on to explain, "Their job is to navigate through the department to find the answers that are needed" (M2). Another minister referred to his staff as his "eyes and ears" and made clear they engaged in bridging:

> We will have discussions on that, and its puts me in a much better position to be better informed and whether we are looking at a change of policy or not, on [a policy area] for example. [The partisan adviser] will do some of the ground work with departmental staff here and will have a series of questions, and we'll have a meeting and see what we can find out from [the deputy minister] or one of the other ADMs, you know. "Here's a series of questions, and let's see if we can get answers to those questions." You know, a lot of the information gathering is done through liaison work. (M1)

Interviews with officials were useful in part to check the descriptions of policy work provided by ministers and partisan advisers themselves, but also to gain a broader perspective of how they saw advisers' contributions and impacts. Senior public servants in New Brunswick confirmed that ministerial-level partisan advisers did indeed serve as bridges. They were transmitting policy-related information bilaterally across political and administrative spheres, which was useful for ministers seeking to increase their political control over the public service and secure policy responsiveness. This is similar to the BC case reviewed above but also rings true in international comparisons within the Westminster family (Eichbaum and Shaw 2010, 2008; OECD 2011; Gains and Stoker 2010). However, again it is important to distinguish that the utility can be based on differences in policy-based resource exchange. That is, the distinction tied to whether it is an advisory or non-advisory form of policy work provides a richer understanding of, and distinctions to, core executive and advisory system configuration and operation. One deputy reported that partisan advisers could be useful to reinforce the "policy message," explaining, "I may use the EA [minister's executive assistant] to just know that the EA is going to be in more frequent contact with the minister than I, because they will be traveling with them and whatever. So, just to make sure they know the messages so that they can just repeat and reiterate and are strong on the messaging" (DM3).

Ministers' office partisan advisers reported almost constant interactions with their ministerial counterparts or through the executive assistant to the Premier's Office. However, these interactions were again cited in the context of constituency problem solving versus activities specific to the department or government. Similarly, when asked about their potential policy interactions with the first minister's office, partisan advisers almost universally characterized them in terms of logistical or constituency casework. Partisan advisers themselves reported more uneven patterns of bridging with exogenous sources of policy advice. Most reported no real activity, but some described maintaining close working relationships with their stakeholder groups. Overall, ministers and their partisan advisers made clear that they relied heavily on departmental officials for such activity. Almost all ministers and deputies described explicit preferences for having departmental officials present to ensure that expertise was on hand if required. Ministers described greater dependence in this case on departmental officials to take notes, ensure that questions from stakeholders were recorded, and provide technical support on policy matters. The universal preference for having officials organize and in essence manage stakeholder consultations and meetings was in large part attributable to the sense that ministers felt the public service had established relationships. A minister, describing the established stakeholder–departmental relationship, made clear a strong dependence on officials: "Because they have been in the department for so long, they probably met the stakeholders beforehand through a previous administration, or they know how to ask the question in a relative way. You know, you always want to have your [departmental] staff there" (M2).

A partisan adviser to a senior minister explained that exogenous-oriented bridging was contingent upon ministerial preference, and any given partisan adviser's level of experience and comfort in such matters. As the adviser put it, "I met with the majority of stakeholders overall and dealt with a number of them quite a bit. Once again, there are other [partisan advisers] that never met with stakeholders" (P9). The adviser further explained that a significant portion of his time was spent relaying information to both the department and the minister from stakeholders. Those who reported any bridging with stakeholders noted it was primarily informational or involved follow-ups to seek out reactions to ensure political stakeholder management was on track. The same partisan adviser explained,

A good EA [ministerial partisan adviser] could really make a difference. But you need to have an EA that the minister obviously trusts in that sort of situation. And I don't, by any means, mean the EA is out there making decisions on behalf of government, but is the perfect conduit for information transfer. One thing I've seen about people or organizations: they believe that when they are talking to the EA that they will be transferring that information to the minister. They have the ear of the minister. (P9)

The New Brunswick case stood out for the degree to which ministers and their staff deferred to the public service in dealing with departmental stakeholders. As was seen above, the federal and BC cases saw partisan advisers much more assertively engaging with stakeholders on a policy-specific basis *apart* from officials. Public servants interviewed in New Brunswick described much more control over stakeholder interaction on departmental policy issues. One official explained, "We've been very careful and the EA and the minister's executive secretary to make sure that any department business that the deputy or myself be aware and that we, or our designated officials, be present" (ADM1). The official continued, "Almost anytime the minister meets with a stakeholder group, an industry or organization, or whatever, either the deputy or myself or at least director-level official would be present with the minister." The New Brunswick case saw departmental officials present at nearly all stakeholder meetings. In the other two cases it was more commonly reported by both political and administrative actors that ministerial partisan advisers engaged with stakeholder groups *without* officials present in addition to joint consultations undertaken with officials.

Conclusion

This chapter has provided evidence that ministers' office partisan advisers can, as buffers and bridges, also be important advisory systems participants. "Political aides" have been long acknowledged as components of such systems (Halligan 1995; Plowden 1987). Yet the traditional locational and control-autonomy dimensions by which these systems are often presented can obscure important content and process aspects of advisory activity. Buffering and bridging, as has been demonstrated in this chapter, provide improved accounts of advisory system dynamics and influence. This was evident in that ministers' office buffering was reported only in two of three cases while, although bridging was notably different, it occurred in all three. These distinctions reveal different propensities for how partisan advisers gained and exerted policy-based influence, and affected core executive policy resource exchanges.

Buffering, where occurring, was described as providing direct content-based policy advice that could span partisan-political and administrative-technical varieties. This involved the provision of policy advice to ministers, officials, or stakeholders, based on substantive or experiential expertise, or assessments of the basic logic or the technical merits or perceived deficiencies of policy advice. As political appointees, partisan advisers were self-aware that they were expected to apply a political lens to policy advice (Head 2008; Esselment, Lees-Marshment, and Marland 2014). This, however, did not discount them from being able to approach policy advice from alternative perspectives as well. Buffering was therefore found to diversify not only the available *quantity* of policy advice to decision-makers, but also the *qualitative* content of that policy advice as well. In each case it was candidly acknowledged by partisan advisers that they were one of many sources of policy advice. Officials, Cabinet, caucus, the first ministers' offices, and non-governmental sources were also circulating within advisory systems. Comparatively, the federal case demonstrated a greater intensiveness, frequency, and sophistication of buffering than either subnational case. This was principally a result of the unique mix of written and oral advisory practices described above, as well as ministerial expectation that their partisan advisers be active advisory-systems participants. Again, a key difference was that both public service and ministerial partisan adviser streams of policy advice were provided at the same time. Ministerial partisan advisers in British Columbia also reported frequent and intensive partisan-political and administrative-technical forms of buffering, but that activity was limited to informal oral advice. No buffering of any kind was reported at the ministerial office level in New Brunswick, again reinforcing the need to pay attention to the actual policy tasks undertaken versus attributions of policy-based influence predicated solely on location. The mere presence of partisan advisers does not mean they are actually important actors in the advisory or policy processes.

Partisan advisers were active as bridges in all three cases, integrating policy advice for ministers and officials from other sources. The BC and federal cases again demonstrated more sophisticated and more intensive bridging along partisan-political and administrative-technical dimensions. In these cases, bridging involved integration of policy advice to *and* from officials, ministers, other partisan advisers, and exogenous actors. The New Brunswick case saw partisan advisers' bridging generally confined to vertical administrative-technical bridging with departmental officials and ministers. In fact, in all cases, ministers' office partisan advisers administrative-technical bridging was confined to their own departments. Interactions with officials outside of their "home" department were facilitated and mediated by their counterparts in those departments. This confirms, as detailed in chapter 3, the pivotal and exclusive function of first ministers' advisers in horizontal "administrative-technical" bridging across government. The BC and federal cases also included horizontal partisan-political bridging among ministerial and first ministers' office advisers. In both cases, ad hoc issue and policy advisory integration supplemented formal "all staff meetings."

Horizontal partisan-political bridging also differed in important ways. The federal case was marked by a greater blend of endogenous and exogenous bridging with other partisan advisers and stakeholders. In contrast, the BC case was marked by a greater tendency towards exogenous horizontality in partisan-political bridging typically reported in conjunction with stakeholders. Strikingly, the New Brunswick case involved departments serving as the primary vehicle for stakeholder-related bridging. Officials in that case explicitly referenced efforts to manage and control how ministers and partisan advisers engaged with exogenous advisory supplies – if at all. Bridging was thus found to increase access for both officials and ministers to other actors and sources of policy advice within the political-administrative nexus. It was a clear means by which partisan advisers could lubricate the advisory systems and increase bilateral integration of policy advice between political and administrative spheres. Interviews with senior officials included direct references to the use of partisan advisers as "conduits" to ministers. For their part, ministers reported using partisan advisers to relay policy preferences to officials and as vehicles to integrate stakeholder policy advice into advisory systems. Combined, these various forms of bridging provide convincing evidence that partisan advisers represent important potential mechanisms for the integration and distribution of policy advice within advisory systems.

This chapter further confirms the important (but not decisive) impact of configuration in determining how, with whom, and with what impact partisan advisers engaged in policy advisory activity. The layered configuration in the federal case again resulted in a greater amount of bridging. For example, senior partisan advisers' buffering was largely supplemental to the preliminary partisan-policy or administrative-technical policy advice of junior partisan advisers. Or, as was noted above, multiple categories of ministerial partisan advisers in the federal case were buffering with other actors in the advisory system. Yet similar configuration within the subnational cases yielded vastly different frequencies and intensities of buffering and bridging. Partisan advisers in BC were quite active sources of content-based policy advice, while those in New Brunswick were clearly not. BC ministers' office partisan advisers were active in exogenous bridging, while those in New Brunswick were not. Such differences, despite similar locational configurations, reinforce the need to focus not only on configuration and spatial attributes of advisory systems, but empirical observations of their actual advisory system participation as well. Together, these considerations provide for more accurate depictions and analysis of partisan advisers' policy work, influence, and core executive activity.

Differences in buffering and bridging can be linked to different propensities of partisan advisers' core executive advisory-based resource exchanges. Ministers' office buffering in the federal and BC cases involved considerable partisan-political advisory-based resource exchanges. The federal case involved pronounced horizontality and verticality with not only more partisan advisers throughout the advisory system, but active ones that were exchanging policy-based resources. Ministers' offices were clearly engaged in such exchanges both vertically with their minister and departmental officials, and with the PMO and in some limited cases the PCO. Partisan advisers in BC were more explicit about their contestation and partisan-political forms of buffering than their first ministers' office counterparts. Further, their buffering tended to be ministry-specific, with their horizontal resource exchanges oriented to their respective stakeholders and, to a lesser degree, counterparts in ministers' offices. New Brunswick demonstrated negligible buffering, suggesting this was simply not a form of policy-based resource exchange being undertaken by partisan advisers. Rather, ministers and officials were left to tend to advisory demand, supply, and brokerage.

Bridging was also an important means by which policy-based resources were exchanged within all three core executives. Senior officials universally reported administrative-technical bridging occurred and was an instrument by which public servants could reinforce or supplement administrative-technical advisory activity. Partisan advisers were conduits by which policy advice could be transmitted. Likewise, partisan advisers engaged bridging with their department and to stakeholders, in varying degrees. This latter form of bridging suggests an important function for these actors in facilitating bilateral exogenous core executive advisory resource exchanges. Further, partisan-political bridging was a clear means by which partisan advisers could provide ministers with improved integration of exogenous political stakeholder policy inputs to which the public service would not have access. Together, these two forms of bridging and the differences in their occurrence in the cases suggest important ways by which partisan advisers' policy-based resource exchanges may facilitate policy legitimacy and improved coherence within the core executive (Wallner 2008; Di Francesco 2002).

These types of resource exchanges are clearly linked to attempts to secure political control and policy responsiveness (Savoie 2004a; Dahlström, Peters, and Pierre 2011). Buffering at the minister's office level diversified the availability of policy advice for the ministers, thus weakening the ability of the public service to monopolize advisory inputs. The federal case demonstrated a greater ability for buffering with its layered configuration and blended written/oral policy advisory practices. This increased the number of actors who were buffering and ensured that all policy advice flowing to the minister was subject to contestation, including but not limited to partisan-political contestation, and ultimately a non–public service recommendation. In the offices examined, the policy practices of ministers' offices providing their policy advice concurrently with that of the department suggest a reduced independence for deputies. However, all respondents were clear that the two types were considered separate, and deputies made clear they had access to ministers, and that at the end of the day the department had provided its free and frank policy advice signed off by the deputy. Conversely, the prominence of officials as opposed to ministers or partisan advisers in New Brunswick stakeholder bridging suggests a much lower capacity to exert political control on this type of policy input. Across the cases, ministerial partisan advisers' administrative-technical bridging with officials increased control by increasing access to departmental sources of policy advice, to varying degrees. Further, as this chapter has demonstrated, the partisan-political bridging described in the federal and BC cases also offered, again to varying degrees, greater access for ministers to variously located sources of partisan-political policy advice. The greater horizontal partisan-political bridging in the federal case points to a much stronger ability to exert coordinated political control. Gatekeeping was also reported in the federal and BC cases. Ministers and their advisers described it as a means to exercise control over ministerial access in general, or for stakeholders and the prioritization of specific advisory supply. Ministers were aware of such activities, with most acknowledging it was a fact of life, given the competing and often overwhelming demands facing their offices. The more direct minister–deputy relationship in New Brunswick, along with a dominant function for departmental officials in stakeholder relations, resulted in no gatekeeping by ministerial partisan advisers.

Senior public servants in all three cases underscored that partisan advisers' provision of partisan-political policy advice was legitimate as a stream of advice but something they could not provide. It was, however, much stronger and more specifically related to traditional conceptions of "policy" broadly cast in the BC and federal cases. In New Brunswick it was clearly more "case specific" or constituent-focused, as opposed to policy-focused. In all three cases, deputies normatively recognized that partisan-political context and factors were part of a minister's world, but that the provision of policy-related advice that took those into consideration was best left to the "experts" at such matters working in ministers' offices. The federal case was marked by a greater insulating effect, despite the combined briefing packages, due to the presence of the parallel written partisan-political policy advice system. In Ottawa, ministers had a clear and separate channel for partisan-political policy advice. As noted in chapter 3, this prevented public servants from having to identify, with careful language, potential political contexts or pitfalls for ministers. Chapter 6 now turns to ministers' office partisan advisers' formulation. Does their privileged position in the political arm translate into substantive or procedural formulation? If so, at what conjuncture in formulation are they most active? How do they compare across the cases or with their first ministers office counterparts? What are the implications for formulation and core executives' operation?

Chapter 6

Movers and Shapers Down the Line

Introduction

Studies from the Westminster family of systems provide evidence that ministerial partisan advisers are also active participants in policy formulation (Eichbaum and Shaw 2010; OECD 2011; LSE GV314 2012; Gains and Stoker 2011). Comparable examinations of Canadian advisers are, however, thin at best (Benoit 2006; Aucoin 2010; Bourgault and Dunn 2012). The moving and shaping concepts are used to examine ministerial partisan advisers' formulation at four sub-phases: appraisal, dialogue, formulation, and consolidation (Howlett, Perl, and Ramesh 2009; Thomas 2001). Attention is also paid to the vertical *intra*-ministerial and horizontal *inter*-ministerial orientation, as well as the partisan-political and administrative-technical nature of such activity. This chapter focuses on if and how ministers' office partisan advisers participated in policy work *formally in development,* as opposed to the broader policy advisory activity previously examined. These actors have a potential "seat at the table" in policy formulation, given their special access to policy resources, proximity to decision-makers and senior public servants, and appointed political status. Following asymmetrical core executives' thinking, these advisers may be endowed with or rely upon types of resources different from those of their first ministerial counterparts (Marsh et al. 2003; Heffernan 2003). They therefore deserve careful analysis as potentially influential policy workers and core executive members.

Ministerial partisan advisers were clearly engaging in moving activities across all three cases and in shaping in two of three cases (federal and BC). The findings presented below illuminate how, when, and with what consequence advisers engaged in formulation. This chapter also highlights how ministers' office advisers' formulation differed across the cases and also compared to their first ministers' office counterparts. These findings highlight that ministerial office partisan advisers' moving and shaping primarily involved the refinement and calibration of policies from pre-existing or established policy direction. That is, ministerial partisan advisers were instrumental to the translation of partisan-political policy direction into concrete programs and policies by departments and ministers, or the refinement and calibration of administrative-technical policy formulation underway in their respective departments. In the BC and federal cases, this involved ongoing and iterative formulation work with officials and exogenous actors, not simply post hoc political analysis of policy.

Of the three cases examined, federal ministers' office partisan advisers were by far the most active in formulation. They demonstrated the most frequent, sophisticated, and multi-staged moving and shaping. It also spanned the partisan-political and administrative dimensions and was much more consistently characterized as horizontal partisan-political moving and shaping than either subnational case. The federal case was also unique in that all categories of respondents acknowledged that partisan advisers were active participants in *formal* policy formulation mechanisms. For example, advisers were actively contributing to the development and analysis of departmental information notes, decision notes, and memoranda to Cabinet and Cabinet / Cabinet committee work. Ministerial partisan advisers in BC were also found to engage in moving and shaping that spanned all four dimensions used in this study to plot such activity (partisan and administrative, horizontal and vertical). However, they were not tied to formal public service policy mechanisms and were reported at fewer formulation sub-phases. New Brunswick ministerial partisan advisers were again found to be the least active in formulation. No shaping at the minister's office level was discernible, with partisan advisers almost exclusively tending to constituency-specific files. They were, however, active in moving, particularly vertical administrative-technical moving involving formulation *with* deputies and other officials. Their formulation was the least horizontal and reported at the fewest formulation phases.

Ministerial partisan advisers were, in some but not all cases, consequential to formulation. Moreover, their formulation varied in how and when they engaged in non-advisory policy work. Not only were

ministerial partisan advisers instrumental for ministerial determinations of political feasibility (Bakvis 1997; Aucoin 2010), they were also
found in the majority of cases to be active participants in the elaboration and refinement of policy options, dialogic sub-stage consultation, and they were important to policy-process management and
coordination. Such substantive and procedural formulation is directly
linked to core executive policy-based resource exchange. This chapter explores how the types and nature of their formulation, and corresponding resource exchanges, affected core executive operation in
each case.

Procedural Policy Work and Ministers' Offices

Federal Ministers' Office "Moving"

Federal partisan advisers in ministers' offices reported a variety of
vertical and horizontal procedural policy formulation, along partisan-
political and administrative-technical dimensions. The greater overall
number and specialization of partisan advisers as detailed in previous
chapters produced more intensive and frequent participation in procedural formulation at a greater number of sub-phases. In interviews,
various categories of respondents clearly articulated that partisan
advisers were active in moving. Ministers and their partisan advisers
emphasized that they took their marching orders from the mandate
letters provided by the PMO/PCO. Policy work that they undertook
was described as flowing largely from the priorities delineated within
these documents. That is, partisan advisers frequently described their
policy formulation functions in relation to *matching* partisan-political
policy priorities to available policy options that were generated in large
measure by departmental officials. When asked to describe the policy
work of partisan advisers, one chief described it as "expected to make
policy changes within the government and within our department that
reflected our policy platform as a party and what we had campaigned
on. To be able then to turn around and say, 'This is what we promised
on the campaign trail and therefore this is what we did when we were
in office.' So the mandate letters that I tried to implement on behalf of
[minister] had very short time frames" (P26). The latter part of this comment speaks to the minority status of the Harper government, that with
the potential of another election on the horizon, advisers were keen
to push the policy agenda to get as much done as possible. Ministers

interviewed generally echoed the importance of mandate letters as direction-setting vehicles. Mandate letters were taken seriously, and partisan advisers were vigilant in ensuring that ministerial policy work matched the policy objective set out in the mandate letters. Most ministers, like partisan advisers, emphasized the function of the "centre" in creating these documents. Partisan advisers were to a large degree monitoring policy development to ensure compliance with centrally set objectives. As former minister David Emerson explained,

> The mandate letter is packed with deliverables that you are expected to deliver on over your annual mandate. That letter is a concoction, typically, of the Privy Council Office and the prime minister's senior staff. So you'll get the mandate letter and your political staff and public service staff will all see that letter. The political staff will be particularly focused on making sure that the, in setting your policy program and the work that you do and the time that you spend. They will be particularly sensitive to the mandate letter. And how you deliver is going to be particularly important to your stature in Cabinet on a go forward basis.

Partisan advisers detailed considerable moving in their descriptions of the types of policy work in which they engaged. Another chief of staff, in explaining the general policy function of a chief, made clear that procedural formulation is a core function, emphasizing that what chiefs do is work *in concert with* the deputy minister to make sure policy files are successfully brought to completion. This, of course, suggests that when it works well, having additional policy workers can serve as a way to provide additional policy capacity to the highest levels of public policymaking and management (Tiernan 2011; Savoie 1983). However, it may also result in challenges or suboptimal outcomes if resource exchanges are inefficient or add complexity or uncertainty (Craft 2015a; Shaw and Eichbaum 2015). When asked to elaborate on how the adviser engaged in policy formulation, the same chief reported a focus on the procedural coordination of policy work, at various formulation sub-phases, occurring along both partisan-political and administrative-technical dimensions. The adviser's response points clearly to activity at appraisal, dialogue, and formulation sub-phases. The chief detailed the three stages at which this occurred and is worth quoting at length:

> The first one is when you do the conceptual work. You sit down and say, "OK, we've been tasked by the Prime Minister's Office and by Cabinet to

do this. What's that project going to look like? What are the parameters? How do we do that?" You deal, you know, primarily with your senior [partisan] staff, with your [partisan] policy staff, and with senior departmental staff. That takes a lot of work because, you know, with the example in [the minister's] office, there might be fifteen different areas that are going at the same time, and so you tend to run around quite a bit, and you have to keep on top of your staff to know what they're doing. The second area would be consultation. The minister's office staff would be meeting, as well as the department, would be meeting with stakeholders right across the country. So, you know, the chief of staff would be responsible for taking the most important of those meetings. The third one, of course, is the writing, the drafting, and I would say, you know, basically making sure that the minister's colleagues on Cabinet are comfortable with the direction, are informed on the direction, and therefore will support her in cabinet. So I spent … I would say I spent most of my time on the design phase and at the end on the networking and liaising with other Cabinet ministers and making sure that the drafts of the materials would be approved and accepted by the prime minister and by the minister's Cabinet colleagues. A lot of human stuff, a lot of talking, a lot of interaction with people and trying to keep them onside or get them onside. (P27)

This type of response reveals the activities that can comprise the "policy work" undertaken by advisers (Colebatch 2006; Colebatch, Hoppe, and Noordegraaf 2010a). That such work may go beyond formal policy analysis, from a partisan-political perspective, to include a diverse set of activities that frequently necessitate policy-based resource exchanges with other policy actors. Sequentially, partisan advisers typically described some limited involvement in initial vertical "front-end" appraisal sub-stage formulation. It was most often described as occurring simultaneously on both partisan-political and administrative-technical fronts. In the former, moving at the early appraisal sub-phase generally consisted of coordination and management of initial assessments by the minister's partisan advisers to determine "fit" with stated political objectives and policy priorities (e.g., platform, throne speech, mandate letter). In administrative-technical moving, partisan advisers emphasized it entailed numerous meetings with department officials to plan and coordinate policy work flowing up from the department, or to deal with pressing issues that may have unexpectedly emerged. Partisan advisers also noted consulting with senior officials (DM/ADM level) about "housekeeping" policy items for medium- and long-term policy.

Vertical moving was reported as subsequently followed by partisan-political horizontal moving, such as signal-checking with the PMO as items were developed, or related to the political management of their items' movement through formal Cabinet processes. The above response from one chief makes clear this involved significant broker-age and coordination with other chiefs (and less frequently, ministers) to ensure proposals had the requisite support for Cabinet/committee ratification. In addition, horizontal partisan-political moving was often characterized by leveraging others to move policy items forward or for dispute resolution. Another chief, when asked to explain who and why she interacted with other ministers' offices' chiefs on policy mat-ters echoed this in responding, "I would relate to other chiefs of staff when perhaps we were having difficulty moving a policy initiative for-ward. You know, sometimes it was our officials slowing things down, sometimes it was another minister's officials who were slowing things down. And so I would interact with my chief-of-staff counterpart" (P28). This again raises the potential costs and benefits of ministerial advisers as core executive members. As process managers they may usefully steer and drive the policy process and exchange policy-based resources with public service and others in the political arm. Con-versely they may in fact produce suboptimal policy processes if their systemic use in policy contexts is not well coordinated (Craft 2015b; Eichbaum and Shaw 2011).

Part of this was the job of chiefs of staff. They were seen by all catego-ries of respondents as engaging in policy work consisting primarily of coordination and management. From a formulation perspective, chiefs described being substantially involved in the coordination of dialogue sub-phase activities involving discussions about feasibility with depart-ment officials and consultations with pertinent external stakeholders or experts (both formal and informal). As the previous chapter on bridg-ing made clear, federal partisan advisers reported frequent policy advi-sory interactions with exogenous actors on policy matters both with *and* apart from officials. This was also true for their policy formulation. However, horizontal administrative-technical moving in the dialogue sub-phase was not reported as involving moving with public service actors outside their "home" departments. Instead, most chiefs charac-terized such horizontal administrative-technical moving as externally oriented towards stakeholders or partisan-political in nature. One min-ister, when asked if and how his partisan advisers played a role in pol-icy, got to the heart of partisan advisers' horizontal moving:

Let's say you get in your mandate letter from the prime minister to address, oh I don't know, housing. So immediately the bureaucracy goes to work and starts to come up with housing ideas. Meanwhile you have all these housing stakeholders coming to you. They don't know that you have housing is in your mandate letter but they're always knocking at the door asking for things. And the political staff starts to engage them, knowing in the back of their mind that this is an issue. But the political staff is also conscious that we've said things in our platform, maybe the prime minister has said something in a speech. So we have some very broad direction on how we want to move forward with these issues. And then based on those interactions with stakeholders, that knowledge of what we've said in the past in political platforms, and this kind of thing will inform our discussions with the bureaucracy about what this should look like, this new policy on housing should look like. And then if political staff are wise, they will also loop in other ministers and PMO about sort of the general direction of where this is going, because the last thing you want to do is surprise people at the end with something that's just not aligned. (M11)

This response confirms an active function for partisan advisers in the policy-based resource exchanges required for alignment or coupling of partisan-political commitments and governmental policy work, and fostering a "no surprises" environment (Craft 2015a; Dahlström, Peters, and Pierre 2011; OECD 2011). The chiefs of staff interviewed tended to focus on the dialogue and formulation sub-phases. They described considerable coordination, management, monitoring, and oversight, as well as "steering" the formulation activities of public servants as well as stakeholders. Simultaneously, they noted they were continuously engaged in signal-checking and coordination with counterparts both vertically and horizontally. Close working relationships involving intensive moving, including process management, sequencing, and coordination with first minister's office partisan advisers were repeatedly reported in interviews. How did it fit with other initiatives that were in progress and the policy priorities of government? How would the timing of the policy development work within broader Cabinet or Cabinet committee processes? Who was affected? Who do we need to consult with? Horizontally, chiefs reported moving through coordination of policy items in relation to their minister's Cabinet business. When asked to describe if and how they involved themselves in policy formulation for Cabinet and

Cabinet committee work, a chief of staff responded that there were typically two aspects:

> You would hold a whole series of meetings with Cabinet colleagues – ones that are affected by this– briefing them on the initiative, you know, ascertaining if there are any concerns, understanding who your allies are, which particular points are of the most interest to Cabinet colleagues and then going back and working with the departmental staff to make sure that presentation that ministers make builds on the strengths of those things, minimizes the weaknesses of those, and attracts the people that it needs to actually get, you know, to get support in the Cabinet. The other thing is that there are regular meetings in the Prime Minister's Office on important bills. So prime minister's policy person would call a meeting of all the five or six implicated people, departments, ministers' offices, and the thing. Go through them, go through the Cabinet agenda. What's your perspective on this, what's your perspective on that, what's your perspective on this, and try and sort out any difficulties and let them know where the prime minister is coming from on these things as well. (P27)

This horizontal partisan-political moving has implications for how partisan advisers may facilitate "policy success" and "political policy success" through policy learning via process management and coordination of partisan-political formulation (Howlett 2012; McConnell 2010a). As the above quotation underscores, moving can facilitate the identification of potential process-related pitfalls, consolidate support at the Cabinet/political level, and/or overcome or avoid information asymmetries through improved policy-process management among ministers and their offices. The limited horizontal administrative-technical moving reported was described as part of inter-ministerial meetings or "four corner meetings."[39] In addition, ministerial chiefs of staff met weekly in the PMO, and chiefs explained this was an opportunity for them to informally network and exchange requests for favours and generally advance various initiatives. Ministers' office directors of policy described much more involvement in the early stages of policy formulation. They were less burdened by the other ministerial office responsibilities and oversight duties that fall upon chiefs of staff. The principal duty of directors of policy was policy work. Procedurally, many reported significant early involvement, particularly on the priority files of their minister or of the government agenda more broadly cast. Again, the ministers' office policy directors frequently reported a distinction between "housekeeping" and "priority" policy work. As one ministerial director of policy characterized it,

> On major projects, projects driven by the ministers' personal interest, legacy projects, high-profile projects, then I will generally keep abreast of it from front to end is maybe a good way to say it. I will invest time in becoming smart on the issue, or the lead [partisan] adviser will in terms of policy background, alongside the department, and be in a position to review advice from both political perspectives and from objective policy perspectives. On more day-to-day issues or issues that don't have a clear political bent, then the team and I will defer to the department and avoid taking a more intimate … unless the minister or the minister on our advice feels as though there's a problem with what's being done, and then we may take personal responsibility for it. (P22)

Most directors of policy described their vertical moving in comparable terms as those used by chiefs of staff. They saw it involving simultaneous partisan-political and administrative-technical formulation. It was described as involving sequencing and coordination of partisan-political and departmental policy work. This is precisely the type policy work captured by Campbell's (1988) notion of amphibians, or those who engage in policy work but maintain explicit partisan links. It speaks to the fact that these actors are at times part of the formal policymaking apparatus of government but again approach that policy work in terms different from those of the permanent public service. Many advisers noted the sheer volume of policy activity occurring and their offices' attempt to systematically apply political perspective and engage with other policy actors within the political arm as well as the public service. Another chief of staff, who had also served in the PMO policy shop, pointed to marked differences in their vertical interactions with public servants, and their policy formulation at the minister's office level compared to that of the PMO. The adviser explained, "I saw that from a PMO perspective one could be forgiven for thinking that, you know, the political side completely drives the agenda of government" (P28). The adviser recounted that there were multiple policy priorities in addition to the policy work that departments undertake, much of which the minister, and thereby their offices, will often not be aware of or interested in. The adviser summed it up, adding, "I found that once I moved into a minister's office, the officials in the bureaucracy themselves had a lot more, there was upward pressure as well as downward pressure on a policy level" (P28).

The same adviser was asked to reflect on his policy experiences at the two locations, PMO and a minister's office. The adviser specified that within a minister's office there was greater dialogue and engagement with officials – the iterative policymaking process was heightened, given that they were getting into the details or the "weeds." He explained that there were differences at the department level, given that a range of officials would be briefing the minister's office, whereas in the PMO it was typically the PCO or deputy ministers who would brief the prime minister and his advisers. At the department level, as the adviser put it, "we would get briefed by more junior officials and by officials who maybe only saw their piece of the overall puzzle. We got briefed by the deputy's office as well, but the more junior officials, you know, all they did all day long was [policy area]. They didn't do the bigger ... they didn't see the bigger picture of [the department], for example. So, again we really got into the weeds there" (P28). The adviser's remarks again suggest a more strategic imperative for ministers' office advisers to move forward the political policy agenda of government while also tending to housekeeping files that emerge and departments are always managing.

This type of vertical administrative-technical dialogue sub-phase activity, occurring within the department, was quite commonly reported by all categories of federal partisan advisers. Ministers and their advisers made clear that, as a general rule, partisan advisers were not there to provide in-depth technical or subject matter expertise. That was the purview of their department. Rather, partisan advisers reported their duties consisted of challenging the veracity of departmental policy work that at times involved their engaging with officials to ensure that formulation included the appropriate degree of consultation and context. Partisan advisers often reported moving that involved coordination and management of policy formulation, ensuring that policy development was unfolding at an acceptable pace, had included appropriate consultation with various actors as required, and was aligned with the policy goal. These process-based interactions were almost always framed as occurring with senior public servants. Partisan advisers described often, but not exclusively, inserting themselves into the formulation stage when policy development became problematic. As such, they would typically consult with senior management to coordinate responses or discuss options for resolutions.

This type of vertical intra-ministerial process-based policy work was described often and represented a core aspect of dialogue or formulation sub-phase activity. When one policy director was asked about his typical policy interactions with officials, he described them as occurring with assistant deputy ministers and directors in the public service. This notwithstanding, he reported that at times he would go deeper into the department and contact lower-level officials if it was a particularly technical subject matter. Across the board, partisan advisers at all levels, from PMO chiefs of staff to those working as "junior" partisan advisers for ministers, recognized that the public service held the "technical expertise" in most if not all instances. In all three cases, partisan advisers mentioned that they would go directly to subject matter experts, and for their part deputies in all cases knew this was occurring. Where they differed was in their tolerance for such practices and the protocols that dictated the unofficial practices. That is, to what level could partisan advisers go? Was it restricted to senior management, directors or managers, or junior departmental personnel? There was variance by office, but universally the last was off limits. Deputies and partisan advisers were aware that once they engaged below the senior management level, public servants may not be accustomed to dealing with political staffs of any kind.

This vertical procedural work extended to significant oversight and coordination in the partisan-political policy-briefing system as well. Most policy directors noted that they might have responsibility for a few key ministerial policy priorities, but their policy shop staff carried most of the load for partisan-political policy analysis. Horizontally, directors of policy, similar to chiefs of staff, reported partisan-political rather than "administrative-technical" moving. Policy directors differed from chiefs in that they almost always interacted with the junior PMO policy adviser who oversaw their policy sector, not the PMO policy director. One director of policy whose minister also had Cabinet committee responsibilities was the exception to the rule. In that case, the director of policy dealt with both the PMO policy director and PCO representatives directly. The adviser interacted with the director of policy in the PMO, as opposed to the junior PMO advisers, and also interacted directly with the PCO Cabinet committee secretary and staff. This adds further clarity to the need to assess the policy work rather than simply the location of partisan advisers. Horizontal partisan-political moving in the federal case was described in terms similar to that reported in the BC case below. Ministerial partisan advisers took the lead in policy interactions with the first minister's office. As one federal minister explained,

> Most of the interaction is between staff. You know, like staff members talking to staff members about the timing of announcements, the sequencing of events, making sure you don't show up on another minister's pet project. PMO is a clearing house for all of that, for all of those things and more. So typically the interactions are between staff who check those things out and then would just say, "Here's how this is likely to roll out," or whatever. But sometimes I would meet with or talk to staff that I needed to. There was nothing to prohibit that, but most of the time I would just leave it to my staff to check that part of it out. (M12)

The most junior partisan advisers in ministers' offices primarily reported vertical moving. They reported significantly less horizontal activity on either partisan-political or administrative-technical dimensions. As can be gleaned from the responses of chiefs and directors of policy set out above, junior partisan advisers did engage in significant partisan-political policy formulation. The more senior partisan advisers tended to engage in broader horizontal and "back-end" policy formulation. Junior partisan advisers were described as the partisan-political subject matter experts. They managed files assigned by the director of policy and kept close tabs on any policy-related developments under their purview. Those interviewed reported more front-end activity in the appraisal and dialogue sub-phases. Junior partisan advisers also provided support in the latter stages of policy formulation, particularly if the minister was presenting at Cabinet committee. One director of policy explained how his policy staff would be involved in consolidation sub-phase activity around Cabinet processes:

> It was the job of the policy adviser and my team to support the presentation of the minister. So they would attend the Cabinet [committee] meeting for that presentation of the item. So let's say it was ... let's go back to [policy area]. Then it would have been one of my team members that would go to the meeting and support the minister. He would have been the one who would sort of brief the minister on what the lay of the land was, if he had any intelligence on whether minister X or minister Y was in support or non-support of the direction we were taking, to try and remove any surprises. Ministers don't like surprises. They don't mind oppositions to their ideas, but they don't like to be surprised by that. (P25)

Deputy ministers interviewed described the policy development of partisan advisers as partisan-political, strategic, and process-related. They reported such activity as most pronounced in the initial appraisal or formulation sub-phases as policy work was more formally fleshed out. Federal deputy ministers, similar to their BC counterparts, also described partisan advisers' formulation activity occurring during dialogue and formulation sub-phases. Partisan advisers were seen as actors who, in light of their regularized interactions with ministers, knew what would be politically feasible and the minister's direction. In short, they could help steer policy development in that direction. Federal deputies were very clear that it was always the minister's directives that were to be sought out, as partisan advisers had no authority to "provide direction" to public servants. Two deputies' responses are indicative of this emphasis and a view that partisan advisers are procedural transmitters of ministerial direction, particularly during appraisal and dialogue sub-phases:

I wouldn't say never. They tend to be more people who would communicate the views on something. So it would be more as communicators as opposed to, if someone on the minister's staff says, "Well, I think you should do it this way instead of this way." The first question you say is, "Is this how the minister feels?" And so sometimes you assume that because they have that day-to-day connection with the minister, they're just communicating it. But if it's their own independent view, then they are kind of not seen as having that role. (ADM2)

Sometimes a political staffer will say to a public servant, "Do this." You know, I teach my staff to say, "Is that the minister's direction that you're giving me, right? Because if it's not, I can't take your direction, right?" That's not the way it works. Usually, that's a sort of, you know … any political staffer with integrity, and they almost all have integrity I think, that kind of catches them short and they say, "Really, is that the minister's wish or just my sort of general impression of that?" (DM8)

Overall, the federal case involved ministers' office partisan advisers moving at all formulation sub-phases. Comparatively, the case stood out in that ministers' office partisan advisers reported significantly greater moving in conjunction with formal policy development. This involved vertical administrative moving via departmental mechanisms, including the development of departmental Cabinet items, and departmental briefing notes, decision notes, and information notes. Horizontally, moving-related activity was heavily reported in conjunction with Cabinet and Cabinet committee activity. This included simple processing of dockets and documents for ministerial signature, as well as ensuring that the minister's Cabinet "decks" (PowerPoint presentations) and memoranda to Cabinet had been properly developed by officials, and received the appropriate partisan-political analysis. A key finding was that partisan advisers, regardless of seniority, reported engaging in exclusively vertical administrative-technical moving. Formulation interactions with the public service, at the minister's office level, were only intra-departmental. Their partisan-political moving, however, spanned both horizontal and vertical dimensions. These included pronounced inter- and intra-ministerial coordination on policy items, gauging and promoting support for Cabinet items, and ongoing signal-checking with pertinent ministerial offices and the PMO. This provides a clear boundary for the types of policy-based resource exchanges that animated policy work in the core executive.

Ministers' Office "Moving" in BC

BC partisan advisers also reported procedural moving and were most commonly reported at the "front end," including activity at the appraisal, dialogue, and formulation sub-phases. Policy formulation was generally described along partisan-political dimensions as opposed to administrative-technical ones. Specifically, as opposed to their federal counterparts, BC partisan advisers reported no vertical involvement in processing departmental policy documents such as decision notes or briefing notes intended for the minister. While they certainly were exposed to and would familiarize themselves with such documents, they had no formal involvement in their development. Similarly, partisan advisers also reported much less administrative-technical moving related to Cabinet or Cabinet committee activity. Horizontal administrative-technical moving was, as reported in the federal case, centred on dealings with external stakeholders in their policy sector rather than public servants outside their "home" department.

Vertical partisan-political and administrative-technical moving was most prominently reported at the appraisal, dialogue, and formulation sub-phases. The smaller contingent of partisan advisers in ministerial offices in BC also resulted in reduced moving within and between ministers' offices. The subnational cases shared this characteristic. When asked to describe if and how the partisan adviser might be involved in the development of policy, one long-time minister's office adviser explained,

> I wouldn't say we'd be completely uninvolved at that point. But in terms of who's doing the evaluation and, you know, gathering information and coming up with options, that's the department that's doing that. But then it comes back with options, and that's when the minister's office gets more involved. You know, are these options sufficient, or do, you know … do they need to look at more options? But whether or not the MA [ministerial assistant] is asked if they're sufficient, you know they're not always asked. They're just … it may be that a briefing is scheduled with the minister and they are presented. And then at that meeting it is decided that we want to see more options or we want more information on this option, or what have you. (P20)

Overall many partisan advisers shared this view and reported that they would engage in policy development during the dialogue and formulation sub-phases. Deputies and partisan advisers largely agreed that on such matters partisan advisers were less consequential at the "front end," again largely deferring to officials. All categories of respondents emphasized that partisan advisers were not there to replace or duplicate public service policy work. In-depth and detailed formal and technical policy analysis were seen as the appropriate function of the public service. For those priority ministerial or governmental policy initiatives, partisan advisers were again reported to undertake moving tasks, such as, at the appraisal sub-stage, relaying the minister's strategic direction, or steering the department away from identified "non-starters" or potential red flags at the outset of policy development. As one long-time partisan adviser explained.

> The ministry stuff, they're the experts on that kind of stuff. You know, by no stretch of the imagination am I an expert on legislation. Those people who write legislation are a strange and wonderful breed of people. I would go nuts, I think, trying to do that. I'm maybe a little different than some of the staffers here, but I tend to be more high level. I tend not maybe to as much detail, but I … you know … and we develop a rapport with the people that we're working with. And like I said, part of our role

especially is to liaise between the deputy minister and the ministry staff and the minister. (P7)

Partisan advisers described significant vertical administrative-technical moving at the dialogue sub-phase. When asked to describe his policy work, one adviser made clear that it included significant procedural policy activity involving multiple actors within the policy domain. Here again the importance of advisers' potential facilitation of resource exchanges within the core executive is apparent. In some cases this involved the exchange of their resources, such as pertinent information or partisan-political analysis or stakeholder information, or their function as conduits or hubs for the exchange of resources from others. As the adviser explained, "A lot of the time we're dealing with not so much policy in a pure sense where you are saying what should our policy be on this, but collecting the data, working with the ministry, and then meeting with the minister and disseminating the information and coming up with a strategy or a policy on how we are going to deal with things." In the BC case, partisan advisers described themselves as heavily involved in ensuring that policy development unfolded without delay. Many referenced a role in keeping the minister apprised of the policies that were "in play" at any given stage of development with the department. Furthermore, horizontal moving was described primarily in relation to dialogue sub-stage activity. This type of moving was, however, focused on particular aspects of specific policies during formulation, as opposed to general discussions about any given policy issue, departmental business, or the policy landscape. Partisan advisers explained that they worked in parallel with officials. Officials would ensure the department was reaching out to the appropriate stakeholders through formal consultations that partisan advisers would monitor. In addition, partisan advisers themselves would reach out, often informally, to consult with stakeholders on partisan-political impacts of policy work. Another long-serving ministerial partisan adviser described her policy formulation activity as occurring throughout the entire process:

I found myself at all levels of the development of policy, from the very germination of ideas. I was lucky enough to see a couple of ideas through from, you know, a sparkle, a twinkle in someone's eyes to a full act passed in the legislation. If you look at [lists various specific policy initiatives], you know, I got to be there at the very start when it was just an idea and help implement it all the way through. Helping follow up with the bure-aucrats, making sure there were no issues related to that, no roadblocks, helping clear the way for talking to stakeholders and other ministries to make sure, even other levels of government to make sure there were no issues blocking the way. On the political side, you do get to help develop policy if you want to. If you as an individual and the minister has the will and vests the authority into you, you can develop policy and see all the way along. (P11)

Significant vertical and horizontal moving for BC partisan advisers was expressed in relation to partisan advisers' ability to coordinate and manage disparate policy inputs during formulation. BC partisan advisers often described their policy work as involving synthesis of policy inputs on specific policies in development. Moreover, while not tied to formal Cabinet instruments as seen in the federal case, many reported involvement in managing the processes of policy formulation. This was particularly the case for key policy priorities as established by their ministers or the government. Ministers and partisan advisers interviewed were quick to point out that government involves clear, politically generated policy priorities, but also a host of ongoing policy and operational concerns or "housekeeping" policy. Their involvement in the former was as drivers of policy development, but one where the policy work was primarily undertaken by officials. With the latter, most explained it was generally limited to formulation sub-phase activ-ity when policy options percolated up that were inconsistent with the political agenda of the minister or the government more broadly. As one ministerial adviser explained,

A lot of the day-to-day work of government, you know, it pretty much runs itself and, you know, you'll get the decision note. You never heard anything about this issue, because government is a big operation, so you've never heard of this issue and you get the decision note and the minister reads it. You have a briefing about it, all the work has already gone into it, and you just have to trust it's accurate and correct, and that the decision is the right decision that the bureaucrats advise, and you go with it, and that's the day-to-day of government. (P11)

Deputies often categorized advisers' formulation work as occurring primarily at a strategic level. This is in part attributable to the fact that they work in ministerial offices, which underscores the importance of location. In jurisdictions and offices where they are active policy work-ers, they are privy to policy at the highest levels, whereas junior public service policy analysts in a department may not have access to par-ticular types of policy work, or ever interact with a minister or deputy. While some noted their minister's partisan advisers had substantive expertise in particular files, most deputies described partisan advisers' moving as strategic, tied to coordination of political policy priorities and departmental work, ensuring departmental work dovetailed with political priorities in content and sequence. With many years of service at the deputy level, one deputy explained that based on experience, partisan advisers were important actors able to reconcile the policy work unfolding in both political and administrative spheres:

> They not only become very knowledgeable about the ministry business, but they become very knowledgeable about getting that back into the poli-tical sphere. The only danger in that is that they [partisan advisers] start doing the strategic thinking, which is probably a good thing in terms of providing advice to the minister in terms on how to handle something politically. But the ministry gets lazy and isn't doing that kind of thinking itself. But I have seen quite a difference, depending on the political staff, as to what the ministry have to adapt to. Because in some cases we have become lazy, because the minister's office is doing some of that strategic thinking for us. (DM5)

Ministers and deputies frequently cited this type of coordination and management at the formulation sub-phase. They fundamentally described it as ensuring the political feasibility of formal policy options as officials developed them, and ensuring that politically established policy direction was followed. This involved steering, coordination, and monitoring types of moving. Ministers reported their partisan advisers' moving as pronounced at the appraisal, dialogue, and for-mulation sub-phases. One minister described his partisan adviser as a proactive contributor to policy development. Again, he emphasized the twin dimensions of administrative and partisan-political policy-related work. The minister elaborated, "He had a proactive role in pol-icy development not only in terms of having the right questions to ask but also often assisting me in getting to both the politically acceptable answer and the practical answer as well" (M9). This response was rep-resentative of ministers' general descriptions of their partisan advisers as having dual partisan-political and administrative-technical duties.

On the one hand, they were part of the departmental policymaking apparatus but served simultaneously as a vehicle for partisan-political oversight for ministers. As such, advisers have become an addition to the traditionally bilateral political-administrative nexus – a nexus that was already difficult to navigate and in which partisan advisers seem to be adding to the wrinkles of policymaking, while at other times ironing them out (Aucoin and Savoie 2009; Aucoin 2010).

In addition, ministers also described their partisan advisers' influence through process management. In a similar way as described at the federal level, minister's office partisan advisers were seen as able to manage and coordinate policy development through control over their schedules and appointments. This type of process management, such as the sequencing of consultation, was reported at the dialogue sub-phase policy formulation. To a limited extent, partisan advisers could affect the sequencing of consultations during formulation or procedurally increase the amount of extra-departmental dialogue sub-phase consultation undertaken during formulation. Ministers in this case made clear they expected their advisers to be in constant contact with external policy communities and other ministerial offices, and to be able to alert the minister to red flags or opportunities related to departmental policy priorities. This type of coordination with exogenous actors was the primary mechanism by which partisan advisers engaged in horizontal moving in BC. It which was predominant in the dialogue sub-phase, but also was a key means by which formulation sub-phase activities were informed.

Horizontal moving was restricted to interactions with their ministerial counterparts or stakeholders. Interviews confirmed that, as in the other cases, partisan advisers' interactions with other ministries were always mediated through their colleagues in other ministers' offices. When asked what typical policy-related interactions were like with their first minister's office counterparts, one adviser responded, "Working with the Premier's Office, usually it's almost entirely information requests. And vice versa, I'll go to them sometimes if I need advice. If I have a problem that I can't figure out what the best response would be, or if it's going to be an issue that the premier is going to have to speak to publicly, then I would call them" (P5).

Horizontal moving from ministerial offices to the first minister's office in British Columbia shared greater similarities to those in the federal case than those reported in New Brunswick. At a basic level, BC partisan advisers, like their federal counterparts, tended to interact with more senior first minister's office staff. Partisan advisers, in a similar sense to their New Brunswick counterparts, also dealt with the premier's EA on logistics or communications. However, they also engaged in interactions on policy matters with the premier's deputy chief of staff. These activities were usually reported as transactional exchanges of information from a policy coordination or issues management perspective, such as raising potentially contentious policy activity or flagging items to the Premier's Office. Most, however, indicated that they would also field requests related to the progress of certain policy work, or for intelligence on stakeholders. As one partisan adviser summarized, "We do have to keep them up to speed on any emerging issues that you may have to deal with. But we probably don't deal with them in the same way we deal with other MAs [ministerial assistants]. Because usually you'll say, 'I need this information on this. Can you help me get it?' Whereas when you're dealing with Premier's Office, you're either giving them information or they're asking for it" (P7). Deputies were also asked if they or their minister's partisan advisers interacted with the first minister's office and what effects this may have on policy formulation. Almost without exception deputy ministers indicated they dealt only with the deputy minister to the premier, leaving partisan advisers to tend to partisan-political aspects of policy formulation. As one deputy explained, partisan advisers existed

> to consistently sit there and look at everything that's coming into his office, and listen to the ... look at the mail, look at the correspondence, set up the kinds of meetings he's going to attend, look at briefing notes and information coming to the minister, make sure he sees all of that in a timely way. But also make sure that a political lens is put on it, and also report back to the [premier's] chief of staff. So, you know, we're putting forward a difficult decision and really there is three other ministries involved, and they need to know, and our minister needs to make sure three other ministries know. Well it would be the [partisan advisers] who would work with the other MAs to make sure everybody's on the same page. (DM7)

While significantly less institutionalized and formal than their federal counterparts, BC partisan advisers did engage in moving, particularly at the dialogue and formulation sub-phases. On a vertical partisan-political level, such activity was more direct with ministers, as a consequence of the smaller complements of ministerial staffs. In the BC case there were no policy teams or formal political policy briefing systems. Moving thus consisted of significant transmission of ministerial direction to officials and ongoing monitoring of development to ensure consistency with such direction. The horizontal moving, both partisan-political and administrative-technical, was less routinized than that reported in the federal case. While partisan advisers did describe coordination between their office and the first minister's office, it was less institutionalized as a practice. As with the federal case, there was little horizontal administrative-technical moving with officials. Horizontal moving was described in partisan-political terms with other ministers' offices and limited moving relating to Premier's Office. Again, the lack of involvement with Cabinet/committee work and formal Cabinet policymaking tools, like memoranda to Cabinet, affected how they engaged in moving. Horizontal administrative-technical moving was reported to consist of formulation involving exogenous policy stakeholders, such as consultations with stakeholders in appraisal and dialogue sub-phases for the legitimation of departmental policy work. Further, clear instances of horizontal partisan-political policy advisory activity with stakeholders were also reported. These involved dialogue and formulation sub-stage activity to gauge stakeholders on their support or the impacts of particular policy decisions.

Ministers' Office "Moving" in New Brunswick

Partisan advisers at the minister's office level in New Brunswick reported the lowest levels of overall policy-related activity of all three cases. Multiple interviewees suggested this was the product of an unmediated political-administrative interface. That is, ministers worked directly with their deputy ministers on all matters of policy and relied almost exclusively on officials as their primary sources of policy advice. Ministers noted they would not hesitate to interact directly or seek out from departmental officials in any policy branch, at mid- to senior levels, whenever necessary. Deputies reported that, in general, partisan advisers were so preoccupied with requests from ministers' constituents that it left little to no time for departmental policy-related work; most deputy ministers hinted that this was probably for the best.

The limited policy-related activity that they did engage in at the formulation sub-phase tended to be highly transactional. Again, ministers and their partisan advisers frequently referenced the electoral platform as having set out what policy would broadly look like, and once they were elected, it was a matter of figuring out the details in conjunction with departmental officials. Partisan advisers described formulation that was most aptly categorized as occurring within the dialogue and formulation sub-phases. Across the board, New Brunswick minister's office partisan advisers described policymaking as a departmental function. One partisan adviser explained the importance of the party platform and how he saw his own policy function. Much like in the federal case it, was articulated to consist of ensuring ministers undertook what had already been set out:

> A lot of the policy is pre-prepared by the party itself and I think [the minister] readily admitted, especially after the fact, that they hadn't read that [platform] when [the minister] was running, going door-to-door. They didn't know what was in that, they hadn't even seen it. It was delayed. It only came on her door like with probably only a week left on the election campaign. So a lot people who ended up being ministers were kind of reading that for the first time when they became ministers. "Oh yeah, exactly what does this say?" I always had it on my desk, I was always quite ... I guess that was part of my job as a political assistant was to know what was in there, you know. "You're going to do this. Well, it says you can't do that." (P9)

The limited moving activity reported by New Brunswick partisan advisers extended to them coordinating updates between ministers and deputies on formal policy development. This would, for example, involve confirming political direction from the minister to the deputy or managing the follow-up of queries to the department. Again, ministers and their staff reported that this was less about partisan advisers being readily involved in policy development and more often the product of busy ministerial schedules. Another partisan adviser recounted having had regular meetings with the deputy about "briefings." When asked to expand on what those briefings involved, the adviser made it quite clear that his interaction was issue specific and the department did the policy work: "When we're talking about a policy change, a regulation change, legislation change, any of those sort of high-level shifts in the way the department operates, the deputy takes care of that. That's sort of how that has happened. Takes care of giving the information on that. I mean, I'm not a staff person in the department per se, implementing the acts and regulations that are set out. If there are any changes on the staff level, the deputy takes care of keeping both of us informed about that" (P34).

Interview respondents were unanimous across categories that partisan advisers' general activities were specific to constituency issues. Ministers often explained that their staff was overwhelmed with responding to such case-specific matters. Even if they wanted to, they simply would not have the time to become more engaged in policy formulation. Ministers may use partisan advisers for basic informational purposes but departments tended to policy. One minister explained, "If there's an email or a letter that comes in and somebody wants answers to questions, you know, I can forward that off to them. [The partisan adviser] goes and contacts the appropriate person in the department and has that information delivered to that person who asked it" (M2). Another minister was even more explicit and clear about her adviser's policy function and approach to policymaking more generally: "The political staffs were not, with me, involved in any policy initiatives or changes. They were to put out fires. So all of the things that I did in policy came, as I say, from the base of the pyramid, where I would then direct the civil service to come up with a way to do it. Political staffs weren't really involved in the policy changes" (M8). Vertical administrative moving was thus limited. However, moving was reported during the dialogue and formulation sub-phases. Deputies explained that, from their perspective, partisan advisers did have a role in moving. Several deputies, again citing the importance of access to ministers, commented on the value of partisan advisers' knowledge of what might be problematic politically. As one deputy put it succinctly, "Where it's helpful, you get a minister and an EA that are really interested in a subject and they will start to say, 'I know who will have trouble with this and I'll meet with them, and I'll do this, and I'll do that,' and then they support and pave the way for you, and that's very helpful" (DM3). Interviews also made clear that, like in the other cases, a significant amount of executive policy work involves vertical moving based on signal-checking with multiple actors and across the political-administrative nexus. How was a particular policy progressing? Were there issues either from a ministerial or public service perspective that needed to be sorted out? With a particular policy example, the same deputy cited above explained what that looked like in practice:

So we are working on some [policy area] and it's a thing that the minister really wants, and we have been trying to get going in the department. He's interested, the department is. You know it's a good match right now. So we are trying to move something forward. So all of our milestones along the way, where this is, where we are, this is how much we got done, are we on the track for what he can support – the EA [partisan adviser] is in on those. So we say, "This is how we are looking at addressing this issue in the bigger issue of [policy area]. You know, are you comfortable with where we are going?" Because we don't want to be at the final end and find out we have taken a left turn and [the minister] wanted us to take a right turn. (DM3)

Horizontal moving on either partisan-political or administrative-technical dimensions was rarely reported. Most partisan advisers interviewed described significant constituency-related work. Ministers confirmed that when it came to policy-related work, they would generally deal with their ministerial counterparts, and then partisan advisers would ensure that whatever action or follow-up work required was then completed. When he was asked if and why he might deal with other partisan advisers, one minister's response is representative of all of the ministers interviewed:

I don't usually deal with the [other] EAs, I let my EA do that. But I certainly will [get] him to work with them. Usually I will work with the minister. I'll tell him, "Look this is the problem I have. I need your help in this. You know, I'm going to talk to my EA, he's going to talk to your EA, and they're going to work this out. But I would like your support on that." This is how I usually deal with that. Make them aware at least that I have a problem here and that I'd appreciate their help. I just had one lately with [the ministry] and that's just what I did. And it worked out well. Worked out well, you know. But it was with the deputy minister. I'll go to the deputy minister sometimes. You know, nobody knows the department better than the DM. But usually that's what I'll do. (M3)

This response was typical of the general responses of ministers on their interactions and perceptions of partisan advisers' formulation. Partisan advisers were involved, albeit in a more limited fashion, in the dialogue sub-phase, moving along both partisan-political and administrative-technical dimensions. They engaged in limited administrative-technical moving vertically, including the transmission and process management of policy information between political and administrative spheres. In very few instances, partisan advisers reported horizontal administrative-technical moving involving stakeholders. Partisan advisers did not report active roles at the front end of policy formulation, as were cited in the federal and BC cases. Their moving was much more narrowly cast to iterative dialogue sub-stage activity along the vertical dimension. Again, these findings reveal a different set of boundaries that govern the types of policy work, and policy-based resources, being wielded and exchanged by advisers within that core executive.

Ministerial "Shaping"

Federal Ministers' Offices' Substantive "Shaping"

Tremendous amounts of partisan-political shaping were reported in interviews with the federal ministerial partisan advisers. This was consistently articulated as applying a political lens to policy as well as iterative and ongoing participation in policy development. Their administrative-technical shaping was described along vertical dimensions, involving successive formulation with their departments and other actors during the development of specific policy measures. At the senior level, ministers' chiefs of staff reported activity along all four dimensions at various sub-phases of policy formulation. Their vertical shaping was often described as involving considerable engagement during appraisal and dialogue sub-phases, involving departmental officials and fellow partisan advisers within their own ministerial policy shop. When asked if and how he might be involved in policy formulation, one chief described his engagement in the substance of policy formulation as "sitting in committee meetings with senior public servants and senior political staff, writing, redacting, editing, briefing the minister, finding out what the minister's perspective is on this." Another chief explained at length her involvement in substantive content-based shaping of specific policies, elucidating that she had to bring a policy initiative into the ministerial office to ensure the policy document was drafted to her satisfaction. However, her description was laden with iterative policy-based resource exchanges:

> The department had drafts but, you know, frankly they weren't good. And the title of it. But we would then go back and forth with the stuff, right? So it all, you know … even at the end of the day, regardless of who's initiating, in the case of [the department] it doesn't work if the two don't come back together in some way. But the [policy] was initiated mostly, well looking back, the department thought it was a good thing to do, the minister

thought it was a good thing to do, and then there's a Cabinet process, PCO, and other things. And then our office, with me in particular, took a strong lead in actually developing it, writing it, you know, *shaping it*, you know sometimes directly with the department and sometimes on our own. Because we thought it was better that way. We'd give them stuff and go back and forth. It's never an exact chart, an exact navigation course. (P14; emphasis added)

Chiefs' shaping was often referenced explicitly in the initial appraisal sub-phase, as well occurring throughout the dialogue and formulation sub-phase, with consolidation occurring politically at the Cabinet level. With very few exceptions, partisan advisers did not characterize their shaping activities as *ab initio*. Rather, most explained they were applying a political lens to formal policy formulation work (i.e., draft policy work including memoranda to Cabinet, budget, or briefing materials) carried out by their departments. As one chief explained, "It's not so much developing core public policy, you know, on a blank sheet of paper. You're responding to what the department is bringing up, but the department is also responding to what you're sending down" (P14). The same chief further explained, "I was more heavily involved. The [policy] was in the first instance very strongly reflective of the party's platform, the incoming government's platform. So those issues were being translated, you know, sent down. They were looking at them" (P14).

Horizontally, ministerial shaping was reported as primarily partisan-political. Respondents explained that they did not engage in administrative-technical shaping with public service officials outside of their "home" department. That type of horizontal administrative-technical shaping was reserved primarily for the PMO-PCO interface around Cabinet committees and memoranda to Cabinet (as detailed in chapter 4). Federal partisan advisers at the ministerial level described their horizontal partisan-political shaping as occurring in concert with their partisan counterparts (typically at their same level) in other ministerial offices. Junior ministerial partisan advisers reported that they engaged with junior PMO partisan advisers who kept a "watching brief" – constantly monitoring a specific policy sectors or files – but that as advisers they tended to interact more substantively and regularly with their counterparts in other ministerial offices. Directors of policy, as with their chief of staff colleagues, shared a focus on both horizontal and vertical shaping along both partisan-political and administrative-technical dimensions. The directors of policy interviewed frequently described holding key policy files themselves and delegating others to their policy teams. They would thus have direct and ongoing shaping interactions with departmental officials related specifically to particular policy initiatives or sectors. This was explained to result in significant vertical administrative-technical shaping in the appraisal, dialogue, and formulation sub-phases. Directors of policy would, at the "front end," set out and confirm the broad parameters of what the minister was looking for, on the basis of their instructions to officials. Subsequently, they would be involved in ongoing interactions with departmental officials at the dialogue and formulation sub-phases as they prepared drafts of formal policy materials. A director of policy, in trying to explain his shaping activity, played out how a typical exchange with a minister would go in the formal elaboration of a memorandum to Cabinet in the department. The scenario lays bare the responsiveness and alignment considerations that drove much of the political arm's activity in this case:

> "You know, minister, the department has drafted the following as per your instructions in the meeting last week. You know, I've looked it over and, you know, I believe it does accord with what you had told them to do, so you can go ahead and sign it. You know, you should read it and be familiar with it, and I'm prepared to brief you in detail on it, but it's OK, you can sign it so it can get processed by the Cabinet papers unit and get on next week's [Cabinet] agenda." Or similarly if it was a problem, then I would point that out: "You know, they got most of it right, but you asked for such-and-such, and I noticed that's not what they did. They did something else. Maybe that's OK, and I can advise, you know ... on balance, I think they have wrestled with it and, you know, they didn't do what you asked, but I think the way they're doing it gets us where we want to be, so that's OK, but I'm drawing it to your attention anyway." Or, you know, say, "No they're trying to get away with something. They don't like what you told them to do and you have to tell them to do it again." (P29)

Vertical administrative-technical shaping was generally an iterative exchange between minister's office partisan advisers and senior officials during the development of MCs or briefing materials. Vertical partisan-political shaping, on the other hand, was first and foremost explained in the context of the partisan-political briefing note system as previously set out. Chiefs of staff and directors of policy referenced an oversight function over this system whereby they would review the partisan-political policy analysis of their subordinates, and, if they were in agreement, would include it in the minister's binder for review. It should be emphasized that the distinction here is that this shaping was directly linked to specific policy proposals formally in development. Most chiefs and policy directors reported very little modification to their junior staff's notes. In general, it was a quick review to ensure they understood the . partisan-political policy analysis and could discuss it, if required, with the minister. They reported infrequently, requesting rewrites or revisions to their policy staff's work. Rather, the picture that emerged from interviews was that, if warranted, they would insert themselves in the policy team's review as it was developed, thus ensuring that senior shaping was brought to bear on more junior staff's partisan-political policy analysis. This was described as typical and occurred primarily at the dialogue and formulation sub-phases and on rare occasion at consolidation sub-phases to resolve disagreements. Additional partisan-political shaping was described as providing departmental officials with the political context or thinking that animated the minister's/government's position. This was reported as occurring primarily within the dialogue and formulation sub-phases. When an adviser was asked to describe how he sought to engage in policy development, the policy director made his partisan-political shaping activities clear. The adviser explained it involved scrutinizing formal policy proposals through a political lens as the department was developing it:

> It's based on having those discussions with the bureaucracy. I don't think I'll be teaching you anything you didn't already observe. If it looked like, smelled like, or sounded like a [policy option], it wouldn't have flown. Even if it was the best idea or not, the department might have packaged it in such a way that it now made sense. Guess what? If it sounds like and walks like a duck, then I don't care. If this thing has the feel of a [policy option], it's not going to get out of the Cabinet alive because of the position the government has taken during a previous election. That would be an example of looking at it from a political lens. Does this smell like a [policy option]? Yes? Then you're wasting my time, and your time, and the minister's time. You're putting the minister at risk from political bullets. (P25)

Vertical partisan-political shaping was described by most respondents as ensuring consistency or "fit" of proposed policy options or fully developed policies with the government's stated positions (in documents such as platforms, throne speeches, or mandate letters). This type of shaping differed from buffering in that it was not simply a matter of providing partisan-political policy advice about any given potential issues, actors, or processes. Rather, it involved direct content-based input into specific policy items that were being developed in their respective departments or going to Cabinet. Partisan advisers used language involving alignment and consistency in explaining how they sought to shape. Ensuring congruence with previously articulated ministerial direction was a recurring theme in interviews and a core activity of partisan advisers, in this case at the formulation sub-phase. Ministerial partisan advisers were politically adjudicating departmental policy work for its feasibility and alignment. Policy directors, like chiefs, also described considerable partisan-political shaping at the appraisal and dialogue sub-phases. Multiple respondents described shaping as involving frank discussions with departmental officials about policy options that were considered to be "non-starters." When asked directly about the distinctions between her functions in procedural versus substantive aspects of policymaking, one policy director was crystal clear:

> In an ideal world, the department would get the process right and we would get the substance right. We obviously advise on substance all the time. It's what we do. But in terms of us getting involved in process, I guess the way I would say it is, we do. Tying back to the fact we're loyal to the minister. We're the ones who know how the minister operates, know his personal wishes, know the wishes of the prime minister in the case of the Cabinet process, know what the prime minister's expectations are. We get involved when there is a … this one I'll put bluntly: if the department has, in the minister's opinion, failed, he will go to us to do better. (P22)

Such frank assessments were not uncommon and point to the direct content-based formulation that partisan advisers undertake. Another junior adviser noted happily that in his most recent position he could focus much more on substantive policy matters. He explained that in a previous ministry his policy role had been more procedural, often in relation to Cabinet submissions. His current position was about the substantive policy the minister had been given the task of generating. As the adviser explained, "For [the policy sector] it was more substance. It was actually really liberating. Before, I was at [the department], and you'd have to try to get things through Cabinet committee, but they weren't things that you felt particularly strong about. They were things you really couldn't care less about, like tech projects and things that cost hundreds of millions of dollars that you didn't understand and you'd have to call around and try and get support for it. And you're like, 'I don't know. I don't really like it either, but it's government, you've got to have these things.' It was a relief to get away from it" (P17).

Ministers concurred that they relied on their staff to provide politically attuned policy formulation rather than subject matter expertise. However, most stated that it was always preferable, if possible, to have someone on staff knowledgeable in the substantive policy field. When he was asked if his political staff played a role in policy development, a minister's response points to the specialization that now characterizes federal partisan advisers as a subset of political staff. The minister explained, "You hire people specifically for policy analysis, and so those people ... and depending on the department and so on, but you'd hire someone with ... that had expertise or that had developed expertise in [one policy sector] and someone else in [another policy sector] and a third one in [another policy sector], and so not everyone weighed in on everything. But you tried to make sure you had somebody who could cover off the different parts of it, of the portfolio" (M12). Ministers in this case described their partisan advisers' policy work as continuously working hand-in-glove with officials, to ensure that any given policy would be technically sound and politically feasible. When asked how the partisan politics of being a minister was reconciled with the public service policy advice in policy development, former minister David Emerson explained, "In my case, the reconciliation at the departmental level would really come in terms of joint meetings that I would have that would include senior public servants and senior political people. And, frankly, I and my deputy and my chief of staff would sort through any conflicting advice that I was getting and land on a particular place." This underscores how partisan advisers in some jurisdictions have become an institutionalized feature, a third party to the traditionally bilateral political-administrative nexus. Ministers largely agreed that for policy development to be sound, it had to include a mix of professional public service and partisan-political perspective. Ministers explained that they used their partisan advisers to, at times, provide a countermeasure to departmental policy work, to challenge the public service during policy development. Moreover, ministers reported using their partisan advisers to ensure that the political context and considerations of any given policy had been well thought through. Shaping for them was generally about their partisan advisers' combining expert policy advice (from whatever source) with an eye to the current partisan-political landscape of government. A minister described partisan-political policy advice and the role of minister's office partisan advisers in policy work as follows,

> You would have to address it [policy] from a Conservative point of view. You would have to figure out what we had said about this, you know, use your political judgment to know what's acceptable to the caucus, the Cabinet, and the base of the party in terms of addressing those issues and take all that into account as you move forward. And really set yourself apart, to some degree, from what the previous government had done. Maybe it's in emphasis or whatever, but you would try and do that. You also had to be, you know, to be as frank and honest as I can be. You also knew enough, or hopefully you did, to know you can't die on every hill. Not every issue would be a red meat issue for the base. Some issues were more of a shield than a sword. Those ones would be issues where you would take some steps in some ways to make sure there was a Conservative imprint on it. But you knew better than to advocate that this was going to be some kind of hill that our party was going to die on. (M11)

Deputies unanimously agreed that partisan advisers were actively involved in policy formulation. Deputies cast the overall formulation contributions of partisan advisers as predominantly partisan-political, but acknowledged that partisan advisers' formulation interaction with senior officials, *and* others in the department, also involved administrative-technical shaping. Deputies interviewed reported interactions primarily with chiefs of staff and occasionally with directors of policy. These partisan advisers were described as engaging in vertical administrative-technical shaping, typically through iterative meetings at the outset of policy development, in the appraisal, dialogue, and formulation sub-phases. While deputies themselves limited their interactions to senior partisan advisers, they readily acknowledged that other senior departmental staff were in regular contact with partisan advisers and generally briefed them prior to briefing the minister. Deputies explained that they spent considerable resources to ensure that ministers' offices were well acquainted and "briefed up" on the departmental policy issues. However, deputies acknowledged that these offices, with their much smaller complement, struggled to keep up with the high volume of policy work that circulated in a department with much larger permanent staffs. It was explained that this sequencing of interaction with partisan advisers prior to ministerial engagement ensured that partisan advisers could complete their political analysis and brief the minister at the same time as the minister receiving the departmental briefing, or subsequently thereafter. This facilitated vertical partisan-political shaping between ministers and their partisan advisers at the formulation sub-phase. Several deputies noted the importance of interactions with the minister's partisan advisers to ensure that they did not become "cross-threaded" on substantive aspects of policy formulation. One deputy explained it well: "I trust [the chief of staff]. If it's an issue that it's appropriate for the department to get involved with, we'll be there. Otherwise we might get cross-threaded. It's OK if we disagree in our advice to the minister, but we have to do it in a way ... and I mean it's very rare, but we have to do it in a way where we explain to him exactly why we disagree" (DM8). These types of policy-based resource exchanges in formulation were significant and evidently a prominent aspect of how policymaking was undertaken. They reveal the consistent and explicit attempts by ministers and their staffs to secure policy responsiveness and political control, often in reference to implementing mandate letter priorities.

BC Ministers' Office "Shaping"

The British Columbia case saw moderate shaping but primarily along the vertical partisan-political dimension. Less frequent horizontal partisan-political shaping can be explained in part by the considerably smaller size of ministerial offices, which reduced the opportunity for senior-junior partisan adviser interactions and produced more "direct" vertical shaping in conjunction with ministers and senior departmental officials. Shaping was most commonly reported at the formulation sub-phase, but also described as appraisal and dialogue sub-phase work. Like their federal counterparts, the provision of partisan-political policy advice and the iterative participation through dialogue sub-phase activity with officials and external stakeholders were the most routinely cited examples of shaping in the BC case. Both political and administrative elites interviewed acknowledged that partisan advisers engaged in partisan-political shaping and described it as a core component of their policy work. When asked about substance versus process dimensions of their policy advisory and formulation activity, a partisan adviser noted that while he certainly applied a political lens to policy development, most also brought substantive "technical" or subject matter expertise to bear:

> I can tell you personally here that most people here have some degree of expertise in their areas and they can offer some advice as to how they, how they think someone should react and work with the minister. The minister is obviously the decision-maker and the policymaker, not the staff. But we try to work with them [officials], and if they need information we help try and get that information. We also talk quite extensively with the stakeholders within the ministry to try to read where they're coming from and try to pass that advice along as well. (P7)

Several BC partisan advisers noted subject matter expertise in their portfolio, either as a product of experience gained in the same ministry over time, or from work experience in the policy sector. Ministers interviewed in the BC case detailed that their partisan advisers could marshal knowledge or substantive expertise applicable to their portfolio. For some, it was described as in-depth policy or sector-specific knowledge. Others noted that their partisan adviser had been in their ministry for longer than they had as a minister and thus could offer significant input on departmental policy work, key stakeholders, and the policy landscape more broadly. More than one minister commented on the utility of their adviser's substantive "administrative-technical" shaping. A minister noted that his adviser had in fact been in the portfolio area longer than he had and had significant expertise that complemented the minister's own. As the minister put it, "I think he plays a fairly significant role. He has expertise in one side of [policy sector] that I don't have, and I have expertise in another side that he doesn't have, so we work very well together as a team" (M7). When asked to elaborate on what that expertise was and how it figured into policy formulation, the minister went on to explain, "I've been over to [a specific country] quite a bit, four times in the last twenty-four months or so. And he [the partisan adviser] has become as knowledgeable about [that country] as I am, and in some ways more so in certain areas. And so on the manufacturing side he has helped steer our policy around working with different companies [in the policy area]. He has a significant expertise in that area. So his advice on where we need to go really helps to shape any policy we take forward in that area" (M7). This type of shaping was obviously not partisan-political in the sense used in this study. The minister relied on expertise and administrative-technical shaping that the adviser could bring to bear in the development and refinement of policy in a specific sector.

Several partisan advisers interviewed framed their shaping as occurring at the appraisal sub-phase. As with their federal counterparts, this was most often expressed as providing the minister's direction at the "front end" of policymaking to ensure that politically suitable options would be generated for considerations. The overarching point was again to avoid any "non-starters." When queried about how he participated in policy development, a ministerial partisan adviser explained that it consisted of a significant amount of formulation occurring in the political sphere, which was subsequently raised with officials in the dialogue sub-phase. The adviser explained, "I would say half of that [policy development] comes from the political side, meaning that it either originates from the minister or myself, or it comes from talking with stakeholders, and we develop it here before going to the bureaucrats asking for more detailed analysis of what we want to do" (P6). Partisan advisers would use bridging to also facilitate shaping that could be administrative-technical or partisan-political, depending on the nature of their exogenous interactions with policy actors. Another minister's office partisan adviser also framed her policy formulation as occurring primarily at the front end. She described significant activity at the appraisal and formulation sub-phases as a regular part of their policy work. When asked at what stage of the policy cycle she was most active, the adviser made it clear:

> I would say it's more in the beginning. So what is it we're trying to achieve? What is it that we want to do, basically? Why is it important enough to be a priority to government? So then, for example, you decide, well [existing policy] isn't really working for everyone. We have these budget constraints. What can we do? A decision is made that we want to try and restructure it somehow to make it more fair. So then that's the overall direction that's given to the ministry, and they go away and work on it. And in some cases, depending on the relationship that an MA would have with senior bureaucrats, there could be interactions there during that process of developing options to kind of bounce ideas off or just to get a little bit of guidance. (P20)

Advisers frequently explained that their policy formulation hinged on the type of policy work in question. A distinction was made, as in the federal case, between policy work that was percolating up through the department and priority policy items that were flowing from ministers and/or the political executive. Partisan advisers in BC shared the view that involvement in the former was during the front-end phases, while considerably more emphasis would be placed at the formulation sub-phase in the latter. As one minister's office partisan adviser suggested,

> It is so variable. If you look at an issue I mentioned [policy issue], so that's a real-life example. As a result of that, you know, we had emerging issues and it needed policy and legislative answers and I was involved in that from start, middle, to end. In other things, more long-term things, you often find that that the ministry comes forward and says, "Oh yeah, we've been working on this for two years and now we are looking for your input." So it's difficult to be involved at the start when nobody told you what was being done. Certainly, that happens within ministries, every ministry I've been in, that if you come to work one day and see a note come forward from the ministry saying, "We just need your input on this." And you say, "Where did that come from? Why are we doing that? Who's idea was it?" There are certain times that things are generated in the ministry from whatever level and then you get involved later in the process. (P10)

This type of response was common. Partisan advisers were involved in sub-phases of formulation but, when pressed, noted that ministers were the decision-makers and the public service took care of the implementation. Partisan advisers' shaping tended to be most pronounced for those "priority" items at the appraisal and dialogue sub-phases in exchanges with officials. These were also informed by ongoing signal-checking with external stakeholders or the first minister's office as needed. When they were presented with policy work that was department-driven, their shaping was described as partisan-political and pronounced in the formulation sub-phase, ensuring that the policy work did not present any political issues that required attention from partisan advisers.

Discussions with DMs painted a picture of partisan advisers as active shapers through policy work occurring at various sub-stages of policy formulation (again in the context of the partisan policy priority versus ongoing housekeeping dynamic described above). However, deputies tended to characterize substantive shaping of partisan advisers as explicit in the latter formulation stages, particularly in partisan-political aspects germane to formulation sub-stage activity. One deputy explained, "Definitely, they provide the political lens to the minister.

In terms of if there are policy recommendations that we are bringing forward to them ultimately for their decision, political staff, in my experience have played a strong role in influencing the thinking of the minister" (DM6). Another, when asked if partisan advisers were perceived as playing a substantive role, suggested they are consequential, albeit in different way:

> I think it's an indirect role. I think they provide advice to the minister from a political perspective. I might query them in terms of their thinking, but in terms of doing the analysis and the development of the policy issue. In terms of their role of providing a political perspective to the minister on decision-making around policy, I think they do have a role. So, in terms of development side, I can't think of them having any, but in terms of decision-making, clearly they have a role because the minister needs to think about things both in terms of what we are telling them is the right thing from a policy perspective and the political consequences of that. We can try to outline some of that, but we can't make those political calls, obviously. (DM5)

Deputies often mentioned, as the quotations above illustrate, interactions with partisan advisers in order to gain a sense of where the minister may stand on policy options. This again suggests the importance of policy-based resource exchanges that flow between political and public service elites. The perspective from deputies was most often that partisan advisers engaged in shaping primarily, but not exclusively, on partisan-political policy dimensions. This was, however, iterative and informal in that it did not involve the formal policymaking instruments that were key to partisan advisers in Ottawa.

New Brunswick Ministers' Office "Shaping"

The interviews with elite political and public service actors confirmed that New Brunswick partisan advisers undertook virtually no substantive shaping. In this case, substantive engagement on policy files was relegated to ad hoc, one-off involvement in individual case-by-case interventions for constituency issues. Advisers themselves made quite clear this was where they engaged. This is, of course, important work but differs dramatically from participation in the development or oversight of a memorandum to Cabinet. Advisers often explained policy work in a much more passive sense, where the department was essentially the lead on any and all policy development, or where their ministers were directly involved, again often described in concert with a heavy reliance on officials. All three categories of respondents interviewed in New Brunswick made sure to emphasize that partisan advisers were hardworking individuals who made a minister's job possible. They dealt with correspondence and constituent cases, and they organized logistics around announcements and legislative activities. They were, however, not described in terms similar to the other cases, as having currency in the policy process. On a more basic level, respondents indicated that partisan advisers would generally be present during briefings with senior officials and interact with departmental officials regularly. They may informally discuss policy with their ministers, but, more typically, their policy formulation was procedural, involving moving across the political-administrative spheres. This type of limited activity on the substantive aspects of policy development was confirmed in interviews with both ministers and deputies. When asked if his partisan advisers contributed to policy formulation, a minister responded, "No," and further elaborated:

> The only thing that political staff would take to the deputy minister or assistant deputy ministers was what we considered to be a solution to a problem and say "[The minister] says that the regulations say this, and this is what he wants to do. Now you tell us, how are we going to accomplish that?" They would not go to the deputy minister or assistant deputy minister and say, "This is the problem. What is the solution?" We would come up with the solution and say, "How do we mould the civil service, or the regulation, or the law around the solution that we found?" (M8)

Deputies were unanimous in stating that ministerial-level partisan advisers did not engage formally in policy development. Most acknowledged that they thought some advice-giving might be occurring between ministers and their advisers but that it was primarily partisan-political. Deputies described partisan advisers as having negligible input with them in shaping the substance of policy. Again, deputies concurred with partisan advisers that their interactions predominantly involved case-specific constituency work. Even on those matters, it was the departmental officials who would inquire into the constituent case and what options there were to address the issue. A senior deputy emphasized that partisan advisers did not shape policy and that this had long been the case in New Brunswick, explaining with reference to specific policies, "In my situation, the two executive assistants have zero role. It's never been any different" (DM1). The comparatively limited formulation work of ministerial partisan advisers in this case was clear, suggesting a much less prominent function for them in core executive policy–based resource exchanges. In this case, as previous chapters have revealed, that was the ambit of ministers, deputies, and first ministers' office advisers. Whether and how this practice may evolve or adapt, or as new administrations seek to organize the political arm, remains to be seen.

Conclusion

The compelling findings presented above confirm that ministerial office partisan advisers were active participants in policy formulation in some but not all cases. This finding is consistent with other recent studies that have found a differentiated pattern of adviser involvement and influence in policy work (Dunn and Bourgault 2012, 2014; Benoit 2006; White 2001, 2005). The findings above further specify that claim by better attending to the substantive and procedural nature of their formulation, the sub-stage(s) of formulation at which it occurred, and its intra- and interdepartmental, partisan-political and/or administrative-technical characteristics. Ministerial partisan advisers were found in all cases to be active in vertical administrative-technical moving at the dialogue sub-phase, such as undertaking monitoring, signal-checking, coordination, or process management as policy actors deliberated, consulted, and developed policy. In the federal and BC cases, "moving" extended to several other formulation sub-phases. Yet only in the federal case were ministerial partisan advisers found to engage in formulation by participation in formal public service policymaking instruments. This included not only activity involving memoranda to Cabinet, but other departmental policy instruments and Cabinet committee processes as well. These provided additional opportunities for these actors to engage in moving and shaping.

Ministerial partisan advisers in the BC and federal cases also described vertical and horizontal partisan-political moving. Other than its more informal nature, vertical partisan-political formulation in the BC case was described in essentially similar terms, often as involving policy process coordination and management. A clear difference in the two cases was how such actors engaged in horizontal partisan-political moving. It was predominantly stakeholder-centric in the BC case, whereas federally the layered configuration of ministerial partisan advisers included that form of shaping but also more frequent and intensive partisan-political moving among advisers throughout the system.

Federal partisan advisers were found to engage in the most frequent and wide-ranging shaping. They consistently described partisan-political and administrative-technical types of shaping at multiple formulation stub-stages. For example, many reported participating in content-based administrative-technical shaping via input into the elaboration, refinement, and calibration of departmental policy development. This was typically described to involve early appraisal sub-stage scrutiny of the policy direction, dialogic activity in the logic underpinning suggested policy options, contributions based on personal knowledge or experience, or transmission of inputs received from other actors in government or stakeholders. Again, this was the *only* case in which partisan advisers provided substantive inputs to ministers through formal policy processes and instruments. "Shaping" in this case had clear partisan-political intentions to increase alignment and consistency of policy direction with previously articulated ministerial/government campaign commitments or policy positions, or to identify potential partisan-political risks and opportunities. Advisers' shaping spanned the greatest number of formulation sub-phases comparatively.

Partisan advisers in British Columbia were reported by ministers and deputies as being able to marshal "expert" or substantive policy knowledge to shape policy, which was attributed to particular skills sets or experience accrued from longstanding participation in policy sectors. Their shaping was, however, decidedly more informal. In no instance did partisan advisers or any other actors report it as including formal written commentary on policy, either in development or after. Partisan-political shaping was also reported but was predominantly vertical with horizontal shaping, similar to moving, being stakeholder-centric and spanning all formulation sub-phases. New Brunswick partisan advisers were not active shapers whatsoever. In that case, shaping was confined to formulation undertaken by ministers, their departments, and partisan advisers at the centre. In all three cases, partisan advisers also regularly articulated that policy agendas had already been set, and that their purpose was to help their ministers, in lock step with their departmental officials, give life to broad policy direction flowing from mandate letters and electoral platforms. This is an important finding in that it confirms the relevance of the formulation stage as a particularly important conjuncture when partisan advisers engage in policy work.

These formulation patterns are only partially explained by differences in the configuration of advisers. Spatial factors such as the layered configuration in the federal case was clearly contributing to how, and with whom, ministerial partisan advisers engaged in formulation. Yet, as with advisory system activity, similar configuration at the subnational level did not yield similar propensities for moving and shaping, with only BC advisers active in formulation. This raises three important implications. First, it solidifies the importance of combining configuration and spatial considerations with a task-based approach to fully appreciate if and how partisan advisers engage in policy work. Second, it reveals that context matters. Differences in the overarching political-administrative arrangements and core executive mode within which partisan advisers operate can affect the nature of their policy work. This was most vividly demonstrated by all categories of New Brunswick respondents universally emphasizing "direct" minister–deputy minister interactions. The two other cases involved more frequent and intensive partisan adviser interactions with both sets of actors. Third, the federal and BC cases demonstrated that moving and shaping also might vary in instrumentality. The lack of participation in formal policymaking mechanisms in the BC case in relation to Cabinet and formal departmental policy instruments reduced ministerial partisan advisers' abilities to insert themselves into *formal* policy development. In contrast, the federal case was replete with references to partisan advisers engaging in activities tied to memoranda to Cabinet and other departmental-specific policy instruments.

Together, these findings reveal a greater diversity of fronts along which core executive policy-based resource exchanges can vary. The prevalence of vertical administrative-technical moving across the cases, particularly dialogic sub-stage activity, emphasizes the importance and endogenous and exogenous nature of policy-based resource exchanges. Partisan advisers were able to leverage extra–core executive policy-based resources to inform core executive policy development. In addition, the activities may also vary in their partisan-political and administrative-technical nature. Signal-checking, monitoring, and process coordination with officials, ministers, and partisan advisers throughout the core executive points to important resource exchange dynamics geared towards improved policy coordination, coherence, and particularly the identification of potential process-related pitfalls. The lack of formulation at the ministerial office level in New Brunswick suggests that ministers, departments, and first ministers' offices can in some cases be wholly responsible for that policy work.

This draws attention to the potential tension between political and process-related policy resource exchanges. For example, in the federal case, if departmental policy documents were not provided to ministers' offices early enough for advisers to analyse, they were *not included* in the minister's reading binder. This suggests an added bilateral resource-exchange imperative in that case. It clearly increases political control and facilitates policy responsiveness but may result in additional procedural delay or policy failure (Howlett 2012; McConnell 2010b). This type of tension is also evident in the layered federal adviser configuration. While it offers opportunities for additional procedural and content-based resource exchanges, it may also result in inefficiencies from the partitocratic or partisan-political "bureaucracy."

Ministerial partisan advisors are also part of the political arm's ability to secure political control and policy responsiveness. The findings document greater variance in the likelihood of such activity at the ministerial office level, as compared to the more consistent findings pertaining to first ministers' offices. The New Brunswick case demonstrates quite clearly that the simple existence of partisan advisers is no guarantee that they will increase political control or responsiveness. By contrast, the federal case involved ministerial office partisan advisers actively moving and shaping along almost all dimensions and multiple formulation sub-phases. In that case, partisan advisers were able to increase political control to a greater degree through combined vertical moving and shaping, along administrative-technical and partisan political formulation dimensions. That case also confirms a variety of techniques and activities by which partisan advisers can increase political control. Their limited horizontal administrative-technical moving and shaping suggests a limited ability to do so in formulation activity *outside* of their own departments. The comparative nature of this study has yielded some important insights into the potential configurations, uses, and impacts partisan advisers raise for core executive operations and the politics of policy work. The concluding chapter of this study now takes a step back to distil and assess the implications of the buffering, bridging, moving, and shaping for the politics of policy work and core executive operation.

Conclusion: Core Executives, Partisan Advisers, and the Politics of Policy Work in Canada

Introduction

It has been more than forty years since Mallory (1967) and Tellier (1968) launched the normative debate as to the purpose and utility of Canadian federal ministerial "exempt" staff. This book's findings make plain that, in many instances, partisan advisers are now active policy workers. Suggesting a return to Mallory's preferred state of affairs is unlikely, if not impractical. We thus need more complete understandings of how partisan advisers, as essential components of the political arm of government, engage in policy work and its impact. The historical perspective and empirical findings provided in the preceding chapters demonstrate that partisan advisers, as a subset of appointed political staffs, have generally evolved through a three-stage process of institutionalization, expansion, and specialization. A principal argument advanced in this book has been that greater care is needed in attributing policy influence to advisers on solely locational grounds or ideal-type "roles." Instead, improved analysis of partisan advisers' influence is gained through focused attention on the *actual* policy work they undertake. To this end, buffering, bridging, moving, and shaping were advanced in a framework to array and examine the substantive and procedural nature of their formulation and advisory activity respectively. This concluding chapter distils the findings detailed above, with a focus on the implications they raise for the configuration and operation of advisory systems, policy formulation, and core executive operation.

Chapters 3 and 4 documented how first ministers' offices in all three cases were found to be consequential to advisory system operation and policy formulation. As buffers and bridges, partisan advisers at the centre were important direct sources of content-based policy advice, and key mechanisms for the integration of policy advice in their respective advisory systems. Their buffering and bridging strengthened political control through quantitative diversification of available policy advice. Their policy advisory activity was also a key means by which the qualitative *content* of available policy advice was diversified thorough the provision of administrative-technical and partisan-political policy advice. In this sense partisan advisers, when deployed appropriately, can add value to policy analysis (Scott and Baehler 2010). Importantly, differences in how buffering was undertaken also further specify distinctions in *how* control and responsiveness are sought and secured, and the potential insulation benefits for the public service from the partisan-political types of core executive resource exchanges that advisers undertake.

Chapter 4 documented how partisan advisers at the centre were also active formulation participants in all cases. As privileged actors in their respective core executives, their moving and shaping occurred throughout formulation, and across almost all dimensions used to plot formulation. As this study has emphasized, first ministers' office advisers were unique in their ability to undertake horizontal administrative-technical and "front-end" formulation work. Further, in some but not all cases, they used formal public service policymaking instruments and participated in formal policymaking processes. Here too, moving and shaping were vehicles by which ministers could seek to increase political control systemically through advisers' work in coordination, process management, and content-based alignment and calibration (Dahlström, Peters, and Pierre 2011; Savoie 1999a).

Chapters 5 and 6 documented that ministerial partisan advisers in the federal and BC cases were also active in advisory systems and formulation activity. They were clear sources of policy advice for ministers and engaged in different but discernible types of bridging. In all three cases, advisers served as important bilateral bridges to officials facilitating important resource exchanges. As has been shown in the federal and BC cases, their bridging also extended to exogenous advisory inputs. These findings suggest that Canadian partisan advisers are, like their international counterparts, important actors who provide contestability to various sources of policy advice and are particularly active in the circulation of supplies and types of policy advice (OECD 2011; Zussman 2009; Eichbaum and Shaw 2011). However, the limited horizontal bridging noted in the New Brunswick case, together with the clear lack of buffering, further supports the need to couple spatial considerations with task-based assessments. It also reveals that important differences can prevail in the types and nature of policy-based resource exchanges. Federal and BC partisan advisers were found to clearly be moving and shaping, while only process-based formulation work was reported in New Brunswick. Again, the federal case dwarfed the subnational cases in the sophistication, frequency, and intensity of formulation. In that case, there was variance at the ministerial office levels in the nature and type of formulation undertaken, when it occurred, with whom, and how, all of which provide improved accounts of how partisan advisers may undertake policy work and affect core executive operation.

Canadian Partisan Advisers and Advisory System Participation

A principal goal of this study was to understand if, how, and with what implications partisan advisers were active within policy advisory systems. The evidence collected confirms that partisan advisers are one of many sources of policy advice. While quite useful, Zussman's (2009) collaborative, gatekeeper, and triangulated ideal-type models of "political advisers" (restated figure 1.1 below) can be further refined.

A greater interaction and overlap among partisan advisers and public service in advisory activity was reported in each case than is suggested

Figure 1.1. Three Models of Political Advisers and the Machinery of Government

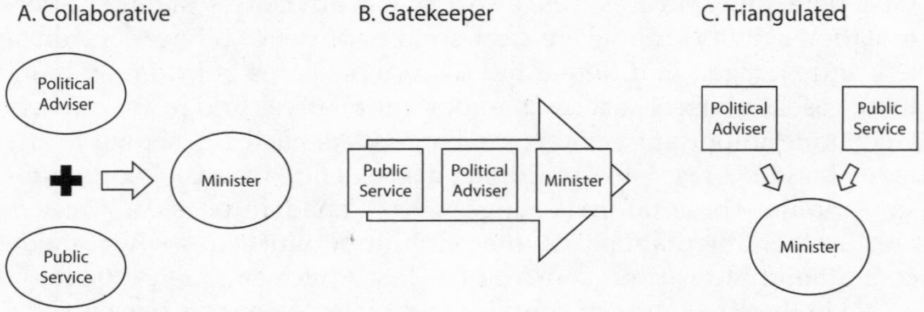

A. Collaborative   B. Gatekeeper   C. Triangulated

Source: Adapted from Zussman (2009)

by the triangulated model. Most respondents described significant independent *and* overlapping policy advisory activities, contrary to the discreet compartmentalization set forth by the triangulated model. This suggests that a mix of the collaborative and triangulation models best characterizes the advisory systems in these cases. Partisan advisers were found to engage in iterative and dialectical policy advisory activity with ministers, deputies, and their fellow advisers. Moreover, the directionality presented in the triangulated model masks the important bidirectional flow of policy advice reported by the actors interviewed. Political and public service respondents in each of the cases acknowledge the existence of firm boundaries, particularly related to partisan-political activity. However, they also described ample instances of administrative-technical policy work. Again, this sheds light on advisory system operation going beyond simply descriptive mapping of such systems to understanding their operating dynamics (Prince 1983; Craft and Howlett 2013). It was clear that while the public service remains the primary source of such advice, partisan advisers were at times subject-matter experts and engaged in advisory activity that contested or supplemented policy advice based on other grounds. Notably, for partisan advisers this was about ensuring that a political lens had been applied, and that sufficient options and sources of advice were made available to decision-makers.

These findings therefore suggest an alternative "dynamic" ideal-type – an advisory system mode in which partisan advisers and public servants work in separate spheres but also engage *regularly* in overlapping policy advisory activities. The dynamic ideal-type recognizes that ministers remain the focal point of advisory activity as the authoritative decision-makers, but that they and partisan advisers are not passive recipients of policy advice (see figure 7.1). This study supports others who have underscored that ministers can be active participants in policy work (Savoie 1999a, 2003; Bakvis 1991, 1997; Campbell and Szablowski 1979; White 2005). Ministers interviewed reported actively seeking out policy advice, not passively waiting for it to be tendered. They were not shy about providing input and direction to officials and reported using their partisan advisers to transmit ministerial direction, feedback, or policy advice of their own. Officials and partisan advisers confirmed such practices as well. The dynamic ideal-type recognizes this active participation, retains the minister as the nodal actor, but acknowledges the multilateral nature of exchanges reported between actors. It also seeks to better leverage core executive thinking in that advisory system activity is fundamentally premised on the exchange of various *types* of advisory-based resources among a plurality of actors.

As set out in chapters 3 and 5, policy advisory activities were not confined solely to political and administrative elite "insiders" within government. All three cases were replete with references to exogenous sources of policy advice. Ministers, senior public servants, and partisan advisers all confirmed that stakeholders' policy inputs are important. As this study detailed, particularly in chapter 5, partisan advisers often integrated external advisory policy feedback and input by formal and informal consultations and interactions. In all three cases, a broad spectrum of respondents made clear that departments also continue to participate in such activities as well. Again, it's not that the public service has been displaced but rather that it must contend with ministerial partisan advisers who are now active on this front and often well integrated with the policy stakeholders and communities of practices for their relevant files. The dynamic ideal-type explicitly recognizes external sources of policy advice as components of advisory systems and partisan advisers as *one* mechanism by which such inputs are contested, integrated, and policy-based resources exchanged.

A key finding from this study is that spatial foundations of policy advisory systems can be improved by coupling them with content and process considerations. Locational approaches can tell us the "where" of advisory sources, but greater specificity can be achieved by marrying location with the "what" (content) and "how" (process) dimension of policy advice. As such, the dynamic ideal-type is provided as a

Figure 7.1. Dynamic Ideal-Type Mode

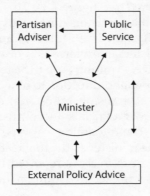

heuristic. In a fashion similar to the various locational models, it provides general contours and parameters (Lindquist 1998; Zussman 2009; Halligan 1995; Maley 2015), leaving the particular operationalization of the model as an empirical question to be addressed through careful analysis. The buffering and bridging concepts used in this book were advanced as a means to do just that. They help clarify that the patterns of interaction and types of advisory system interactions can be further specified, such as revealing that the public service can be disaggregated into departmental and central agency advisory system participants and similarly that ministers' offices and first ministers' offices can also be composed of multiple actors, variously configured, with implications for how partisan advisors engage in advisory-related activity. When combined, buffering and bridging, along with the locational and operational particularities of the cases, reveal distinct advisory system operating modes. The differences in the three cases allow this to be illustrated and paint a picture of three distinct types of advisory systems.

The Federal Dynamic Advisory System Configuration: Comprehensive-Differentiated and Layered-Dispersed

The federal case suggests a comprehensive, differentiated, dispersed, and layered configuration of advisers within the advisory system. From a locational perspective, partisan advisers were dispersed, in that they were deployed at the ministerial and first minister's office levels. This arrangement produced ample policy advisory activity within and among ministers' offices and the first minister's office, as well as between partisan advisers and a range of public service officials and external actors. They were also "layered" in that they operated at multiple levels within the two institutional locations (e.g., junior/senior partisan advisers). As detailed in chapter 3, at the first ministers' office level, junior and senior partisan advisers often interacted and exchanged advisory-based resources among themselves and with senior PCO officials.

Ministers' offices were organized in a similar hierarchical structure, also resulting in multi-level interactions between partisan advisers and departmental officials. Routine policy advisory interactions were also reported between junior-level partisan advisers and senior partisan advisers at the ministerial and first ministerial office levels. Ministers' office partisan advisers reported engaging in policy advisory activity directly with the minister. However, at the PMO level, only senior partisan advisers reported regular in person advisory interactions with the prime minister. For their part, junior PMO advisers described more mediated advisory activity, often occurring with senior PMO partisan advisers. At both institutional locations junior partisan advisers, in concert with their respective directors of policy, undertook the detailed partisan-political analysis. In contrast, chiefs of staff reported engaging in that activity as well but characterized their overall advisory activity in coordination and management terms. Chiefs were the point of contact for the deputy minister and also managed advisory inputs that flowed up from their policy teams and external policy communities. Crucially, the ministers' offices studied, and most others by accounts from those interviewed, typically functioned in such a way so that ministers received the officially signed off departmental policy advice along with their offices' partisan-political policy advice *at the same time*.

On content-based grounds, federal partisan advisers' advisory activity was found to be comprehensive and differentiated – *comprehensive* in that partisan advisers at all locations were found to engage in both buffering and bridging along the partisan-political and administrative-technical dimensions. Differences were clear in how and with whom bridging was focused, with, for instance, exogenous bridging occurring principally at the ministerial office level, but all were involved in the direct provision and integration of policy advice. Uniquely, in Ottawa partisan-political policy advice was provided discreetly through a separate or *differentiated* partisan-political written and oral briefing system. This was supplemental to partisan advisers' participation, in concert with officials, in the development of departmental "administrative-technical" policy advice. As per figure 7.2 below, this can be used to map out the basic operation of that advisory system.

Junior partisan advisers in ministers' offices described engaging in partisan-political policy advisory activity with fellow partisan advisers in their own offices, or at times with the more junior partisan advisers in the PMO policy shop. Interactions with the PMO chief of staff were described as restricted to the ministerial chief of staff–level and / or directly occurring with ministers. At the minister's office level, both junior and senior partisan advisers reported ongoing administrative-technical advisory activity with departmental officials. This was most commonly described as involving discussions about the proposed policy options being considered. Conversely, deputies and senior PCO officials interviewed all emphasized that they and departmental officials

Figure 7.2. Federal Partisan Advisers and the Dynamic Policy Advisory System

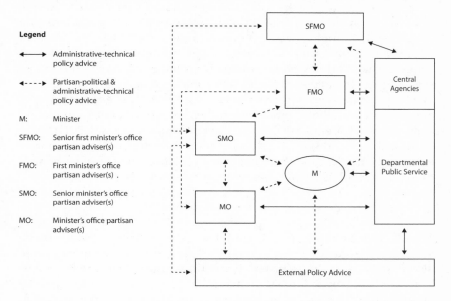

provided only non-partisan "administrative-technical" forms of policy advice. This is depicted through the use of solid line linkages between actors. Minister's office partisan advisers' policy advisory interactions were limited to their senior departmental–level officials.

For their part, first minister's office partisan advisers described almost exclusive policy advisory interactions as occurring with senior PCO and central agency officials. As detailed in this study, PMO buffering and bridging was animated by attempts to ensure that partisan-political overlays were provided to the PCO clerk's notes that would make their way up *separately* to the prime minister. This required both procedural coordination and content-based alignment to ensure that partisan-political considerations of the policy in question were provided. Much less advisory interaction was reported between PMO partisan advisers and departmental deputy ministers. Of course there were instances where it would occur, but the standard operating procedure was for PMO partisan advisers to engage with their ministerial counterparts or senior PCO officials in their day-to-day activity. PMO partisan advisers also reported that they explicitly "pushed out" policy-specific stakeholder engagements to ministers' office partisan advisers. While they indicated meeting with groups or policy sector–based stakeholders, they would always ensure that ministers' offices were the lead actors. This was to avoid "end runs" around ministers or complications due to "cross threading" between offices and the public service. This is an important insight into how exogenous policy inputs are integrated. It suggests that advisory-based resource exchanges occurred with ministers' office staff and department's, who, in turn, would inform the "centre." This again points to an important policy resource that ministers and their departments could bring to bear on policy development and core executive operation (Craft 2015b; Eichbaum and Shaw 2011; Shaw and Eichbaum 2014). This advisory system configuration is sophisticated and complex, and it involves the circulation and coupling of multiple types of advisory inputs from multiple locations.

BC: LIMITED-DISPERSED AND INTEGRATED ADVISORY SYSTEM CONFIGURATION

The BC case demonstrates a limited-dispersed and integrated advisory-system configuration. From a spatial perspective, partisan advisers were also dispersed at the ministerial and first minister's office locations. They were, however, limited, in that they were confined to a single tier at the ministerial office level[40] and two or three partisan advisers within the first minister's office. This limited-dispersed locational configuration greatly reduced the number of reported intra-ministerial partisan advisory resource exchanges compared to those described in the federal case. It resulted in a markedly different pattern of advisory system interaction and core executive policy-based resource exchanges. As for the content basis of their advisory activity, ministerial partisan advisers reported administrative-technical and partisan-political activity but informally and iteratively with officials. They were explicit about their application of a political lens to departmental policy advice and again emphasized ensuring consistency with the policy direction of their minister and government. Ministers' office partisan advisers also reported advisory-based interactions with the first minister's office, on both partisan-political and administrative-technical fronts, but to a much lesser degree than federally. The single-tiered configuration at the ministerial office level and smaller first minister's office reduced the frequency and intensity of such activity. This suggests a less systematic pattern of advisory resource exchanges and one where ministerial and first minister's partisan advisers played significant roles, but in discreet areas. For ministers' offices' advisers, buffering and bridging were heavily oriented to the department, with much less input sought or provided to the "centre."

First minister's office partisan advisers reported much less coordination in their exchanges with ministerial counterparts but were clearly key advisory actors at the centre, serving to buffer and bridge policy advice. BC first minister's office partisan advisers were much less comfortable in acknowledging partisan-political policy advisory activity. They preferred instead to paint their advisory activities as focused on the "public interest." However, their description of their own policy work, and accounts from others, are clearly in keeping with the definition advanced here of partisan-political policy advice. It was characterized by a focus on ensuring consistency of policy work with politically articulated and electorally mandated policy positions and commitments. As per figure 7.3, partisan advisers at the centre reported a mix of departmental deputy-level and central agency (primarily the deputy minister to the premier) interactions. This was described as involving the synthesis of considerable sources of policy advice, and the content-based integration or "knitting together" of partisan-political and public service policy advice. At the minister's office level, partisan advisers described policy advisory interactions that were predominantly with departmental officials. These involved providing administrative-technical policy advice often in relation to clarifying their minister's direction, or integrating policy advice flowing from external stakeholders.

Figure 7.3. BC Partisan Advisers' Dynamic Policy Advisory System

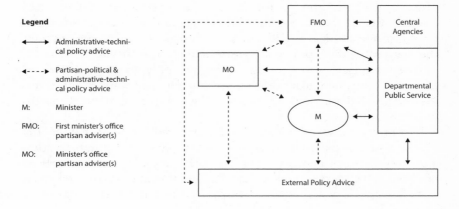

Compared to the situation in Ottawa, ministers' office advisers' partisan-political bridging consisted far more of the integration of exogenous sources of policy advice. This was often described as integrating key stakeholders' policy preferences into the policy advisory system and consulting (formally or informally) with stakeholders on what reception formal policy options might elicit. Ministerial partisan advisers reported ongoing consultations with stakeholders that were explicitly partisan-political. Ministers and deputies in this case also widely confirmed that such activities were common and consequential to policy work. There was consensus that partisan advisers frequently engaged in such interaction with stakeholders *without* the minister or departmental representatives present. BC first minister's office partisan advisers also reported limited "group" types of exogenous policy advisory integration. However, they too shared the preference and practice of "pushing out" almost all stakeholder advisory integration activities to ministers, their offices, and departmental officials.

NEW BRUNSWICK DYNAMIC ADVISORY SYSTEM: LIMITED–DISPERSED AND CENTRALIZED–INTEGRATED CONFIGURATION

As this study documented, partisan advisers at the ministerial level in New Brunswick were found to be far less active than their counterparts in both policy advisory and formulation activity. Supporting theory about size and scale, respondents all attributed this more limited engagement to the smaller size of government that resulted in more direct and unmediated relationships between ministers and deputies (White 1990). Spatially, the configuration was limited-dispersed. Partisan advisers were present at the ministers' and first minister's offices but shared the BC format. That is, they were configured in a single tier at the ministerial office level and a limited two-tiered first minister's office. However, as per figure 7.4, when coupled with the content of their policy advisory activity, ministerial office–level partisan advisers were found to engage only in limited vertical administrative-technical bridging. All categories of respondents interviewed painted ministerial partisan advisers as marginal direct sources of policy advice.

In contrast, those interviewed all underscored the point that the first minister's office partisan advisers were heavily involved in both advisory and non-advisory forms of policy work. New Brunswick partisan advisers at the centre readily acknowledged that at times they engaged in policy advisory activity that was partisan-political. This was, as in

Figure 7.4. New Brunswick Partisan Advisers and the Dynamic Policy Advice System

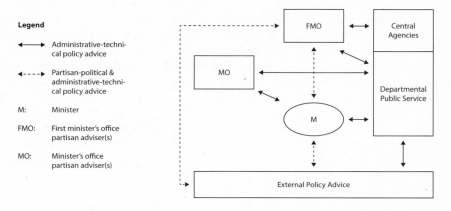

the federal case, explicitly described as an application of a political perspective to ensure consistency with their platform – a compass by which they oriented their policy advice. There was no formal partisan-political policy advisory briefing system in place in New Brunswick. Interviews with first minister's office partisan advisers made clear that contestation and scrutiny were undertaken through verbal partisan-political advisory activity with the first minister and Cabinet through strategy meetings and the like. However, their input was always integrated by the public service into the "final" or formal advisory product. The public service would provide its own free and frank advice, but would contextualize that by informal discussions and consultations with senior Premier's Office partisan advisers. This content integration and signal-checking mirrored the process that was described in the BC case. Partisan advisers at the centre in New Brunswick reported limited exogenous policy advisory integration. However, as detailed above, the bulk of stakeholder integration in New Brunswick was dealt with directly by ministers, and uniquely by departmental officials in particular.

The variance within and among cases in partisan advisers' advisory system participation supports the claims that components of policy-advice supply systems are often combined in different ratios (Prince 1983; White 2001; Howlett 2011). It also provides new insights that go beyond locational and control-autonomy approaches, confirming that the content of policy advice generated and integrated within advisory systems is also variable (Craft and Howlett 2012). Returning to the currents of change set out in the introductory chapter, the findings confirm that sharing truth with multiple actors of influence is a more accurate way of understanding contemporary advisory work. However, it is perhaps useful to think of that work as part of a broader conversation, a dialectic that involves multiple voices espousing different perspectives, that carry different weight, and are themselves highly dynamic and contingent. Partisan advisers invite, and to a degree compel, a reappraisal of longstanding questions in the study and practice of public administration and policymaking: How are the partisan-political and public service aspects of governing reconciled? Where are the boundaries between the two spheres, and how firm or porous are they, and should they be? It is not novel to suggest that governing and the policy process involve a conversation of which an aspect is partisan-political. However, tackling these difficult questions can benefit from more fulsome appraisal of what newer actors, like partisan advisers, and the longstanding and shifting governance contexts mean for how public service and political elites go about the work of policy and governance. There is no doubt that partisan advisers politicize the policy process – that is what they are appointed to do – and official government documents have long recognized this (Canada 2011). However, they must not contribute to the politicization of the public service, whose free and frank advice to decision-makers remain essential (Rhodes, Wanna, and Weller 2010; Scott and Baehler 2010; Aucoin and Savoie 2009). This is an important but difficult distinction to draw in theory, and even more so in practice.

Many interviewed recognized this, and as one senior public servant interviewed emphasized, what is crucial is that the public service continue to have a seat at the table and be *able* to provide their free and frank policy advice. However, the government is under no obligation to heed it. Comparable studies in other systems with Westminster traditions have noted similar tensions and challenges, but the conclusions are similar. In general, advisers provide political inputs into the policy process that the public service cannot and should not provide, which help insolate public servants from the more explicit partisan-political aspects of policy work (Eichbaum and Shaw, 2007b, 2008). This is not to say that exceptions to norms, rules, and official standards of practice do not occur. Interviews revealed these tensions certainly exist but are perhaps best understood not only as a fundamental driver of Canada's adaptation of responsible government (Aucoin 1995a), but also as animating forces of policy work itself. As a former prime ministerial principal secretary put it, "Partisans bring creativity; public servants provide perspective. The political arm makes things move; bureaucratic routines prevent errors. Both kinds of counsel are necessary but in Canada we are now in danger of doing permanent damage to the concept of a neutral civil service. Paradoxically, a strongly partisan personal office is the best way to defend an apolitical public service. Good advice necessitates different kinds of expertise" (Axworthy 1988, 248).

This speaks to the adaptive force of advisers within the political-administrative nexus, a traditionally bilateral relationship that is now increasingly multilateral. The advent, expansion, and particularly the specialization of partisan advisers, as policy workers, make more visible these tensions and adaptations. Many accounts have already pointed to the changing role of the public service, and that its utility and function ebbs and flows with different governments, and the context within which it operates (Aucoin 1986; Prince 2007; Savoie 2003, 2015; Zussman 2015). To claim the public service is now completely marginalized seems unfair and inaccurate. This and other studies provide evidence that it continues to be a leading voice in all three cases examined, and remains an essential component of the policy process (Dunn and Bourgault 2014; Bernier, Brownsey, and Howlett 2005). Has the political arm in these cases flexed its muscle more? Certainly in Ottawa there is evidence that partisan-political perspective and input occupied a more prominent place in the Harper government than in previous administrations. This is clear with the establishment of a discreet partisan-political advisory process and advisers' clear insertion into advisory activity more generally, at multiple locations within government. Partisan advisers in Ottawa have certainly become full-fledged partners in the policy conversation. Yet, in keeping with other studies of advisers, they themselves, along with all categories of respondents, were quick to describe them as a supplementary, and ideally complementary voices to those of the public service and others (Esselment, Lees-Marshment, and Marland 2014). The policy advisory work of partisan advisers is important for all of the reasons listed above but paints only a partial picture of them as policy workers. Indeed, another basic aim of this book was to explore if, how, and with what consequence partisan advisers were meaningful participants in policy formulation.

Canadian Partisan Advisers as Formulation Participants

The evidence from the cases examined provides new insights detailing that (1) current accounts elide important procedural aspects of partisan advisers' formulation; (2) partisan advisers substantive and procedural participation in formulation extends beyond determinations of political feasibility; and (3), the instrumentation and actors with which moving and shaping occur can differ in meaningful ways.

Process Dimensions of Partisan Advisers' Formulation Activity

As we have seen, procedural formulation or "moving" was a key means by which partisan advisers participated in formulation. When plotted together, the moving activities from the cases span multiple formulation sub-phases and across partisan-political and administrative-technical dimensions. Given their "whole of government" responsibility, the finding that horizontal administrative-technical moving was restricted to first ministers' office partisan advisers is unsurprising. Such actors have long been (implicitly) suggested to have such procedural types of responsibilities (Savoie 1999a; White 2005, 2001). However, beyond this obvious general observation, the findings that such activity was found to often span all formulation sub-phases is important. As emphasized in chapter 4, partisan advisers at the centre were key participants in concert with senior officials in the appraisal sub-stage involving determination of the initial policy parameters during formulation. In addition, they were also active process managers as policy was formalized through a formal political and public service channels (e.g., Cabinet). Partisan advisers were also important to "back-end" horizontal administrative-technical formulation with actors at the consolidation sub-phase. They almost exclusively adjudicated contentious policy issues, conflicts between competing policy priorities, and sequencing determinations. This was a key means by which they wielded additional policy-based influence. In addition, the moving of these actors, in all cases and categories used to plot them, were heavily associated with formal public service policymaking instruments. These actors were pivotal to formal government-wide process management and coordination. In sum, they were important actors whose policy-based influence is particularly salient for contemporary governance practices, given the emphasis accorded to collaboration and horizontality in policymaking (Bakvis and Julliet 2004; Dahlström, Peters, and Pierre 2011; Peters 1998; Peach 2004).

A subsidiary finding was that this horizontal moving was a product of partisan advisers' leveraging other actors' resources and capabilities. This speaks directly to asymmetrical notions of core executive resource exchange. At the "centre" in Ottawa, formulation activity was heavily PMO- and PCO-centric, whereas the two subnational cases included greater mixes of central agencies *and* deputy minister–based interactions. Regardless of their preferred approach, this finding weakens the argument that partisan advisers are usurping or overtaking public service actors as the dominant force in formulation. Their effective engagement in policy work was based in large part on their ability to leverage the public service, and central agencies in particular, in the case of Ottawa. Similar resource dependence and exchanges were also clear in that case in horizontal partisan-political moving. The reality is that while "the centre" may remain well resourced and uniquely positioned to exert tremendous influence, the PMO depended upon and exchanged resources with ministerial partisan advisers stationed throughout the core executive.

While such findings support the fact that, in short, configuration matters, as detailed in chapter 5, it had limited explanatory purchase. Despite similar subnational configurations, the cases varied dramatically in how advisers engaged in formulation. Moreover, the BC and federal cases demonstrate that extra-departmental or horizontal partisan-political moving can also vary in its orientation towards actors within government or policy communities outside of it. The two cases included a stakeholder component, the federal case was characterized by a much stronger and institutionalized pattern of horizontality between ministers' offices and the PMO. Such differences may lead to variation in dialogic activities as well as the "open" or "closed" nature of policy subsystems (Howlett, Perl, and Ramesh 2009; Howlett and Ramesh 1998). These differences also suggest different propensities or needs for policy coordination among partisan advisers themselves. Finally, the federal and BC cases involved ministerial partisan advisers' horizontal partisan-political activities extending beyond the formulation sub-phase. Partisan-political moving is thus not confined to this sub-stage but rather can be pivotal to any one or combination of formulation sub-phases.

The combination of a layered configuration and a "policy shop" within the PMO fuelled a broader array of verticality along all fronts and formulation sub-phases. As detailed in chapter 5, it resulted in considerable vertical partisan-political moving among PMO staff. It also increased vertical administrative-technical moving as junior and senior PMO staff coordinated and managed the formulation they engaged in with PCO counterparts. The best example of this was the repeated references to vertical intra-PMO administrative-technical policy work in relation to Cabinet committees and MCs as they worked their way through the PMO-PCO nexus. This type of moving was much less commonly reported in the two subnational cases, with no such policy shops in existence and operating with a much smaller complement of only two partisan advisers. Respondents did point to limited vertical moving at the appraisal and dialogue sub-phases in both cases, with additional vertical partisan-political moving produced by the sharper distinction between "policy" and "politics" in New Brunswick.

Across all three cases at the ministers' office level, vertical moving was reported along multiple formulation sub-phases. A wide spectrum of political and administrative respondents described signal-checking with officials during formulation, monitoring departmental policy formulation, or process management and sequencing. Vertical moving at the dialogue sub-stage along both administrative-technical and partisan-political categories was the only formulation consistently reported in all three cases. It was described not only by partisan advisers but also explicitly by deputies and ministers, who noted it as a key aspect of partisan advisers' formulation contribution. As detailed in chapter 6, the BC and federal cases included a broader range of moving along a greater number of sub-phases. The layered configuration in the federal case again produced greater opportunity for partisan-political and administrative-technical moving at various formulation sub-phases. This was due in part to greater specialization in policy functions among partisan advisers and the more specific division of adviser labour. Moving was more pronounced in the federal case, given that the unique opportunity for ministerial partisan advisers to actively participate in formal public service policymaking instruments. In the BC case, moving was a much more informal and dialectical process. The procedural moving documented at various sub-phases and dimensions in these cases points to the increased specialization that now distinguishes partisan advisers from broader "political staffs." That is, increased vertical and horizontal specialization[41] among partisan advisers themselves, as well as with other core executive members and the wider policy community, supports the notion that advisers are increasingly engaged in specialized policy work (Lægreid and Verhoest 2010; Bouckaert, Peters, and Verhoest 2010).

"Shaping": Beyond Determinations of Political Feasibility

Partisan advisers' shaping was described in many instances as extending beyond determinations of political feasibility to involve substantive formulation, at various sub-phases, and along partisan-political and administrative-technical dimensions. First ministers' advisers dominated in horizontal non-advisory work as they were the only actors who engaged in horizontal administrative-technical shaping. This was reported as spanning the formulation sub-phases, with "front-end" instruments such as mandate letters and budgets being key shaping instruments. Across the cases, respondents noted that first ministers' offices were essential to appraisal sub-stage formulation involving determinations of initial policy direction and setting parameters in concert *with officials*. As noted in chapter 5, shaping occurred throughout formulation, particularly in relation to Cabinet and Treasury / Management board submissions and in relation to other items requiring attention. First ministers' office partisan advisers reported decidedly different preferences in the instruments by which they sought to shape policy. As detailed, the federal case featured a clear emphasis on the development and use of mandate letters, with some mention of this in New Brunswick and little reported in the BC case. In addition, as already explored, there were decidedly different orientations to their shaping as either central agency–focused or more deputy minister–focused.

Horizontal administrative-technical shaping was also described as ongoing and undertaken at all of the sub-phases involving, for example, formal and informal consultations with officials consisting of advancing recommendations and refining policy options being considered; contestation or challenge functions based on knowledge of related or pending policy initiatives; scrutiny of the internal logic and consistency or, less frequently, technical merits of any policy being developed. The federal case included additional horizontal administrative-technical formulation flowing from bidirectional shaping between first minister and ministers' office partisan advisers throughout formulation. This was described largely as involving similar activities as delineated above, such as with both sets of actors jointly discussing Cabinet submissions being drafted or departmental policy recommendations or potential initiatives, or using their counterparts to provide a second opinions for proposed policy in development.

Divisions of labour within first ministers' offices were again partially responsible for variance in degree, intensity, and type of vertical shaping in the three cases. The hierarchical structure of the PMO policy shop, for example, necessitated greater intra-PMO administrative-technical policy shaping. Junior and senior levels of partisan advisers reported engaging (at level) with PCO officials and working with PMO policy shop colleagues on content aspects and "nuts and bolts" of memoranda to Cabinet, and Cabinet and cabinet committee items and policy documents. Both subnational cases were found to have much less intensive overall verticality in their shaping, which can be explained, in part, by their respective divisions of labour. In New Brunswick, the agreed upon political/policy division of labour between chief and principal secretary resulted in some verticality in shaping stemming from determination of who tackled what items and engaging in collaborative work in the 20 per cent of policy situations where their purviews overlapped. The BC case had no principal secretary, only a deputy chief of staff (policy coordination and issues management), but interviews widely supported the suggestion of a near monopoly of policy formulation by chief of staff Martyn Brown. The BC case also included some vertical partisan-political shaping that was most commonly reported at the formulation sub-stage but also described in the context of appraisal and dialogue sub-stage activity. As with their federal counterparts, this involved providing the minister's direction at the "front-end" appraisal sub-phase of policymaking to ensure that politically suitable options were generated for considerations. It was also reported to involve external stakeholders at the appraisal and dialogue sub-phases.

A key finding emanating from interviews was that, irrespective of location or case, partisan advisers characterized partisan-political shaping in essentially similar terms. It was described as (1) involving the translation of partisan-political policy positions into concrete policies and programs, (2) the adjudication of policy recommendations from the public service to ensure consistency with previously articulated policy positions and commitments, and (3) the identification of partisan-political risks/benefits for elected officials. The cases all abounded with references to "translation," "alignment," and "consistency." This activity was also not confined to the formulation sub-stage but was also found to span formulation sub-phases. This is an important finding for two reasons: first, it suggests that partisan advisers in these cases approached partisan-political formulation in similar ways; and second, it underscores that partisan-political shaping can occur not only in the formulation sub-stage but throughout formulation. How policy is initially framed, how and from whom data are collected, who is involved in dialogue sub-stage activity and the nature of the input they provide, and what options are excluded can all involve advisers contributing towards the coherence and coordination of policy work. As one New Brunswick first minister's partisan adviser made plain, constant vigilance throughout formulation was required to avoid policy getting "lost in translation." The shaping activities documented in this study provide evidence of a unique form of "expertise" provided by partisan advisers that supplements and complements other forms of "expertise" (Head 2008; Page 2010; Peters and Barker 1993; MacRae and Whittington 1997). This further supports the argument of an evolution towards greater specialization in partisan advisers' formulation activities, as well as distinct core executive policy-based resource exchange dynamics.

Partisan Advisers, Core Executive Operation, and the Politics of Policy Work

Implicit in the rationale for the institutionalization of partisan advisers was the logic that they may serve as a means to improve governance. When deployed effectively, advisers could increase ministerial involvement in policymaking, provide additional policy capacity for ministers, ensure closer alignment of policy outcomes with democratic mandates, and prevent ministerial "overload" (Savoie 1983; White 2005; Tellier 1968). This study used the core executive approach to examine if and how partisan advisors engaged in policy-based resource exchanges. What are the implications of the key differences set out above for the types and nature of resource exchanges? Core executive theory has been used to analyse the particular resource endowments of various actors. As noted at the outset of this book, with the exception of first ministers' offices, partisan advisers have not figured prominently in such analysis. As per table 7.1, some examples of partisan advisors' resource endowments can be added to those typically attributed other core executive members.

The elaboration of the term *partisan-political policy advice* was not intended as an exercise in esoteric academic nomenclature development. It seeks to capture and analytically explore partisan advisers' ability to engage in recognized "political" forms of policy work (Majone 1975; Esselment, Lees-Mashment, and Marland 2014; May 1981; Webber 1986; Head 2008). A central argument of this study is that, as political appointees, advisers are privileged not only because

Table 7.1. Core Executive Actor Resources

Officials	Prime Minister	Ministers	Partisan Advisers
Permanence	Patronage	Political support	Increased contestability in policy work
Knowledge	Authority	Authority	"Boundary spanning" policy work
Time	Political support / party	Department	Endogenous networks (partisan-political and public service)
Public service network	Political support / electorate	Knowledge	Exogenous networks
Control over information	Prime Minister's Office and central agency support	Policy networks	Policy coordination for ministers and/or other core executive actors
Keepers of the constitution	Bilateral policymaking	Policy success	Policy responsiveness and alignment of policy with stated partisan-political policy objectives

Source: Adapted from Smith (1999)

of their institutional proximity to ministers but also because they may engage in explicitly partisan-political activities to support their ministers as elected officials. Such activity has a direct bearing on core executive policy-based resource exchange in that it supports the exchange of partisan-political resources involved in Cabinet decision-making and individual ministerial activity. It also supports the ability of ministers to exert political control and avoid so-called bureaucratic capture, improve credit claiming and blame avoidance, and legitimation with citizens and stakeholders (Hood 2002a; Wallner 2008; Peters 2001; Howlett 2012). It may also facilitate securing electoral/reputational benefit for political actors through advancing stated political direction, objectives, or commitments; or increased avoidance of political traps or negative political consequences (Hood 2002b; Weaver 1986). This study's findings draw attention to partisan advisers' policy work in the "translation" or alignment of partisan-political policy goals to concrete public programs, services, and decisions. This is an important type of resource exchange undertaken by the political arm and deserves greater attention to improve our understanding of core executive operation.

The types of resource exchange dynamics charted in these three cases reveal potential for conflict among types of resources. This is pertinent to core executive scholarship that recognizes that core executives "pull together and integrate central government policies, or act as final arbiters within the executive of conflicts between different elements of the government machine" (Dunleavy and Rhodes 1990, 4). First ministers' office partisan advisers continue to be crucial actors in conflict arbitration and coordination. This is equally so for advisory and non-advisory policy work. Importantly, these two functions are well suited to analysis along the substantive and procedural categories used in this study. As arbiters, partisan advisers at the centre served as key actors in the adjudication and calibration of content-based policy work, whether it was in the substance of policy advice or the elaboration of particular policy in development. This extends to both their functions as partisans and the policy work that is undertaken with officials and other policy actors. In addition, on procedural grounds partisan advisers' policy work also suggests that they can be quite significant for "pulling together" or coordinating policy. Partisan advisers at the centre were particularly active in this regard, but ministers' offices were also found to engage in such activity. In the federal case, it was a much more systematic affair with the PMO and ministers' offices wielding and exchanging policy-based resources to facilitate such practices. This was less prevalent in the subnational cases, with first ministers' offices, ministers, and officials driving those dynamics.

Deputies and senior central agency officials also continue to serve as policy arbiters and coordinators for the public service (Savoie 1999a). Interviews were full with references to these actors engaging in activities that ensured coordination and coherence of policy across government, as well as the weaving advisory and non-advisory policy work required for "housekeeping" and the government's policy priorities. Those interviewed gave no impression that they were now subject to partisan pressure that jeopardized their non-partisan professional public service values. There were grey areas, times of conflict, and tensions, but these were articulated to be healthy and part of what makes the system work. Several deputies noted that if they had a problem with a partisan adviser, they had several avenues by which to ensure functions were clarified and there was proper comportment of ministers' offices. Partisan advisers' policy work was clearly linked to attempts to increase policy responsiveness and exert political control. The many quotations from respondents themselves make this abundantly clear.

As partisans, they engage in types of policy work that are out of bounds for public servants. There are certainly documented instances where partisan advisers have acted inappropriately (Sutherland 1991; Benoit 2006; Aucoin 2010). This study's findings suggest that, while such instances occur and will likely continue, they are the exception rather than the rule. Respondents point to a reality that is much more akin to the findings of King (2003) and others, who conclude that policy work is certainly more contested with the presence of advisers, but "there is little evidence that political advisers have supplanted the core adviser role of the public service, systematically thwarted the access of departmental officials to ministers, or undermined important civil service norms" (Boston and Nethercote 2012, 202). Many officials across the cases described processes in place to clarify roles and activities, and a continued understanding and appreciation of their non-partisan functions and obligations. Officials expressed an ability to effectively provide their "free and frank" advice to ministers and to "push back" and clarify in the situations where tensions and conflict emerged, knowing all the while that if ministers did not accept their advice, that was fine, as long as they were still able to provide it.

It is not just a matter of what types of resources core executive actors may possess. Resource exchanges occur in an institutional context and involve the agency of those who possess and exchange them (Smith 1999; Heffernan 2003; Marsh et al. 2003). As has been detailed already, the configuration of advisers themselves can affect policy-relevant resource exchanges. This was clear in the federal case, where multiple partisan advisers at ministerial and first ministers' offices organized hierarchically produced a particular pattern of policy-based resource exchanges. However, the lack of similar patterns in the subnational cases, despite similar configurations, demonstrates that this variable, while important, is insufficient for determinations of partisan advisers' policy work and core executive influence.

A second structural feature was the location of partisan advisers. Clear differences were discernible in the types of policy work that partisan advisers at different locations undertook, along with access to specific resources, and their patterns of resource exchange with others. This was clearly demonstrated by the prominent and exclusive ability of first ministers' offices to undertake horizontal administrative-technical policy work, their access to central agencies and Cabinet, and particular policy instruments like mandate letters and throne speeches. Ministerial partisan advisers, however, had their own location-specific policy-based resources. These included the day-to-day policy work and thinking of their departments and ministers, and in some cases established relationships and access to pertinent stakeholder inputs. A final structural feature is the "open" or "closed" nature of ministers' offices – that is, differences in their propensities and patterns of resource exchange can be linked to whether they are willing and able to engage in advisory or non-advisory policy work. This was perhaps most clearly demonstrated by the differences in the integration of exogenous stakeholder inputs, and minister–first ministers' office interactions (see table 7.2).

Operationally, the three cases have been shown to feature distinct policy-based resource exchanges. One important but often overlooked

Table 7.2: Structural and Operational Criteria of Partisan Advisers' Core Executive Resource Exchanges

Factors	Components	Variations
Structural	Configuration	Single or layered at first ministers' and/or ministers' offices
	Institutional location	First minister's office–centric, ministers' office–centric, "systemic"
	Accessibility	Openness or closeness of ministerial office to other policy actors
Operational	Policy work undertaken	Advisory, non-advisory, or mix Procedural, substantive, or mix Partisan-political, administrative-technical, or mix Intra- or extra-departmental orientation
	Ministerial preferences	Direct, mediated, or mixed ministerial relations with public service, and policy work
	Partisan advisers' desire/ability to engage in policy work	Complete, partial, non-existent
	Instrument availability/preference	Formal, informal, or mix Front end, back end, ongoing, or mix
	Sequence and conjuncture of policy work	Front end, back end, ongoing, or mix

distinction pertains to differences in the actual policy work being under-taken. These have been set out in detail in the preceding pages and need not be restated here. They reveal that partisan advisers can be engaged in some, all, or no appreciable policy work with corresponding impli-cations for core executive operation, and that, where occurring, core executive resource exchanges can be advisory or non-advisory based, or a mix thereof. As partisan-political appointees, advisers were found to be able to engage in types of resource exchanges that other policy workers could not. This is an important insight in that understanding core executive operation compels attention to the types of resources that are being exchanged.

This study did not include sufficient interview questions or fieldwork with all federal central agencies and ministers required to systemati-cally evaluate the court government thesis. The findings do, however, support the point that "governance from the centre" depends in part on PMO leveraging and using the PCO for policy-based resource exchanges (Savoie 1999a, 2003). As seen above, the PMO and minis-ters' office advisers were frequently engaged in policy-based resource exchanges that increased overall policy coherence for the political arm and ensured the PMO had the ability to engage itself, as needed, in policy work that required its attention. For their part, ministerial office advisers knew the benefits of keeping their PMO counterparts "looped in" and often saw PMO as helpful rather than a hindrance. It also points to the increasing function of ministerial partisan advis-ers in the federal case as systematic features that facilitate core execu-tive resource exchange and policy coordination (Maley 2011; Craft 2015b). The two provincial cases, however, involved much less use and reliance by the "centre" on ministerial partisan advisers. In the BC case, interactions were central agency–focused with the public service, while the New Brunswick case involved much more direct deputy minister–first minister's office interactions on policy files. These differences add further nuance to attempts to understand how the "centre" can operate and distinctions in its interactions with oth-ers and their policy resources. On the one hand, by making available additional personnel and policy resources, partisan advisers through-out the core executive can be used instrumentally to further empower and enable first ministers and their offices. In contrast, as seen in the subnational cases, first minister's office advisers without ministerial office counterparts can be influential figures in their own right. They can drive the political arm's ability to shape and advance government's policy agendas through greater policy work directly involving ministers, senior officials, and Cabinet.

Additional operational considerations linked to ministerial preferences, and partisan advisers' capabilities to undertake policy work, are also noteworthy dynamics. The more direct political-public service relationship in New Brunswick was salient to the lack of policy work at the ministers' office level in that case, whereas the opposite was clear in the federal and BC cases, which were characterized by greater mediation by partisan advisers but also with their ministers expecting them to engage in partisan-political and administrative-technical forms of policy work. Stylistic or personality-driven preferences have long been noted to be important for executives and policy work (Bernier, Brownsey, and Howlett 2005; Doern 1971; Aucoin 1986). Partisan advisers can be added to this literature as extensions of such idiosyncratic stylistic preferences, and as actors with stylistic preferences in their own right. Relatedly, partisan advisers can logically be expected to have different degrees of policy capability based on training, education, experience, and the like. It was clear that, for a variety of reasons, some partisan advisers were better able to contribute to certain forms of policy work than others. This finding is not only in keeping with studies that have suggested "role types" for partisan advisers (Maley 2000; Connaughton 2010a), but also speaks to the more cynical notions of some being considered "hacks" or "kids in short pants" and others high-calibre policy workers.

Lastly, sequencing and instrumentality deserve greater scrutiny as core executive dynamics. As has been discussed at length in this book, participation in formal policymaking instruments and processes, Cabinet and Cabinet committee orientation, and the presence or absence of separate partisan-political advisory mechanisms were important. Differences in instrumentality may facilitate or impede resource exchanges and have implications for core executive operation. The prominence of partisan advisers' references to Cabinet submissions and the partisan-political written advisory system in the federal case, and lack thereof in either subnational case, illustrates this well. The prominence of first ministers' partisan advisers' involvement in "front-end" policy instruments including mandate letters, throne speeches, and budgets further buttresses the point. In addition, it raises the importance of temporal variables and sequence. When is it that partisan advisers are engaging in resource exchange? This was a concrete distinction in the cases with distinct sequencing in Ottawa for partisan-political policy advice, with the prime minister receiving formal PCO advice separately and before partisan-political advice, whereas ministers' offices saw a practice of ministers receiving the advice concurrently. Likewise, the tracing of formulation sub-stage dynamics in non-advisory policy work revealed the prominence of dialogic sub-stage activity across the cases. This and other sub-stage characteristics further emphasize not only the importance of partisan advisers' resource exchanges, but also when it is actually occurring. In all, these structural and operational distinctions provide additional nuance and help refine thinking and analysis of partisan advisers, policy work, and core executives. Importantly, illuminating that partisan advisers' core executive activities, and influence therein, can vary along multiple fronts. Coupling spatial variables with other important considerations, like the types of policy work in question, is required to accurately depict and understand advisers' participation and policy influence.

Conclusion

The complexities of contemporary policymaking confront not only the public service but also the political arm of government. The latter, however, receives much less attention in thinking through how it seeks to manage, cope, or exert influence in shifting governance contexts (Dahlström, Peters, and Pierre 2011). Tackling the challenges of governance head on, while also contributing to an effective and appropriate political-public service relationship, is complex and fraught with challenges (Peters 1987; Pickersgill 1972; Osbaldeston 1987; Aucoin and Savoie 2009). Each set of actors has official and practical responsibilities and obligations. Each engages in discreet sets of activities but by necessity also often overlap. The advent and expanded use of partisan advisers has transformed the traditionally bilateral relationship into one that is trilateral, and in some cases multilateral. Are partisan advisers influential policy workers? This study suggests they certainly can be, but draws attention to the fact that attributions of policy-based influence must carefully account for how that influence is gained and exercised. Throughout interviews with all categories of respondents, it was clear that partisan advisers were not *dominant* policy actors. Rather, they were one of many, predominantly serving in supporting roles. They were not, as one adviser put it, there to "out-bureaucrat the bureaucrats."

They knew full well that the public service more often than not possessed the substantive and procedural experience and skills required for optimal policy development. That said, as partisan-political appointees advisers often engaged in forms of policy work that other core executive members could not. Ultimately, policymaking is a political activity. Understanding how the political arm organizes itself and undertakes policy work, and how its constituent elements interact with other policy actors provides improved accounts of policymaking and core executive dynamics. A final tantalizing thought to leave readers with is that the differences in these cases, historical and empirical, raise the possibility of a Dupré-Dunn-Savoie-like evolution for the political arm itself (Bernier, Brownsey, and Howlett 2005) – that is, that the organization and practices of the more muscular federal political arm of government may foreshadow developments to come in other Canadian jurisdictions. This, of course, will be evident only in time and with additional study. The 2015 election of a Liberal majority government in Ottawa has been accompanied by promises of a new style of governing, one rooted in a collaborative approach to its relations with the public service, the restoration of the primacy of cabinet, and a less partisan, more transparent and evidence-based approach to policymaking. It remains to be seen if Canada's twenty-third prime minister will be able to reverse the trend of governing from the centre associated with his father, Canada's fifteenth prime minister. Likewise, new premiers and governments have also taken the helm in many Canadian provinces, all of which may have important implications for advisers and the politics of policy work. For now, this book's findings are clear – as buffers and bridges, and movers and shapers – Canadian partisan advisers are policy workers with currency in backrooms and beyond.

Appendix A: Federal Exempt Staff by Department (31 March 2001 to 31 March 2014)

Organization	Year													
	2001	2002	2003	2004	2005	2006	2007	2008	2009	2010	2011	2012	2013	2014
Atlantic Canada Opportunities Agency	6	19	13	9	9	1	–	–	4	5	6	5	5	6
Canadian International Development Agency	9	10	7	4	11	3	12	10	12	9	8	11	13	9
Department of Aboriginal Affairs and Northern Development	13	13	11	15	18	4	17	12	14	14	15	14	18	16
Department of Agriculture and Agri-Food	16	17	20	8	12	9	15	19	18	16	17	18	17	16
Department of Canadian Heritage	24	17	29	15	17	4	16	18	26	20	17	21	23	23
Department of Citizenship and Immigration	13	10	14	13	2	2	11	12	22	22	28	25	26	23
Department of Finance	18	18	26	16	14	2	14	21	20	20	24	27	28	28
Department of Fisheries and Oceans	11	3	14	12	12	–	13	14	12	16	13	16	16	14

(Continued)

Organization	Year													
	2001	2002	2003	2004	2005	2006	2007	2008	2009	2010	2011	2012	2013	2014
Department of Foreign Affairs and International Trade	35	34	41	30	23	9	33	27	30	27	30	31	33	30
Department of Human Resources and Skills Development	31	27	25	33	47	5	26	24	22	27	27	32	29	45
Department of Industry	21	18	15	17	19	6	16	22	20	31	26	28	30	34
Department of Justice	15	13	24	13	17	10	9	12	16	15	18	17	18	20
Department of National Defence	12	13	12	14	9	9	14	20	19	21	20	24	22	14
Department of Natural Resources	11	15	16	13	11	6	8	10	9	5	17	12	15	16
Department of Public Safety and Emergency Preparedness	–	–	–	–	–	6	11	14	9	14	16	19	19	15
Department of Public Works and Government Services	21	19	14	11	8	4	15	15	17	24	11	11	16	21
Department of the Environment	13	10	15	15	10	8	18	15	13	15	8	14	14	21
Department of the Solicitor General	12	11	9	19	19	–	–	–	–	–	–	–	–	–
Department of Transport	14	15	15	7	25	7	18	21	25	18	19	24	30	20
Department of Veterans Affairs	9	9	14	8	10	3	10	9	10	11	13	12	11	13

Organization	Year													
	2001	2002	2003	2004	2005	2006	2007	2008	2009	2010	2011	2012	2013	2014
Department of Western Economic Diversification	–	–	4	9	6	–	–	–	5	8	5	5	6	6
Economic Development Agency of Canada for the Regions of Quebec	1	5	6	3	6	1	–	–	6	10	8	6	5	9
Federal Economic Development Agency for Southern Ontario	–	–	–	–	–	–	–	–	–	–	–	–	–	5
Health Canada	10	16	16	21	13	3	10	11	12	15	15	16	15	20
Office of Infrastructure of Canada	–	–	–	5	14	–	–	–	–	–	–	–	–	–
Office of the Coordinator Status of Women	–	–	–	–	–	–	–	–	–	7	3	3	5	3
Privy Council Office	51	56	38	43	47	15	27	26	31	38	38	36	38	27
Treasury Board (Secretariat)	12	12	13	11	14	7	14	13	10	11	12	14	17	16
Office of the Prime Minister (employees)	83	81	77	64	68	65	79	92	94	112	99	95	101	96
CPA total	461	461	488	428	461	189	406	437	476	531	513	536	570	566

Source: Adapted from two tables provided by the Office of the Chief Human Resources Officer, Treasury Board of Canada Secretariat, 24 October 2011 and 27 March 2014, in response to request no. 31029 and no. 87685. Figures include employees on leave without pay. Data are presented as of 31 March of each year, with the exception of the last column, which presents data as of 28 February 2014. The information provided is for the Core Public Administration (CPA) only. CPA departments and agencies as detailed in schedules I and IV of the Financial Administration Act. Data include all employment tenures, active employees, and employees on leave without pay.

Appendix B: Organization of BC Premier's Office (2001)

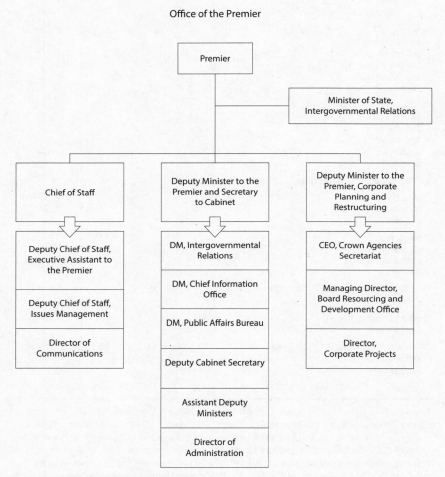

Office of the Premier

Premier

Minister of State, Intergovernmental Relations

Chief of Staff
- Deputy Chief of Staff, Executive Assistant to the Premier
- Deputy Chief of Staff, Issues Management
- Director of Communications

Deputy Minister to the Premier and Secretary to Cabinet
- DM, Intergovernmental Relations
- DM, Chief Information Office
- DM, Public Affairs Bureau
- Deputy Cabinet Secretary
- Assistant Deputy Ministers
- Director of Administration

Deputy Minister to the Premier, Corporate Planning and Restructuring
- CEO, Crown Agencies Secretariat
- Managing Director, Board Resourcing and Development Office
- Director, Corporate Projects

Source: Office of the Premier (2002, 5).

Appendix C: Organization of BC Premier's Office (2011)

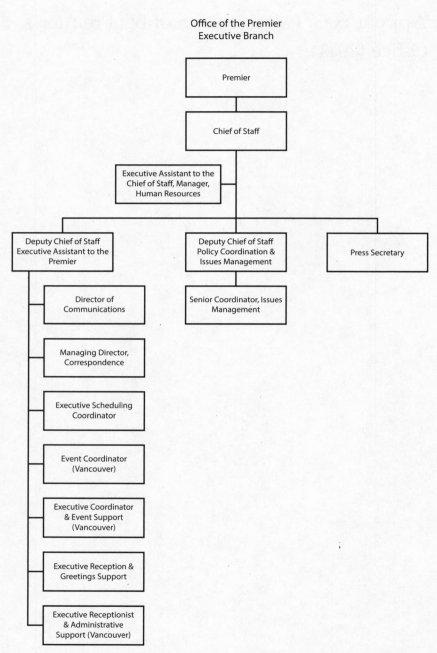

Office of the Premier
Executive Branch

Premier

Chief of Staff

Executive Assistant to the
Chief of Staff, Manager,
Human Resources

Deputy Chief of Staff
Executive Assistant to the
Premier

Deputy Chief of Staff
Policy Coordination &
Issues Management

Press Secretary

Director of
Communications

Senior Coordinator, Issues
Management

Managing Director,
Correspondence

Executive Scheduling
Coordinator

Event Coordinator
(Vancouver)

Executive Coordinator
& Event Support
(Vancouver)

Executive Reception &
Greetings Support

Executive Receptionist
& Administrative
Support (Vancouver)

Source: Accessed online, 12 April 2015, http://www.bcbudget.gov.bc.ca/2011/sp/pdf/
ministry/charts/Executive_Branch_2011.pdf

Appendix D: BC Ministers' Office Staff by Department and Classification (1996–2001)

Job title	Year																
	1996	1997	1998	1999	2000	2001	2002	2003	2004	2005	2006	2007	2008	2009	2010	2011 (01/01)	2011 (11/18)
Administrative coordinator	17	14	15	18	20	21	22	21	22	21	21	24	23	23	25	26	19
Administrative officer R14	1	–	–	–	–	–	1	–	–	–	–	–	–	–	–	–	–
Administrative officer R18	–	1	–	–	1	–	2	2	–	–	2	2	2	3	3	3	3
Administrative officer R21	–	–	–	–	–	–	–	–	–	–	–	1	1	1	–	–	–
Band A	–	–	–	–	–	–	–	–	–	–	30	30	34	35	36	28	26
Band B	–	–	–	–	–	–	–	–	–	–	–	26	26	28	20	23	26
Band C	–	–	–	–	–	–	–	–	–	–	–	1	1	1	1	1	1
Band D	–	–	–	–	–	–	–	–	–	–	–	2	2	2	2	2	3
Band E	–	–	–	–	–	–	–	–	–	–	–	–	–	2	2	1	3
Clerk R11	6	9	7	12	19	11	7	5	6	10	2	2	1	2	2	–	–
Clerk R14	15	23	25	22	26	36	11	11	11	9	17	14	13	9	11	10	9
Clerk R9	3	5	6	14	9	11	14	16	14	11	6	7	11	13	10	6	10
Clerk stenographer R9	9	4	3	1	–	2	–	–	–	–	–	–	–	–	–	–	–

Clerk stenographer R11	3	3	3	1	3	1	1	1	–	–	–	–	–	–	–	–	–
Clerk stenographer R14	6	–	–	–	–	–	–	–	–	–	–	–	–	–	–	–	–
Executive assistant	21	14	15	16	20	21	24	22	24	21	22	–	–	–	–	–	–
Ministerial assistant	21	22	22	26	27	52	27	27	24	29	26	–	–	–	–	–	–
Office assistant R7	4	–	1	2	1	–	–	–	–	–	–	–	–	–	–	–	–
Senior executive assistant	–	2	2	–	1	2	–	–	–	–	–	–	–	–	–	–	–
Senior executive secretary	2	–	–	–	–	–	–	–	–	–	–	–	–	–	–	–	–
Special assistant	–	–	3	3	13	2	–	–	–	–	–	–	–	–	–	–	–
Total	108	97	101	115	140	159	109	105	101	101	96	109	114	119	112	100	100

Source: Provided to author 8 November 2011 by the BC Public Service Commission

Appendix E: Interview Index

Identifier	Characteristic (name, title)	Date of interview/consultation
	Ian Brodie, former PMO chief of staff to Stephen Harper	14 October 2011
	Stockwell Day, former minister, Government of Canada	21 July 2011
	David Emerson, former minister, Government of Canada	8 September 2011
	Guy Giorno, former PMO chief of staff to Stephen Harper	14 October and 15 November 2011
	Tim Murphy, former PMO chief of staff to Paul Martin	20 October 2011
	Alan Seckle, deputy minister to the premier, BC	14 November 2011
ADM1	New Brunswick assistant deputy minister	10 August 2010
ADM2	Assistant deputy minister, Government of Canada	30 August 2011
BCO1	Senior Cabinet office official, Government of BC	29 September 2011
BCO2	Senior cabinet office official, Government of BC	29 September 2011
DM1	Deputy minister, New Brunswick	6 August 2010
DM2	Deputy minister, New Brunswick	4 August 2010
DM3	Deputy minister, New Brunswick	August *XXX*
DM4	Deputy minister, BC	2 February 2011

Identifier	Characteristic (name, title)	Date of interview/consultation
DM5	Deputy minister, BC	28 January 2011
DM6	Deputy minister, BC	6 January 2011
DM7	Deputy minister, BC	13 July 2011
DM8	Deputy minister, Government of Canada	13 July 2011
DM9	Deputy minister, Government of Canada	18 July 2011
DM11	Deputy minister, Government of Canada	19 September 2011
M1	Minister of the Crown, New Brunswick	3 August 2010
M2	Minister of the Crown, New Brunswick	4 August 2010
M3	Minister of the Crown, New Brunswick	5 August 2010
M4	Minister of the Crown, BC	21 February 2011
M5	Minister of the Crown, BC	23 February 2011
M6	Minister of the Crown, BC	4 March 2011
M7	Minister of the Crown, BC	7 March 2011
M8	Minister of the Crown, New Brunswick	1 June 2011
M9	Minister of the Crown, BC	7 September 2009
M11	Minister of the Crown, Government of Canada	25 August 2011
M12	Minister of the Crown, Government of Canada	1 September 2011
P1	New Brunswick Premier's Office partisan adviser	3 August 2010
P2	New Brunswick Premier's Office partisan adviser	3 August 2010
P3	BC Premier's Office partisan adviser	11 May 2011
P4	BC Premier's Office partisan adviser	24 August 2011
P5	BC ministerial partisan adviser	25 February 2011
P6	BC ministerial partisan adviser	25 February 2011
P7	BC ministerial partisan adviser	16 March 2011

(*Continued*)

Identifier	Characteristic (name, title)	Date of interview/consultation
P8	New Brunswick minister's office partisan adviser	2 August 2010
P9	New Brunswick minister's office partisan adviser	28 July 2010
P10	BC ministerial partisan adviser	11 July 2011
P11	BC ministerial partisan adviser	12 September 2011
P12	Former Harper director of policy, PMO	2 September 2011
P13	Former director of policy, PMO	23 August 2011
P14	Minister's office chief of staff	16 September 2011
P15	PMO policy adviser	21 September 2011
P16	Minister's office policy director	23 August 2010
P17	Minister's office policy adviser	23 September 2011
P18	PMO policy adviser	8 September 2011
P20	BC ministerial partisan adviser	20 September 2011
P21	Partisan adviser, minister's office	21 September 2011
P22	Minister's office director of policy	7 October 2011
P25	Minister's office director of policy	17 October 2011
P26	Minister's office deputy chief of staff	10 August 2011
P27	Minister's office chief of staff	2 September 2011
P28	Minister's office chief of staff	21 September 2011
P29	Minister's office policy director	23 August 2011
P30	Mark Cameron, former PMO director of Policy	14 December 2011
P31	Former Chrétien senior PMO partisan adviser	15 September 2011
P32	Former Chrétien PMO partisan adviser	18 July 2011
P33	Former Chrétien PMO chief of staff	25 August 2011
P34	New Brunswick, minister's office partisan adviser	4 August 2010
P35	New Brunswick, minister's office partisan adviser	5 August 2010
PCO1	Senior Privy Council Office official	12 January 2011

Identifier	Characteristic (name, title)	Date of interview/consultation
PCO2	Senior Privy Council Office official	12 January 2011
PCO3	Former senior Privy Council Office official	20 September 2011
PCO4	Former senior Privy Council Office official	26 July 2010

Notes

Introduction

1 The limited studies that have examined political staffs as policy workers paint a mixed and evolving portrait at the federal level. Campbell (1988) detailed limited capacity for partisan advisory policy, even in the PMO (see also Campbell and Szablowski 1979). One frequently cited assessment claims that, by Westminster standards, "as sources of policy advice political staff in Canada probably rank among the weakest. By and large a typical minister's office tends to be unduly pre-occupied with picayune political matters" (Bakvis 1997, 114). King simply cites Savoie (1999a) in explaining the ministerial executive assistant as "a relatively junior position and enjoys neither the salary nor the status that the chief of staff position enjoyed in the Mulroney years" (King 2003, 40). Other studies, almost exclusively federal, are significantly more generous in their interpretations of Canadian partisan advisers' purchase in policymaking. Benoit (2006, 146) finds that exempt staff are "well placed to influence both the bounce and bobble of bureaucratic political interface and the pace and progress of public policy in Canada." Additionally, Zussman (2009), Savoie (1999a, 2003), Aucoin (2010), and Thomas (2008, 2010) all underscore significant advisory and policy-related activity and influence.

2 The term *partisan advisers* is used to define remunerated political appointees employed by a minister of the Crown at the federal or provincial level with an officially acknowledged policy role. It excludes other types of "exempt" political staff (i.e., clerical staff, communications staff). The term also excludes political staff employed in non-ministerial offices such as the Senate (save those who work for a senator appointed to Cabinet), for backbench members of legislatures, or in the constituency offices of elected

officials. The term *partisan* is used to distinguish between policy work-ers (including the public service) who may engage in "policy-politics" or "small *p*" politics, whereas professional non-partisan public servants are precluded from engaging in "big *P*" or "partisan-politics" (see Kernaghan 1986; Overeem 2005; Rhodes 2015).

3 For historical overview see Mallory (1967). The Public Service Employ-ment Act (2003) states, "A minister, or a person holding the recognized position of Leader of the Opposition in the House of Commons or Leader of the Opposition in the Senate, may appoint an executive assistant and other persons required in his or her office."

4 Governance is defined in various ways (see Robichau 2011). As the term is used in this book, *public* governance is "about establishing, promoting and supporting a specific type of relationship between governmental and non-governmental actors in the governing process" (Howlett and Ramesh 2014, 318).

5 Aucoin (2008b) did not include the integrating of governance and cam-paigning that does, however, appear in a revised work (Aucoin 2012). For the purposes of this study they are both included as part of the NPG model.

6 Rhodes revised the concept to "the complex web of institutions, networks and practices surrounding the prime minister, cabinet, cabinet commit-tees and their official counterparts, less formalised ministerial "clubs" or meetings, bilateral negotiations and interdepartmental committees. It also includes coordinating departments, chiefly the Cabinet Office, the Treasury, the Foreign Office, the law officers and the security and intelli-gence services" (Rhodes 1995, 12). For thoughtful analysis of the executive, including core executive theory, see Elgie (1997, 2011).

Chapter 1

7 It should be noted that Baccigalupo (1973) provided similar models over thirty years prior in a pioneering study on the role and functions of "chiefs of staffs" in Quebec. His three possible configurations included "*écran*" (akin to Zussman's "gatekeeper" model) "braintrust" (akin to Zussman's collaborative model), and "staff *spécialisé*" (akin to the triangulated model).

8 Partisans and partisanship have been various used within the political science and policy literatures (see, for example, Lindblom 1965; Duverger 1965; Rosenblum 2008). Following Esselment (2009) the term *partisan* is used in this study as it pertains to politically appointed staffs in minis-ters' offices, defining such actors as *professional activists*. That is, it shares

Esselment's (2009) and Webb and Kolodny's (2006, 338) categorization of political professionals who are remunerated by the state but engage in work inside of government that is considered partisan. Partisanship can apply to an individual's support of a particular leader or policy issue and not simply their formal membership in a political party.

 9 The degree to which senior public servants are aware of political context and poses "political acumen" in policymaking and governance has long been recognized and debated (see, for example, Campbell and Szablowski 1979; Heclo and Wildavsky 1974; Simon 1957; Suleiman 1984; Rhodes 2015). Even allowing for such political awareness, appointed political staffs are hired to engage in partisan-political forms of policy work that public servants in Westminster systems cannot (see Prasser 2006; Eichbaum and Shaw 2010; LSE GV314 2012).

10 This is not to say that no analysis has been undertaken, but treatments have focused on particular sets of political staff (e.g., ministers' chiefs of staff) or have not included focused assessments of them as policy workers. For those interested in earlier accounts of federal exempt staff more generally, see Lee (1971), Jeffrey (1978), and Flemming (1997). On the provinces, see White (2001), Marley (1997), Dutil (2006), Plassé (1981), Baccigalupo (1973), and Maltais and Harvey (2007).

11 Pronoun attribution was also randomized for grammatical and anonymity purposes for all categories of respondents.

Chapter 2

12 Mallory (1967, 28) cites P.C. 30/1188, dated 8 March 1950. It allowed for executive assistant to the minister, head clerk, secretary to the executive, clerk grade 4 or stenographer grade 3, clerk grade 3, stenographer grade 2B, stenographer grade 2A or clerk grade 2A or messenger, and confidential messenger.

13 Statutes of Canada, 166–7, chapter 71, section 37.

14 See PCO (1965) for a review of the minutes where the policy is outlined as "the generally accepted policy had been to establish certain limits on the numbers of exempt staff allowed to individual ministers and the pattern had developed that each minister was provided with an establishment of 11 exempt positions with a considerable degree of variation in grades and salaries of the positions at the lower level." The Cabinet conclusion also notes that this matter was referred to an ad hoc committee for review. See PCO (1966) for the Cabinet agreement of the increase to ministerial office budgets to $78,000.

15 Prime Minister Trudeau appointed the first ever deputy prime minister in 1977. The position was expanded and formalized with the creation of its own "office" under Mulroney.

16 This was confirmed in an interview with a senior Chrétien PMO adviser, P31.

17 See Treasury Board (2003, appendix C).

18 Interview with Tim Murphy, 20 October 2011.

19 Interview with former Harper PMO director of policy, P12, 2 September 2011.

20 Interview with former Harper PMO chief of staff, Ian Brodie, 14 October 2011.

21 While written memos have been used in the past (see Mallory 1967, 30), their use as described by a number of partisan advisers employed in the Harper years involved more than a summary of the docket or policy document in question. They provided written partisan-political analysis as well as a *recommendation* to the minister/prime minister.

22 Interview with former Harper PMO chief of staff, Ian Brodie, 14 October 2011.

23 See Treasury Board Secretariat (2011), Appendix A: Exempt Staff Position Structure, for a detailed breakdown of the exempt staff categories.

24 Ruff (2005, 229) does, however, note that Premier Vander Zalm (1986–91) had only a chief of staff and no deputy minister to the premier. Premier Christina Clark adopted a more elaborate Premier's Office structure: a principal secretary located in the legislative precinct and a senior policy adviser and other senior staff located in her Vancouver office.

25 See Ruff (2005, 228) for an account of the various "styles" of such premiers.

26 Because there is a shortage of information on the chiefs of staff in various provinces, it is generally accepted that Mr Brown was the longest-serving chief of staff in the modern sense.

27 These two advisory bodies would remain housed in the Office of the Premier until 2009, when they were moved to the Ministry of Small Business, Technology and Economic Development (Ruff 2009).

28 Interview with senior Premier's Office staff, 11 May 2011.

29 The 2011 figures are only partial, as Premier Gordon Campbell resigned and a new premier, Christina Clark, was sworn in, in March 2011.

30 Provided in correspondence to the author by the director, Compensation, Classification & Corporate Research, Office of Human Resources, Government of New Brunswick, 22 November 2011.

31 Ibid.
32 Interviews with two long-serving deputy ministers in Fredericton, New Brunswick, 6 August 2010.
33 See section 27.2(1)(a).

Chapter 3

34 Documents written by partisan advisers or used within ministerial offices only, including those drafted and/used in the PMO, are not subject to access-to-information legislation. Ministers (and their offices) are not deemed "institutions," and thus any documents under their control are not subject to access-to-information legislation. Great care is thus taken to ensure partisan-political policy advice is drafted, utilized, and maintained strictly by partisan advisers to ensure it does not become subject to access-to-information provisions. This was notably confirmed in a 2011 Supreme Court of Canada decision on access to Prime Minister Jean Chrétien's PMO scheduling agenda (Supreme Court of Canada 2011). Court rulings have noted, however, that the Access to Information Act could be amended to explicitly include ministers' offices as subject to the provisions of the act. The Harper government did not adopt such revisions when the Act was amended to include additional non-departmental organizations in 2006 (Thomas 2010, 109).
35 Schacter (1999, 9) explains that upon Cabinet committee approval, the recommendation from memorandum to Cabinet is passed to full Cabinet in the form of a committee report, which is attached as an annex item to the agenda of a meeting of the full Cabinet. Cabinet would normally accept the committee's recommendation without significant discussion. The minister in the anecdote was surprised that the prime minister new detailed aspects of the annex items in question that day in Cabinet.
36 See Clark (2009) and Macdonald (2009). Interviews with Guy Giorno and other senior PMO partisan advisers made clear that Mr Lynch favoured a centralized PCO approach. Both senior PMO and PCO respondents consulted described his preference for PMO-PCO interactions to be run strictly through his office.

Chapter 4

37 Consultation with multiple senior partisan advisers from the Chrétien and Martin PMOs (Tim Murphy, P31, P32, P33).

Chapter 5

38 It should be noted there is a distinct tolerance of senior appointment politicization in some provinces, including New Brunswick. Many respondents noted that some deputy minister appointments were considered "political," and this was widely understood by both political and public service elites. For instance, with some senior deputy minister appointments, changing with the election of a new government (see CBC 2014).

Chapter 6

39 These include ministers and their staff, deputies, as well as PMO and PCO staff. These meetings were, however, reported to be rare. More typically, like in all the other cases in this study, horizontal administrative-technical moving would be coordinated through their counterparts in the respective ministerial office.

Chapter 7

40 The one exception was the minister of health's office that later employed two ministerial assistants.

41 Vertical specialization is meant to denote "differentiation of responsibility on hierarchical levels describing how political and administrative tasks and authority are allocated between forms and affiliations" (Bezes et al. 2013, 4). Horizontal specialization implies "how tasks and authorities are allocated between organizations at the same hierarchical level, for example between ministerial areas" (ibid.).

References

Aberbach, J.D., and B.A. Rockman. 1994. Civil Servants and Policymakers: Neutral or Responsive Competence? *Governance* 7 (4): 461–9. http://dx.doi. org/10.1111/j.1468-0491.1994.tb00192.x.

Althaus, C. 2008. *Calculating Political Risk*. Sydney: University of New South Wales Press.

Althaus, C., P. Bridgman, and G. Davis. 2013. *The Australian Policy Handbook*. Sydney: Allen & Unwin Australia.

Anderson, G. 2006. Ministerial Staff: New Players in the Policy Game. In *Beyond the Policy Cycle: The Policy Process in Australia*, ed. H.K. Colebatch, 166–83. Sydney: Allen & Unwin.

Andrews, R., G.A. Boyne, K.J. Meier, L.J. O'Toole, Jr, and R.M. Walker. 2012. Vertical Strategic Alignment and Public Service Performance. *Public Administration* 90 (1): 77–98. http://dx.doi. org/10.1111/j.1467-9299.2011.01938.x.

Aucoin, P. 1986. Organizational Change in the Machinery of Canadian Government: From Rational Management to Brokerage Politics. *Canadian Journal of Political Science / Revue canadienne de science politique* 19 (1): 3–27.

———. 1990. Administrative Reform in Public Management: Paradigms, Principles, Paradoxes and Pendulums. *Governance* 3 (2): 115–37. http:// dx.doi.org/10.1111/j.1468-0491.1990.tb00111.x.

———. 1991. Cabinet Government in Canada: Corporate Management of a Confederal Executive. In *Executive Leadership in Anglo-American Systems*, ed. S.J. Campbell and M.J. Wyszomirski, 139-160. Pittsburgh: University of Pittsburgh Press.

———. 1995a. *The New Public Management: Canada in Comparative Perspective*. Montreal and Kingston: McGill-Queen's University Press.

———. 1995b. Politicians, Public Servants, and Public Management: Getting Government Right. In Peters and Savoie 2000, 138–72.

―――. 2008a. New Public Management and New Public Governance: Finding the Balance. In *Professionalism and Public Service: Essays in Honour of Kenneth Kernaghan*, ed. D. Siegel and K. Rasmussen, 16–35. Toronto: University of Toronto Press.

―――. 2008b. New Public Management and the Quality of Government: Coping with the New Political Governance in Canada. Paper presented at conference entitled "New Public Management and the Quality of Government," Structure and Organization Government and the Quality of Government Institute, University of Gothenburg, Sweden, 13–15 November.

―――. 2010. Canada. In *Partisan Appointees and Public Servants: An International Analysis of the Role of the Political Adviser*, ed. C. Eichbaum and R. Shaw, 64–93. Boston: Edward Elgar. http://dx.doi.org/10.4337/9781849803298.00008.

―――. 2012. New Political Governance in Westminster Systems: Impartial Public Administration and Management Performance at Risk. *Governance* 25 (2): 177–199. http://dx.doi.org/10.1111/j.1468-0491.2012.01569.x.

Aucoin, P., M. Jarvis, and L. Turnbull. 2011. *Democratizing the Constitution: Reforming Responsible Government*. Toronto: Emond.

Aucoin, P., and D.J. Savoie. 2009. The Politics-Administration Dichotomy: Democracy versus Bureaucracy? In *The Evolving Physiology of Government: Canadian Public Administration in Transition*, ed. O.P. Dwivedi, B.M. Sheldrick, and T.A. Mau, 97–117. Ottawa: University of Ottawa Press.

Axworthy, T. 1988. Of Secretaries to Princes. *Canadian Public Administration* 31 (2): 247–64. http://dx.doi.org/10.1111/j.1754-7121.1988.tb01316.x.

Baccigalupo, A. 1973. Vie administrative à l'étranger: Les cabinets ministériels dans l'administration publique québécoise. *Revista ADM* 26 (153): 317–19, 321–5, 327–8.

Bakvis, H. 1988. *Regional Ministers: Power and Influence in the Canadian Cabinet*. Toronto: University of Toronto Press.

―――. 1989. Regional Politics and Policy in the Mulroney Cabinet, 1984–88: Towards a Theory of the Regional Minister System in Canada. *Canadian Public Policy / Analyse de Politiques* 15 (2): 121–34.

―――. 1991. *Regional Ministers: Power and Influence in the Canadian Cabinet*. Toronto: University of Toronto Press.

―――. 1997. Advising the Executive: Think Tanks, Consultants, Political Staff and Kitchen Cabinets. In *The Hollow Crown: Countervailing Trends in Core Executives*, ed. P. Weller, H. Bakvis, and R.A.W. Rhodes, 84–125. Basingstoke, UK: Macmillan.

―――. 2000. Rebuilding Policy Capacity in the Era of Fiscal Dividend: A Report from Canada. *Governance* 13 (1): 71–103. http://dx.doi.org/10.1111/0952-1895.00124.

———. 2001. Prime Minister and Cabinet in Canada: An Autocracy in Need of Reform? *Journal of Canadian Studies / Revue d'Études Canadiennes* 35 (4): 60–79.

Bakvis, H., and Jarvis, M.D., eds. 2012. *From New Public Management to New Political Governance: Essays in Honour of Peter C. Aucoin.* Montreal and Kingston: McGill-Queen's University Press.

Bakvis, H., and L. Julliet. 2004. *The Horizontal Challenge: Line Departments, Central Agencies and Leadership.* Ottawa: Canada School of Public Service.

Bakvis, H., and S.B. Wolinetz. 2005. Canada: Executive Dominance and Presidentialization. In *The Presidentialization of Politics: A Comparative Study of Modern Democracies,* ed. T. Poguntke and P. Webb, 199–220. Oxford: Oxford University Press. http://dx.doi.org/10.1093/0199252017.003.0009.

Bardach, E. 2009. *A Practical Guide for Policy Analysis.* Washington: CQ.

Benoit, L. 2006. Ministerial Staff: The Life and Times of Parliament's Statutory Orphans. In *Commission of Inquiry into the Sponsorship Program and Advertising Activities, Restoring Accountability, Research Studies* 1:145–252. Ottawa: Public Works and Government Services Canada.

Bernier, L., K. Brownsey, and M. Howlett, eds. 2005. *Executive Styles in Canada: Cabinet Structures and Leadership Practices in Canadian Government Institute of Public Administration of Canada.* Toronto: University of Toronto Press.

Bevir, M. and R.A.W. Rhodes. 2006. Interpretive Approaches to British Government and Politics. *British Politics* 1:84–112.

Bezes, P., A.L. Fimreite, P. Le Lidec, and P. Lægreid. 2013. Understanding Organizational Reforms in the Modern State: Specialization and Integration in Norway and France. *Governance* 26 (1): 147–75. http://dx.doi.org/10.1111/j.1468-0491.2012.01608.x.

Bingham, L.B., T. Nabatchi, and R. O'Leary. 2005. The New Governance: Practices and Processes for Stakeholder and Citizen Participation in the Work of Government. *Public Administration Review* 65 (5): 547–58. http://dx.doi.org/10.1111/j.1540-6210.2005.00482.x.

Birkland, T. 2001. *An Introduction to the Policy Process: Theories, Concepts, and Models of Public Policy Making.* New York: M.E. Sharpe.

Boston, J., and J.R. Nethercote. 2012. Reflections on "New Political Governance in Westminster Systems." *Governance* 25 (2): 201–7. http://dx.doi.org/10.1111/j.1468-0491.2012.01568.x.

Bouchard, G. 1999. Les sous-ministres du Nouveau-Brunswick: de l'ère des technicians à l'ère des gestionnaires. *Canadian Public Administration* 42 (1): 93–107. http://dx.doi.org/10.1111/j.1754-7121.1999.tb01549.x.

———. 2014. New Brunswick's Deputy Ministers: Out of the Ordinary and Close to the Premier. In *Deputy Ministers in Canada: Comparative and*

Jurisdictional Perspectives, ed. J. Bougault and C. Dunn, 100–22. Toronto: University of Toronto Press.

Bouckaert, G., B.G. Peters, and K. Verhoest. 2010. *The Coordination of Public Sector Organizations: Shifting Patterns of Public Management.* Basingstoke, UK: Palgrave Macmillan. http://dx.doi.org/10.1057/9780230275256.

Bourgault, J. 2002. The Role of Deputy Ministers in Canadian Government. In *The Handbook of Canadian Public Administration,* ed. C. Dunn, 430–49. Toronto: Oxford University Press.

Bourgault, J., and C. Dunn. 2012. Deputy Ministers and Policy Advice in Times of a Conservative Government in Canada. Paper presented at International Political Science Association Annual Conference, 8–12 July, Madrid.

———. 2014. *Deputy Ministers in Canada: Comparative and Jurisdictional Perspectives.* Toronto: University of Toronto Press.

Brady, H.E., and D. Collier. 2004. *Rethinking Social Inquiry: Diverse Tools, Shared Standards.* Lanham, MD: Rowman and Littlefield.

Brans, M., C. Pelgrims, and D. Hoet. 2006. Comparative Observations on Tensions between Professional Policy Advice and Political Control in the Low Countries. *International Review of Administrative Sciences* 72 (1): 57–71. http://dx.doi.org/10.1177/0020852306061617.

Brodie, I. 2012. *In Defence of Political Staff: The 2012 Tansley Lecture.* Regina, SK: Johnson-Shoyama Graduate School of Public Policy.

Brown, M. 2012. Towards a New Government. In *Towards a New Government in British Columbia.* http://www.amazon.ca/Towards-New-Government-British-Columbia-ebook/dp/B009033J10.

Burney, D. 2005. *Getting It Done.* Montreal and Kingston: McGill-Queen's University Press.

Campbell, C. 1988. The Political Roles of Senior Government Officials in Advanced Democracies. *British Journal of Political Science* 18 (2): 243–72. http://dx.doi.org/10.1017/S0007123400005081.

———. 2007. Spontaneous Adaptation in Public Management: An Overview. *Governance* 20 (3): 377–400. http://dx.doi.org/10.1111/j.1468-0491.2007.00363.x.

Campbell, C.J., and B.G. Peters. 1988. The Politics/Administration Dichotomy: Death or Merely Change? *Governance* 1 (1): 79–99. http://dx.doi.org/10.1111/j.1468-0491.1988.tb00060.x.

Campbell, C., and G.J. Szablowski. 1979. *The Superbureaucrats: Structure and Behaviour in Central Agencies.* Toronto: Macmillan of Canada.

Campbell, C., and G.K. Wilson. 1995. *The End of Whitehall: Death of a Paradigm?* Oxford: Blackwell.

Canada. 2011. (Information Commissioner) v Canada (Minister of National Defence). SCC 25, 2 SCR 306.

CBC News. 2013. PMO Asked Staff to Supply "Enemy" Lists to New Ministers. 16 July. http://www.cbc.ca/news/politics/pmo-asked-staff-to-supply-enemy-lists-to-new-ministers-1.1361102.

———. 2014. David Alward's Tory Deputy Ministers Face Unclear Future: Invest NB's Robert MacLeod, Efficiency NB's Margaret-Ann Blaney Will Be Laid Off, Brian Gallant Say. 3 October. http://www.cbc.ca/news/canada/new-brunswick/david-alward-s-tory-deputy-ministers-face-unclear-future-1.2786369.

Carson, B. 2014. *14 Days: Making the Conservative Movement in Canada.* Montreal and Kingston: McGill-Queen's University Press.

Clark, C. 2009. Workaholic Out, "Mechanic" In at Privy Council. *Globe and Mail,* 8 May.

Colebatch, H.K. 1998. *Policy.* Buckingham: Open University Press.

———. 2006. What Work Makes Policy? *Policy Sciences* 39 (4): 309–21. http://dx.doi.org/10.1007/s11077-006-9025-4.

Colebatch, H.K, R. Hoppe, and Mirko Noordegraaf. 2010a. Understanding Policy Work. In *Working for Policy,* ed. H.K. Colebatch, R. Hoppe, and M. Noordegraaf, 11–30. Amsterdam: Amsterdam University Press.

———, eds. 2010b. *Working for Policy.* Amsterdam: Amsterdam University Press.

Connaughton, B. 2010a. "Glorified Gofers, Policy Experts or Good Generalists": A Classification of the Roles of the Irish Ministerial Adviser. *Irish Political Studies* 25 (3): 347–69. http://dx.doi.org/10.1080/07907184.2010.497636.

———. 2010b. "Minding" the Minister: Conceptualising the Role of the Special Adviser in Ireland. *Administration* 58 (1): 55–76.

Conteh, C. and I. Roberge. 2013. *Canadian Public Administration in the 21st Century.* Boca Raton, FL: CRC. http://dx.doi.org/10.1201/b15343.

Craft, J. 2013. Appointed Political Staffs and the Diversification of Policy Advisory Sources: Theory and Evidence from Canada. *Policy and Society* 32 (3): 211–23. http://dx.doi.org/10.1016/j.polsoc.2013.07.003.

———. 2014. Policy Advice and New Political Governance: Revisiting the Orthodox. In *Canadian Public Administration in the 21st Century,* ed. Roberge and Conteh, 41–59. Boca Raton: CRC.

———. 2015a. Conceptualizing Partisan Advisers as Policy Workers. *Policy Sciences Journal* 48 (2): 135–58.

———. 2015b. Revisiting the Gospel: Appointed Political Staffs and Core Executive Policy Coordination. *International Journal of Public Administration* 38 (1): 56–65. http://dx.doi.org/10.1080/01900692.2014.928316.

Craft, J., and M. Howlett. 2012. Policy Formulation, Governance Shifts and Policy Influence: Location and Content in Policy Advisory Systems. *Journal of Public Policy* 32 (2): 79–98. http://dx.doi.org/10.1017/S0143814X12000049.

———. 2013. The Dual Dynamics of Policy Advisory Systems: The Impact of Externalization and Politicization on Policy Advice. *Policy and Society* 32 (3): 187–97. http://dx.doi.org/10.1016/j.polsoc.2013.07.001.

Dahlström, C., B.G. Peters, and J. Pierre. 2011. *Steering from the Centre: Strengthening Political Control in Western Democracies*. Toronto: University of Toronto Press.

Dawson, M. 1922. *The Principle of Official Independence*. London: S. King and Son.

D'Aquino, T. 1974. The Prime Minister's Office: Catalyst or Cabal? Aspects of the Development of the Office in Canada and Some Thoughts about Its Future. *Canadian Public Administration* 17 (1): 55–79. http://dx.doi.org/10.1111/j.1754-7121.1974.tb01655.x.

Davis, J. 2010. PMO Budget Largely Stable since 1975. *Hill Times*, 8 February.

Di Francesco, M. 2000. An Evaluation Crucible: Evaluating Policy Advice in Australian Central Agencies. *Australian Journal of Public Administration* 59 (1): 36–49.

———. 2002. Process Not Outcomes in New Public Management? Policy Coherence in Australian Government. *Australian Review of Public Affairs* 1 (3): 103–16.

Dobuzinskis, L., M. Howlett, and D. Laycock, eds. 2007. *Policy Analysis in Canada: The State of the Art*. Toronto: University of Toronto Press.

Doern, G.B. 1971. The Development of Policy Organization in the Executive Arena. In *The Structures of Policy-making in Canada*, ed. G.B. Doern and P. Aucoin, 38–78. Toronto: Macmillan of Canada.

Doern, G.B., and R.W. Phidd. 1992. *Canadian Public Policy: Ideas, Structure, Process*, 2nd ed. Scarborough, ON: Nelson Canada.

Doyle, Arthur T. 1984. *The Premiers of New Brunswick*. Fredericton: Brunswick.

Dunleavy, P., and R.A.W. Rhodes. 1990. Core Executive Studies in Britain. *Public Administration* 68 (1): 3–28.

Dunn, C. 1995. *The Institutionalized Cabinet: Governing the Western Provinces*. Montreal and Kingston: McGill-Queen's University Press.

———. 2006. Premiers and Cabinets. In *Provinces: Canadian Provincial Politics*, ed. C. Dunn, 2nd ed., 215–44. Peterborough, ON: Broadview.

———. 2010. The Central Executive in Canadian Government: Searching for the Holy Grail. In *The Handbook of Canadian Public Administration*, ed. C. Dunn, 2nd ed., 85–105. Don Mills, ON: Oxford University Press.

Dunn, C., and J. Bourgault, eds. 2014. *Deputy Ministers in Canada: Comparative and Jurisdictional Perspectives.* Toronto: IPAC / University of Toronto Press.

Dutil, P. 2006. *Working with Political Staff at Queen's Park: Trends, Outlooks, Opportunities.* Toronto: Institute of Public Administration of Canada.

Duverger, M. 1965. *Political Parties: Their Organization and Activity in the Modern State*, 2nd ed. New York: Wiley.

Eichbaum, C., and R. Shaw. 2007a. Ministerial Advisers and the Politics of Policy-making: Bureaucratic Permanence and Popular Control. *Australian Journal of Public Administration* 66 (4): 453–67. http://dx.doi.org/10.1111/j.1467-8500.2007.00556.x.

——. 2007b. Ministerial Advisers, Politicization and the Retreat from Westminster: The Case of New Zealand. *Public Administration* 85 (3): 609–40. http://dx.doi.org/10.1111/j.1467-9299.2007.00666.x.

——. 2008. Revisiting Politicization: Political Advisers and Public Servants in Westminster Systems. *Governance* 21 (3): 337–63. http://dx.doi.org/10.1111/j.1468-0491.2008.00403.x.

——, eds. 2010. *Partisan Appointees and Public Servants: An International Analysis of the Role of the Political adviser.* Cheltenham, UK: Edward Elgar. http://dx.doi.org/10.4337/9781849803298.

——. 2011. Political Staff in Executive Government: Conceptualising and Mapping Roles within the Core Executive. *Australian Journal of Political Science* 46 (4): 583–600. http://dx.doi.org/10.1080/10361146.2011.623668.

Elgie, R. 1997. Models of Executive Politics: A Framework for the Study of Executive Power Relations in Parliamentary and Semi-Presidential Regimes. *Political Studies* 45 (2): 217–31.

——. 2011. Core Executive Studies Two Decades On. *Public Administration* 89 (1): 64–77.

Esselment, A.L. 2009. Family Matters: The Role of Partisanship in Federal-Provincial Relations in Canada. PhD diss., University of Western Ontario, London, ON.

Esselment, A.L., J. Lees-Marshment, and A. Marland. 2014. The Nature of Political Advising to Prime Ministers in Australia, Canada, New Zealand and the UK. *Commonwealth & Comparative Politics* 52 (3): 358–75.

Evetts, J. 2003a. The Construction of Professionalism in New and Existing Occupational Contexts: Promoting and Facilitating Occupational Change. *International Journal of Sociology and Social Policy* 23 (4/5): 22–35. http://dx.doi.org/10.1108/01443330310790499.

——. 2003b. The Sociological Analysis of Professionalism: Occupational Change in the Modern World. *International Sociology* 18 (2): 395–415. http://dx.doi.org/10.1177/0268580903018002005.

Fawcett, P., and O. Gay. 2010. United Kingdom. In *Partisan Appointees and Public Servants: An International Analysis of the Role of the Political Adviser*, ed. C. Eichbaum and R. Shaw, 24–63. Cheltenham, UK: Edward Elgar. http://dx.doi.org/10.4337/9781849803298.00007.

Flemming, J. 1997. Le rôle de l'adjoint exécutif d'un ministre fédéral. *Optimum: La Revue de gestion du secteur public* 27 (2): 70–6.

French, R.D., and R. Van Loon. 1984. *How Ottawa Decides: Planning and Industrial Policy-making 1968–1984*, 2nd ed. Toronto: James Lorimer.

Gains, F., and G. Stoker. 2011. Special Advisers and the Transmission of Ideas from the Policy Primeval Soup. *Policy and Politics* 39 (4): 485–98. http://dx.doi.org/10.1332/030557310X550169.

Giorno, G. 2009. *Response from the Prime Minister's Office to "Who Is Getting the Message," Report by Paul G. Thomas, Office of the Prime Minister*. Ottawa: Government of Canada.

Goldenberg, E. 2006. *The Way It Works: Inside Ottawa*. Toronto: McClelland & Stewart.

Goldhamer, H. 1978. *The Adviser*. New York: Elsevier.

Good, D.A. 2003. *The Politics of Public Management: The HRDC Audit of Grants and Contributions*. Toronto: University of Toronto Press.

Gow, I.J. 2004. *A Canadian Model of Public Administration?* Ottawa: Canada School of Public Service.

Granatstein, J.L. 1982. *The Ottawa Men: The Civil Service Mandarins, 1935–1957*. Toronto: Oxford University Press.

Halligan, J. 1995. Policy Advice and the Public Service. In *Governance in a Changing Environment*, ed. B.G. Peters and D.J. Savoie, 138–72. Montreal and Kingston: Canadian Centre for Management Development and McGill-Queen's University Press.

Hamburger, P., B. Stevens, and P. Weller. 2011. A Capacity for Central Coordination: The Case of the Department of the Prime Minister and Cabinet. *Australian Journal of Public Administration* 70 (4): 377–90. http://dx.doi.org/10.1111/j.1467-8500.2011.00739.x.

Head, B.W. 2008. The Three Lenses of Evidence-Based Policy. *Australian Journal of Public Administration* 67 (1): 1–11. http://dx.doi.org/10.1111/j.1467-8500.2007.00564.x.

Heclo, H., and A. Wildavsky. 1974. *Private Government of Public Money*. Berkeley: University of California Press.

Heffernan, R. 2003. Prime Ministerial Predominance? Core Executive Politics in the UK. *British Journal of Politics and International Relations* 5 (3): 347–72. http://dx.doi.org/10.1111/1467-856X.00110.

Hill, M. 2012. *The Public Policy Process*, 6th ed. London: Routledge

Hood, C. 2000. Relationships between Ministers/Politicians and Public Servants: Public Service Bargains Old and New. In *Governance in the Twenty-First Century: Revitalizing the Public Service*, ed. B.G. Peters and D.J. Savoie, 178–206. Montreal and Kingston: Canadian Centre for Management Development / McGill-Queen's University Press.

———. 2002a. Control, Bargains, and Cheating: The Politics of Public-Service Reform. *Journal of Public Administration: Research and Theory* 12 (3): 309–32. http://dx.doi.org/10.1093/oxfordjournals.jpart.a003536.

———. 2002b. The Risk Game and the Blame Game. *Government and Opposition* 37 (1): 15–37. http://dx.doi.org/10.1111/1477-7053.00085.

———. 2010. *The Blame Game: Spin, Bureaucracy, and Self-Preservation in Government*. Princeton: Princeton University Press. http://dx.doi.org/10.1515/9781400836819.

Hoppe, R. 1999. Policy Analysis, Science and Politics: From "Speaking Truth to Power" to "Making Sense Together." *Science & Public Policy* 26 (3): 201–10.

Howlett, M. 2000. Managing the "Hollow State": Procedural Policy Instruments and Modern Governance. *Canadian Public Administration* 43 (4): 412–31. http://dx.doi.org/10.1111/j.1754-7121.2000.tb01152.x.

———. 2011. *Designing Public Policy: Principles and Instruments*. New York: Routledge.

———. 2012. The Lessons of Failure: Learning and Blame Avoidance in Public Policy-making. *International Political Science Review* 33 (5): 539–55.

Howlett, M., and B. Cashore. 2014. Conceptualizing Public Policy. In *Comparative Policy Studies: Conceptual and Methodological Challenges*, ed. I. Engeli and C. Rothmayr, 17–34. Colchester, UK: ECPR.

Howlett, M., A. Perl, and M. Ramesh. 2009. *Studying Public Policy: Policy Cycles and Policy Subsystems*, 3rd ed. Toronto: Oxford University Press.

Howlett, M., and M. Ramesh. 1998. Policy Subsystem Configurations and Policy Change: Operationalizing the Postpositivist Analysis of the Politics of the Policy Process. *Policy Studies Journal* 26 (3): 466–81. http://dx.doi.org/10.1111/j.1541-0072.1998.tb01913.x.

———. 2014. The Two Orders of Governance Failure: Design Mismatches and Policy Capacity Issues in Modern Governance. *Policy and Society* 33 (4): 317–27.

Howlett, M., S. Tan, A. Migone, A. Wellstead, and B. Evans. 2014. The Distribution of Analytical Techniques in Policy Advisory Systems: Policy Formulation and the Tools of Policy Appraisal. *Public Policy and Administration* 29 (4): 271–91.

Howlett, M., and A. Wellstead. 2011. Policy Analysts in the Bureaucracy Revisited: The Nature of Professional Policy Work in Contemporary Government. *Politics & Policy* 39 (4): 613–33.

Hyson, S. 2005. Governing from the Centre in New Brunswick. In *Executive Styles in Canada: Cabinet Structures and Leadership Practices in Canadian Government*, ed. L. Bernier, K. Brownsey, and M. Howlett, 75–90. Toronto: University of Toronto Press.

Ivision, J. 2012. Conservative Backbench Has Lost Its Fear of Stephen Harper. *National Post*, 2 October.

Jann, W., and K. Wegrich. 2007. Theories of the Policy Cycle. In *Handbook of Public Policy Analysis: Theory, Politics and Methods*, ed. F. Fischer, G.J. Miller and, M. S. Sidney, 43–62. Boca Raton: CRC.

Jeffrey, B. 1978. *A Comparison of the Role of the Minister's Office in France, Britain and Canada*. Ottawa: Research Branch, Library of Parliament. Canada.

–––––. 2010. *Divided Loyalties: The Liberal Party of Canada, 1984–2008*. Toronto: University of Toronto Press.

Jordan, A.J., and J.R. Turnpenny, eds. 2015. *The Tools of Policy Formulation: Actors, Capacities, Venues and Effects*. Cheltenham, UK: Edward Elgar. http://dx.doi.org/10.4337/9781783477043.

Kaufman, Herbert. 1956. Emerging Conflicts in the Doctrines of Public Administration. *American Political Science Review* 50 (4): 1057–73.

Kellermanns, F.W., J. Walter, C. Lechner, and S.W. Floyd. 2005. The Lack of Consensus about Strategic Consensus: Advancing Theory and Research. *Journal of Management* 31 (5): 719–37. http://dx.doi.org/10.1177/0149206305279114.

Kemp, D.A. 1986. The Recent Evolution of Central Political Control Mechanisms in Parliamentary Systems. *International Political Science Review* 7 (1): 56–66. http://dx.doi.org/10.1177/019251218600700106.

Kernaghan, K. 1986. Political Rights and Political Neutrality: Finding the Balance Point. *Canadian Public Administration* 29 (4): 639–52. http://dx.doi.org/10.1111/j.1754-7121.1986.tb00205.x.

Kernaghan, K., and D. Siegel. 1995. *Public Administration in Canada*, 3rd ed. Scarborough, ON: Nelson Canada.

King, S. 2003. *Regulating the Behaviour of Ministers, Special Advisers and Civil Servants*. London: Constitution Unit, School of Public Policy, University College London.

Krause, G.A. 1996. The Institutional Dynamics of Policy Administration: Bureaucratic Influence over Securities Regulation. *American Journal of Political Science* 40 (4): 1083–1121. http://dx.doi.org/10.2307/2111744.

————. 1999. *A Two-Way Street: The Institutional Dynamics of the Modern Administrative State*. Pittsburgh: University of Pittsburgh Press.

Lægreid, P., and K. Verhoest, eds. 2010. *Governance of Public Sector Organizations: Proliferation, Autonomy and Performance*. London: Palgrave Macmillan. http://dx.doi.org/10.1057/9780230290600.

Lalonde, M. 1971. The Changing Role of the Prime Minister's Office. *Canadian Public Administration* 14 (4): 509–37. http://dx.doi.org/10.1111/j.1754-7121.1971.tb00296.x.

Larson, P. 1999. The Canadian Experience. In *Redefining Management Roles: Improving the Functional Relationship between Ministers and Permanent Secretaries*, ed. S. Agere, 55–74. Toronto: University of Toronto Press / Commonwealth Association for Public Administration and Management.

Laswell, H. 1971. *A Pre-view of the Policy Sciences*. New York: American Elsevier.

Lee, W.M. 1971. The Executive Function: A Ministerial Assistant's View. *Quarterly of Canadian Studies* 1 (1): 141–4.

Lenoski, G. 1977. Ministerial Staffs and Leadership Politics. In *Apex of Power*, 2nd ed., ed. T.A. Hockin, 165–75. Scarborough, ON: Prentice Hall.

Lewis, J.P. 2013. Elite Attitudes on the Centralization of Power in Canadian Political Executives: A Survey of Former Canadian Provincial and Federal Cabinet Ministers, 2000–2010. *Canadian Journal of Political Science* 46 (4): 799–819. http://dx.doi.org/10.1017/S0008423913000905.

Lindblom, C. 1965. *The Intelligence of Democracy*. New York: Free Press.

Lindquist, E. 1998. A Quarter Century of Canadian Think Tanks: Evolving Institutions, Conditions, and Strategies. In *Think Tanks across Nations: A Comparative Approach*, ed. D. Stone, A. Denham, and M. Garnett, 127–44. Manchester: Manchester University Press.

Lindquist, E., and T. Vaskil. 2014. Government Transitions, Leadership Succession, and Executive Turnover in British Columbia, 1996–2006. In *Deputy Ministers in Canada: Comparative and Jurisdictional Perspectives*, ed. J. Bourgault and C. Dunn, 283-308. Toronto: University of Toronto Press.

Lodge, M. 2010. Public Service Bargains in British Central Government: Multiplication, Diversification and Reassertion? In *Traditions and Public Administration*, ed. M. Painter and B.G. Peters, 99–113. New York: Palgrave Macmillan.

LSE GV314 Group. 2012. New Life at the Top: Special Advisers in British Government. *Parliamentary Affairs* 65 (4): 1–18.

Macdonald, L.I. 2009. A Palace Coup in the PMO. *National Post*, 8 May.

MacRae, D., Jr, and D. Whittington. 1997. *Expert Advice for Policy Choice: Analysis and Discourse*. Washington, DC: Georgetown University Press.

Majone, G. 1975. On the Notion of Political Feasibility. *European Journal of Political Research* 3 (3): 259–74. http://dx.doi.org/10.1111/j.1475-6765.1975.tb00780.x.

———. 1989. *Evidence, Argument and Persuasion in the Policy Process*. New Heaven, CT: Yale University Press.

Maley, M. 2015. The Policy Work of Australian Political Staff. *International Journal of Public Administration* 38 (1): 46–55.

———. 2000. Conceptualizing Advisers' Policy Work: The Distinctive Policy Roles of Ministerial Advisers in the Keating Government, 1991–96. *Australian Journal of Political Science*, 35 (3): 449–70. http://dx.doi.org/10.1080/713649346.

———. 2002. *Partisans at the Centre of Government: The Role of Ministerial Advisers in the Keating Government 1991–96*. Unpublished thesis, School of Social Sciences, Australia National University.

———. 2011. Strategic Links in a Cut-Throat World: Rethinking the Role and Relationships of Australian Ministerial Staff. *Public Administration* 89 (4): 1469–88. http://dx.doi.org/10.1111/j.1467-9299.2011.01928.x.

Mallory, J.R. 1967. The Minister's Office Staff: An Unreformed Part of the Public Service. *Canadian Public Administration* 10 (1): 25–34. http://dx.doi.org/10.1111/j.1754-7121.1967.tb00962.x.

———. 1984. *The Structure of Canadian Government*. Toronto: Gage Publishing.

Maltais, D., and M.E. Harvey. 2007. Les gestionnaires de l'ombre: Les directeurs de cabinets ministériels québécois. *Canadian Public Administration* 50 (1): 53–78. http://dx.doi.org/10.1111/j.1754-7121.2007.tb02003.x.

Marley, D.O. 1997. Life in the Shadows: Political Exempt Staff in Canadian Cabinet Government. Master of Business Major Research Project, University of British Columbia.

Marsh, D., D. Richards, and M. Smith. 2003. Unequal Plurality: Towards an Asymmetric Power Model of British Politics. *Government and Opposition* 38 (3): 306–32.

Martin, L. 2006. Ottawa's "Bubble Boy" Is Courting Conflict. *The Globe and Mail*, March 20, 2006. http://www.theglobeandmail.com/globe-debate/ottawas-bubble-boy-is-courting-conflict/article1097026/.

———. 2010. *Harperland: The Politics of Control*. Toronto: Viking.

Matheson, G. 2000. Policy Formulation in Australian Government: Vertical and Horizontal Axes. *Australian Journal of Public Administration* 59 (2): 44–5.

May, P.J. 1981. Hints for Crafting Alternative Policies. *Policy Analysis* 7 (2): 227–44.

———. 2005. Policy Maps and Political Feasibility. In *Thinking like a Policy Analyst: Policy Analysis as a Clinical Profession*, ed. I. Geva-May, 127–51. London: Palgrave Macmillan.

McConnell, A. 2010a. Policy Success, Policy Failure and Grey Areas In-Between. *Journal of Public Policy* 30 (3): 345–62. http://dx.doi.org/10.1017/S0143814X10000152.

———. 2010b. *Understanding Policy Success: Rethinking Public Policy.* New York: Palgrave Macmillan.

Meyer, M.W. 1987. The Growth of Public and Private Bureaucracies. *Theory and Society* 16 (2): 215–35. http://dx.doi.org/10.1007/BF00135695.

Miljan, L. 2008. *Public Policy in Canada: An Introduction.* 5th ed. Toronto: Oxford University Press.

Moe, T.M. 1989. The Politics of Bureaucratic Structure. In *Can the Government Govern?* ed. John Chubb and Paul Peterson, 267–329. Washington, DC: Brookings.

Montpetit, É. 2011. Between Detachment and Responsiveness: Civil Servants in Europe and North America. *West European Politics* 34 (6): 1250–71.

Morley, T.J. 1993. From Bill Vander Zalm to Mike Harcourt: Government Transitions in British Columbia. In *Taking Power: Managing Government Transitions*, ed. D.J. Savoie and J. Bourgault, 187–212. Toronto: Institute of Public Administration of Canada, Canadian Centre for Management Development.

Öberg, P., M. Lundin, and J. Thelander. 2015. Political Power and Policy Design: Why Are Policy Alternatives Constrained? *Policy Studies Journal*, 43 (1): 93–114. http://dx.doi.org/10.1111/psj.12086.

O'Connor, L.J. 1991. Chief of Staff. *Policy Options* 12 (3): 23–6

OECD. 2007. Political Advisors and Civil Servants in European Countries. SIGMA Paper no. 38, GOV/SIGMA(2007)2/REV1. Paris: OECD.

———. 2011. *Ministerial Advisers: Role, Influence and Management.* Paris: OECD.

Office of the Premier. 2002. *2001/02 Annual Report: A New Era Update.* Victoria: Government of British Columbia. http://www.bcbudget.gov.bc.ca/Annual_Reports/2001_2002/premier.pdf.

———. 2006a. Backgrounder: New Compensation Framework Announced for Senior Political Staff. News release, 21 July. http://www2.news.gov.bc.ca/news_releases_2005-2009/2006OTP0129-000973-Attachment1.htm.

———. 2006b. New Compensation Framework Announced for Senior Political Staff. News release, 21 July. http://www2.news.gov.bc.ca/news_releases_2005-2009/2006OTP0129-000973.htm.

———. 2010. *2010/11–2011/12 Service Plan, Office of the Premier.* Victoria: Government of British Columbia.

O'Malley, E. 2007. The Power of Prime Ministers: Results of an Expert Survey. *International Political Science Review* 28 (1): 7–27. http://dx.doi.org/10.1177/0192512107070398.

Osbaldeston, G. 1987. The Public Servant and Politics. *Policy Options* 8 (1): 3–7.

Osborne, S. 2006. The New Public Governance? *Public Management Review* 8 (3): 377–87. http://dx.doi.org/10.1080/14719030600853022.

Overeem, P. 2005. The Value of the Dichotomy: Politics, Administration, and the Political Neutrality of Administrators. *Administrative Theory & Praxis* 27 (2): 311–29.

Page, E.C. 2010. Bureaucrats and Expertise: Elucidating a Problematic Relationship in Three Tableaux and Six Jurisdictions. *Sociologie du Travail* 52 (2): 255–73.

Parsons, W. 2004. Not Just Steering but Weaving: Relevant Knowledge and the Craft of Building Policy Capacity and Coherence. *Australian Journal of Public Administration* 63 (1): 43–57. http://dx.doi.org/10.1111/j.1467-8500.2004.00358.x.

Peach, I. 2004. *Managing Complexity: The Lessons of Horizontal Policy-making in the Provinces. Saskatchewan Institute for Public Policy.* http://www.schoolof publicpolicy.sk.ca/_documents/_outreach_event_announcements/SIPP_ archived_publications/the_scholar_series/Peach_ScholarSeries.pdf.

Peters, B.G. 1987. Politicians and Bureaucrats in the Politics of Policy-making. In *Bureaucracy and Public Choice*, ed. J. Lane, 255–82. New York: Sage.

———. 1998. Managing Horizontal Government: The Politics of Coordination. Research Paper no. 21. Ottawa: Canadian Centre for Management Development, Minister of Supply and Services Canada.

———. 2001. *The Politics of Bureaucracy*. 5th ed. New York: Routledge.

Peters, B.G., and A. Barker. 1993. *Advising West European Governments: Inquiries, Expertise and Public Policy.* Edinburgh: Edinburgh University Press.

Peters, B.G., and D.J. Savoie. 1994. Civil Service Reform: Misdiagnosing the Patient. *Public Administration Review* 54 (5): 418–25.

Peters, B.G., and J. Pierre, eds. 2004. *Politicization of the Civil Service in Comparative Perspective: The Quest for Control.* New York: Routledge.

Peters, B.G., R.A.W. Rhodes, and V. Wright. 2000. Staffing the Summit – The Administration of the Core Executive: Convergent Trends and National Specificities. In *Administering the Summit: Administration of the Core Executive in Developed Countries*, ed. B.G. Peters, R.A.W. Rhodes, and V. Wright, 3–22. Basingstoke, UK: Macmillan.

Peters, B.G., and D.J. Savoie. 2000a. Administering the Summit from a Canadian Perspective. In *Administering the Summit: Administration of the Core Executive in Developed Countries*, ed. B.G. Peters, R.A.W. Rhodes, and V. Wright, 43–58. Basingstoke, UK: Macmillan.

———. 2000b. *Governing in the Twenty-First Century: Revitalizing the Public Service.* Ottawa: Canadian Centre for Management Development.

Pickersgill, J.W. 1972. The W. Clifford Clark Memorial Lectures, 1972 (no 1): Bureaucrats and Politicians. *Canadian Public Administration* 15 (3): 418–27. http://dx.doi.org/10.1111/j.1754-7121.1972.tb01248.x.

Plassé, M. 1981. Les chefs de cabinets ministériels au Québec: La transition du gouvernement libéral au gouvernement péquiste (1976–1977). *Canadian Journal of Political Science / Revue canadienne de science politique* 14 (2): 309–35.

———. 1994. *Ministerial Chiefs of Staff in the Federal Government in 1990: Profiles, Recruitment, Duties, and Relations with Senior public Servants*. Ottawa: Canadian Centre for Management Development.

Plowden, W., ed. 1987. *Advising the Rulers*. Oxford: Basil Blackwell.

Plumptre, T. 1987. New Perspectives in the Role of the Deputy Minister. *Canadian Journal of Public Administration* 30 (3): 376–98.

Pollitt, C., and G. Bouckaert. 2011. *Public Management Reform: A Comparative Analysis*, 3rd ed. London: Oxford University Press.

Prasser, S. 2006. *Providing Advice to Government*. Papers on Parliament. Canberra: Senate of Australia. Accessed September 1, 2014. http://www.aph.gov.au/binaries/senate/pubs/pops/pop46/providing-advice.pdf.

Prince, M. 2007. Soft Craft, Hard Choices, Altered Context: Reflections on Twenty Five Years of Policy Advice in Canada. In *Policy Analysis in Canada: The State of the Art*, ed. L. Dobuzinskis, M. Howlett, and D. Laycock, 163–85. Toronto: University of Toronto Press.

Prince, M.J. 1983. *Policy Advice and Organizational Survival*. Aldershot: Gower.

Privy Council Office. 1960a. Cabinet Conclusion "Ministers' Staffs," meeting 12 October 1960, RG2, Privy Council Office, series A-5-a, vol. 2747, no. 20087, Library and Archives Canada.

———. 1960b. Cabinet Conclusion "Ministers' Staffs," meeting 17 October 1960, RG2, Privy Council Office, series A-5-a, vol. 2747, no. 20095, LAC.

———. 1965. Cabinet Conclusion "Exempt Staff from Minister's Offices," meeting 22 December 1965, RG2, Privy Council Office, series A-5-a, vol. 6271, no. 27213, LAC.

———. 1966. Cabinet Conclusion "Exempt Staff from Minister's Offices," meeting 13 October 1966, RG2, Privy Council Office, series A-5-a, vol. 6321, no. 29015, LAC.

———. 1967. Cabinet Conclusion "Exempt Staff from Minister's Offices: Staff of Minister of Justice," meeting 21 December 1967, RG2, Privy Council Office, series A-5-a, vol. 6323, Item no. 30141.

———. 1968a. *Manual of Official Procedure of the Government of Canada*. Ottawa: LAC.

———. 1968b. Cabinet Conclusion "Exempt Staff of Ministers' Offices," RG2, meeting 17 August 1968, RG2, Privy Council Office, series A-5-a, vol. 6338, no. 4561, LAC.

———. 1971. Cabinet Conclusion "Exempt Staff from Ministers' Offices," meeting 25 November 1971, RG2, Privy Council Office, series A-5-a, vol. 6381, LAC.

———. 1973. Cabinet Conclusion "Conflict of Interest: Public Servants, Order in Council Appointees and Exempt Staff," meeting 13 December 1973, RG2, Privy Council Office, series A-5-a, volume 6422, no. 38678, LAC.

———. 2011. *Accountable Government: A Guide for Ministers and Ministers of State*. Ottawa: Privy Council Office.

The Public Service Employment Act (SC 2003, c 22, ss 12, 13) 2003. http://laws-lois.justice.gc.ca/eng/acts/p-33.01/.

Pullen, K. 2014. With Friends Like Harper: How Nigel Wright Went from Golden Boy to Fall Guy. *Toronto Life*. http://www.torontolife.com/informer/features/2014/03/25/nigel-wright-golden-boy-to-fall-guy/.

Punnett, R.M. 1977. *The Prime Minister in Canadian Government and Politics*. Toronto: Macmillan of Canada.

Radin, B.A. 2000. *Beyond Machiavelli: Policy Analysis Comes of Age*. Washington, DC: Georgetown University Press.

Radwanski, G. 1978. *Trudeau*. Toronto: Macmillan of Canada.

Rhodes, R.A.W. 1995. From Prime Ministerial Power to Core Executive. In *Prime Minister, Cabinet and Core Executive*, ed. R.A.W. Rhodes and P. Dunleavy, 11–37. London: Macmillan.

———. 1997. The New Governance: Governing without Government. *Political Studies* 44 (4): 652–67. http://dx.doi.org/10.1111/j.1467-9248.1996.tb01747.x.

———. 2007. Understanding Governance: Ten Years On. *Organization Studies* 28 (12): 43–64.

Rhodes, R.A.W., and A. Tiernan. 2014. *The Prime Ministers' Gatekeepers*. Melbourne: Melbourne University Press.

———. 2015. Recovering the Craft of Public Administration. *Public Administration Review*. DOI: 10.1111/puar.12504.

Rhodes, R.A.W., and J. Wanna. 2007. The Limits to Public Value, or Rescuing Responsible Government from the Platonic Guardians. *Australian Journal of Public Administration* 66 (4): 406–21. http://dx.doi.org/10.1111/j.1467-8500.2007.00553.x.

Rhodes, R.A.W., J. Wanna, and P. Weller. 2010. *Comparing Westminster*. Oxford: Oxford University Press.

Rhodes, R.A.W., and P. Weller, eds. 2001. *The Changing World of Top Officials: Mandarins or Valets?* Buckingham, UK: Open University Press.

———. 2003. *Localism and Exceptionalism: Comparing Public Sector Reforms in European and Westminster Systems in Modernizing Civil Services,* ed. Boucher and Massey, 16–36. Cheltenham: Edward Elgar.

Robichau, R.W. 2011. The Mosaic of Governance: Creating a Picture with Definitions, Theories, and Debates. *Policy Studies Journal* 39:113–31. http://dx.doi.org/10.1111/j.1541-0072.2010.00389_8.x.

Rockman, B.A. 2000. Administering the Summit in the United States. In *Administering the Summit. Administration of the Core Executive in Developed Countries,* ed. G. Peters, R.W.A. Rhodes, and V. Wright. London: Palgrave Macmillan.

Rosenblum, N.L. 2008. *On the Side of the Angels: An Appreciation of Parties and Partisanship.* Princeton, NJ: Princeton University Press.

Ruff, N.J. 2005. The West Annex: Executive Structure and Administrative Style in British Columbia. In *Executive Styles in Canada: Cabinet Structures and Leadership Practices in Canadian government,* ed. L. Bernier, K. Brownsey, and M. Howlett, 225–41. Toronto: Institute of Public Administration of Canada / University of Toronto Press.

———. 2009. Executive Dominance: Cabinet and the Office of Premier in British Columbia. In *British Columbia Politics and Government,* ed. M. Howlett, D. Pilon, and T. Summerville, 205–16. Toronto: Emond Montgomery.

Sabatier, P.A. 2007. The Need for Better Theories. In *Theories of the Policy Process,* ed. P.A. Sabatier, 3–17. Boulder, CO: Westview.

Savoie, D.J. 1983. The Minister's Staff: The Need for Reform. *Canadian Public Administration* 26 (4): 509–24. http://dx.doi.org/10.1111/j.1754-7121.1983.tb01042.x.

———. 1989. Governing a "Have-Less" Province: Unraveling the New Brunswick Budget Process in the Hatfield Era. In *Budgeting in the Provinces: Leadership and the Premiers,* ed. A. Malsolve, 31–54. Toronto: Institute of Public Administration of Canada.

———. 1994. *Thatcher, Reagan, Mulroney: In Search of a New Bureaucracy.* Toronto: University of Toronto Press.

———. 1999a. *Governing from the Centre: The Concentration of Power in Canadian Politics.* Toronto: University of Toronto Press.

———. 1999b. The Rise of Court Government in Canada. *Canadian Journal of Political Science* 32 (4): 635–64. http://dx.doi.org/10.1017/S0008423900016930.

———. 2000. New Brunswick: A "Have" Public Service in a "Have-less" Province. In *Government Restructuring and Career Public Service,* ed. E. Lindquist, 260–84. Toronto: Institute of Public Administration of Canada.

———. 2003. *Breaking the Bargain: Public Servants, Ministers, and Parliament.* Toronto: IPAC /University of Toronto Press.

———. 2004a. The Search for a Responsive Bureaucracy in Canada. In *Politicization of the Civil Service in Comparative Perspective: The Quest for Control*, ed. B.G. Peters and J. Pierre, 139–56. New York: Routledge.

———. 2004b. Searching for Accountability in a Government without Boundaries. *Canadian Public Administration* 47 (1): 1–26.

———. 2006. The Canadian Public Service Has a Personality. *Canadian Public Administration* 49 (3): 261–81. http://dx.doi.org/10.1111/j.1754-7121.2006. tb01983.x.

———. 2008. *Court Government and the Collapse of Accountability in Canada and the United Kingdom*. Toronto: Institute of Public Administration of Canada / University of Toronto Press.

———. 2010. *Power: Where Is It?* Montreal and Kingston: McGill-Queen's University Press.

———. 2011. Steering from the Centre: The Canadian Way. In *Steering from the Centre: Strengthening Political Control in Western Democracies*, ed. C. Dahlström, B.G. Peters, and J. Pierre, 147–65. Toronto: University of Toronto Press.

———. 2015. The Canadian Public Service: In Search of a New Equilibrium. In *The International Handbook of Public Administration and Governance*, ed. A. Massey and K. Johnson, 182–98. Cheltenham: Edward Elgar.

Schacter, M.P.H. 1999. *Cabinet Decision-Making in Canada: Lessons and Practices*. Ottawa: Institute on Governance.

Scott, C., and K. Baehler. 2010. *Adding Value to Policy Analysis and Advice*. Sydney: University of New South Wales Press.

Shaw, R., and C. Eichbaum. 2014. Ministers, Minders and the Core Executive: Why Ministers Appoint Political Advisers in Westminster Contexts. *Parliamentary Affairs* 67 (3): 584–616. http://dx.doi.org/10.1093/pa/gss080.

———. 2015. Following the Yellow Brick Road: Theorizing the Third Element in Executive Government. *International Journal of Public Administration* 38 (1): 66–74.

Sidney, M. 2007. Policy Formulation: Design and Tools. In *Handbook of Public Policy Analysis: Theory, Politics, and Methods*, ed. F. Fischer, G.J. Miller, and M. Sidney, 79–87. Boca Raton: CRC.

Simon, H.A. 1957. *Administrative Behavior*. New York: Macmillan.

Simpson, J. 2001. *The Friendly Dictatorship*. Toronto: McClelland & Stewart.

Seymour-Ure, C. 1987. Institutionalization and Informality in Advisory Systems. In *Advising the Rulers*, ed. W. Plowden, 175–84. Blackwell.

Smith, D. 1970. President and Parliament: The Transformation of Parliamentary Government in Canada. In *The Canadian Political Process*, ed. O. Kruhlak, R. Schultz, and S. Pobihushchy, 367–82. Toronto: Holt, Rinehart and Winston.

Smith, M.J. 1999. *The Core Executive in Britain*. London: Macmillan.

Sossin, L. 2006. Defining Boundaries: The Constitutional Argument for Bureaucratic Independence and Its Implication for the Accountability of the Public Service. In *Canada, Commission of Inquiry into the Sponsorship Program and Advertising Activities, Restoring Accountability: Research Studies*, vol. 2, *The Public Service and Transparency*. Ottawa: Queen's Printer.

Stebbins, R.A. 2001. *Exploratory Research in the Social Sciences*. Thousand Oaks, CA: Sage.

Suleiman, E.N. 1984. *Bureaucrats and Policy-making*. London: Holmes and Meier.

Sutherland, S.L. 1991. The Al-Mashat Affair: Administrative Accountability in Parliamentary Institutions. *Canadian Public Administration* 34 (4): 573–603. http://dx.doi.org/10.1111/j.1754-7121.1991.tb01487.x.

Svara, J. 2006. Introduction: Politicians and Administrators in the Political Process – A Review of Themes and Issues in the Literature. *International Journal of Public Administration* 29 (12): 953–76. http://dx.doi.org/10.1080/01900690600854555.

Tellier, P. 1968. Pour une réforme des cabinets de ministres fédéraux. *Canadian Public Administration* 11 (4): 414–27. http://dx.doi.org/10.1111/j.1754-7121.1968.tb00601.x.

Tenbensel, T. 2006. Policy Knowledge for Policy Work. In *The Work of Policy: An International Survey*, ed. H. Colebatch, 199–216. Lanham, MD: Lexington Books.

Tennant, P. 1977. The NDP Government of British Columbia: Unaided Politicians in an Unaided Cabinet. *Canadian Public Policy* 3 (4): 489–503. http://dx.doi.org/10.2307/3549569.

Thomas, H. 2001. Towards a New Higher Education Law in Lithuania: Reflections on the Process of Policy Formulation. *Higher Education Policy* 14 (3): 213–23. http://dx.doi.org/10.1016/S0952-8733(01)00015-0.

Thomas, P. 2008. Political-Administrative Interface in Canada's Public Sector. *Optimum Online* 38 (2): 21-29.

———. 2010. Who Is Getting the Message? Communications at the Centre of Government. In *Public Policy Issues and the Oliphant Commission: Independent Research Studies*, ed. C. Forcese, 77–133. Ottawa: Minister of Public Works and Government Services Canada.

Tiernan, A. 2006a. Advising Howard: Interpreting Changes in Advisory and Support Structures for the Prime Minister of Australia. *Australian Journal of Political Science* 41 (3): 309–24. http://dx.doi.org/10.1080/10361140600848937.

———. 2006b. Overblown or Overload? Ministerial Staff and Dilemmas of Executive Advice. *Social Alternatives* 25 (3): 7–12.

————. 2007. *Power without Responsibility*. Kensington: University of New South Wales Press.

————. 2011. Advising Australian Federal Governments: Assessing the Evolving Capacity and Role of the Australian Public Service. *Australian Journal of Public Administration* 70 (4): 335–46.

Treasury Board Secretariat. 2006. Expenditure Review of Federal Public Sector. Vol. 2, Compensation Snapshot and Historical Perspective, 1990 to 2003. Ottawa: Treasury Board Secretariat. http://www.tbs-sct.gc.ca/report/orp/2007/er-ed/vol2/vol212-eng.asp#Toc158090277.

————. 2008, November. Policies and Guidelines for Ministers' Offices. Ottawa: Treasury Board Secretariat.

————. 2011, January. Policies for Minister's Offices. Ottawa: Treasury Board Secretariat.

Tushman, M.L., and T.J. Scanlan. 1981. Boundary Spanning Individuals: Their Role in Information Transfer and Their Antecedents. *Academy of Management Journal* 24 (2): 289–305. http://dx.doi.org/10.2307/255842.

Wallner, J. 2008. Legitimacy and Public Policy: Seeing beyond Effectiveness, Efficiency, and Performance. *Policy Studies Journal* 36 (3): 421–43. http://dx.doi.org/10.1111/j.1541-0072.2008.00275.x.

Walter, J. 1986. *The Ministers' Minders: Personal Advisers in National Government*. Melbourne: Oxford University Press.

————. 2006. Ministers, Minders and Public Servants: Changing Parameters of Responsibility in Australia. *Australian Journal of Public Administration* 65 (3): 22–7. http://dx.doi.org/10.1111/j.1467-8500.2006.00491a.x.

Wanna, J. 2005. New Zealand's Westminster Trajectory: Archetypal Transplant to Maverick Outlier. In *Westminster Legacies: Democracy and Responsible Government in Asia and the Pacific*, ed. H. Patapan, J. Wanna, and P. Weller, 153–85. Sydney: University of New South Wales Press.

Weaver, R.K. 1986. The Politics of Blame Avoidance. *Journal of Public Policy* 6 (4): 371–98. http://dx.doi.org/10.1017/S0143814X00004219.

Weaver, R.K., and P. Stares. 2001. Overview. In *Guidance for Governance: Comparing Alternative Sources of Public Policy Advice*, ed. R.K. Weaver and P. Stares, 71–88. Tokyo: Japan Center for International Exchange.

Webb, P., and R. Kolodny. 2006. Professional Staff in Political Parties. In *Handbook of Party Politics*, ed. R.S. Katz and W.J. Crotty, 337–47. London: Sage Publications. http://dx.doi.org/10.4135/9781848608047.n28.

Weber, D.J. 1986. Analyzing Political Feasibility: Political Scientists' Unique Contribution to Policy Analysis. *Policy Studies Journal* 14 (4): 545–53. http://dx.doi.org/10.1111/j.1541-0072.1986.tb00360.x.

Weller, P. 1987. Types of Advice. In *Advising the Rulers*, ed. W. Plowden, 149–57. Oxford: Basil Blackwell.

———. 2002. *Don't Tell the Prime Minister*. Melbourne: Scribe Publications.

Weller, P., H. Bakvis, and R.A.W. Rhodes, eds. 1997. *The Hollow Crown: Countervailing Trends in Core Executives*. London: Macmillan.

Wells, P. 2006. *Right Side Up: The Fall of Paul Martin and the Rise of Stephen Harper's New Conservatism*. Toronto: McClelland & Stewart.

———. 2013. *The Longer I'm Prime Minister: Stephen Harper and Canada 2006–*. Toronto: Random House.

West, W.F. 2005. Neutral Competence and Political Responsiveness: An Uneasy Relationship. *Policy Studies Journal* 33 (2): 147–60. http://dx.doi. org/10.1111/j.1541-0072.2005.00099.x.

White, G. 1990. Big Is Different from Little: On Taking Size Seriously in the Analysis of Canadian Governmental Institutions. *Canadian Public Administration* 33 (4): 526–50. http://dx.doi.org/10.1111/j.1754-7121.1990.tb01416.x.

———. 2001. Adapting the Westminster Model: Provincial and Territorial Cabinet in Canada. *Public Money & Management* 21 (2): 17–24. http://dx.doi. org/10.1111/1467-9302.00255.

———. 2005. *Cabinets and First Ministers*. Vancouver: UBC Press.

Wicks, N. 2003. *Defining the Boundaries within the Executive: Ministers, Special Advisers and the Permanent Civil Service*. Ninth Report of the Committee on Standards in Public Life. https://www.gov.uk/government/publications/ defining-the-boundaries-within-the-executive-ministers-special-advisers- and-the-permanent-civil-service.

Wildavsky, A. 1979. *Speaking Truth to Power: The Art and Craft of Policy Analysis*. Boston: Little, Brown.

Williams, B. 1980. The Para-Political Bureaucracy in Ottawa. In *Parliament, Policy and Representation*, ed. H.D. Clark, 215–29. Toronto: Methuen.

Williams, P. 2002. The Competent Boundary Spanner. *Public Administration* 80 (1): 103–24. http://dx.doi.org/10.1111/1467-9299.00296.

Young, W., and T. Morley. 1983. The Premier and the Cabinet. In *The Reins of Power: Governing British Columbia*, ed. J.T. Morley, N.J. Ruff, N.A. Swainson, R.J. Wilson, and W.D. Young, 45-82. Vancouver: Douglas and McIntyre.

Zussman, D. 2009. *Political Advisers*. Paris: OECD.

———. 2013. *Off and Running: The Prospects and Pitfalls of Government Transitions in Canada*. Toronto: University of Toronto Press / Institute of Public Administration of Canada.

———. 2015. Public Policy Analysis in Canada: A Forty-Year Overview. In *A Subtle Balance: Expertise, Evidence, and Democracy in Public Policy and Governance*, ed. E.A. Parson, 11–36. Montreal and Kingston: McGill-Queen's University Press.

Index

Page references followed by *fig* indicate figures; page references followed by *t* indicate tables.

advice: political (hot) *vs.* rational (cold), 33, 33*t*
advisers: types of, 44
advisory system. *See* policy advisory system
advisory work, 236
Alboim, Elly, 56
Alward, David, 67
Aucoin, Peter, 11, 17, 37, 40, 267n1, 268n5
Australia: policy advisory practices in, 33
Axworthy, Lloyd, 49

Baccigalupo, Alain, 268n7
Benoit, Liane, 7, 57, 267n1
Birkland, Thomas, 30
Bouchard, Gert, 69
bridging activity: at British Columbia ministers' office, 169–74; characteristics of, 72; in comparative perspective, 101–2, 178–9, 180; concept of, 25, 27, 28, 71; definition of, 145; at federal ministers' office level, 162–9;

gatekeeping as form of, 36, 90, 167; at New Brunswick ministers' offices, 174–7; political control and, 36; in Prime Minister's Office, 86–92; types of, 71–2
British Columbia: appointment of ministerial staff, 272n40; Cabinet committee system, 61; deputy ministers' role in policy work, 134; evolution of administrative style, 61–2; ministerial office budgets, 62; partisan advisers' buffering in, 154–9; partisan advisers under Campbell government, 63–7, 95; policy decision-making, 118; political arm of government, 83; political staff in, 62, 63*t*, 270n24; "unaided" Cabinet style of Bennett government, 61
British Columbia ministers' office: advisory role of ministerial assistants, 170, 172–3; bridging activity in, 172–3, 179; buffering activity in, 81, 155; deputy ministers' interactions, 170–1, 218;

gatekeeping, 173–4; growth and specialization of, 62; interaction with external stakeholders, 172–3; moving activity in, 196–7; policy formulation, 116–17, 118; policy work, 156; role of partisan advisers, 154, 156–7, 170, 171–2, 174, 217–18; shaping activity in, 214, 217–18

British Columbia ministers' office partisan advisers: advisory function of, 159, 170; bridging activity of, 169–70, 171; buffering activity of, 155–6; interactions with ministries, 201–2; interactions with Premier's Office, 202, 232; interaction with deputy ministers, 218; involvement in policy development, 197, 198–9, 216; liaison role of, 197–8; moving activity of, 184, 198, 200–1, 202–3; policy expertise of, 221; policy formulation work of, 199–200, 216–17; provision of policy advice, 156, 157; responsibilities of, 202; shaping activity of, 184, 214, 216, 217–18; as strategic thinkers, 200; subject matter expertise of, 215–16

British Columbia policy advisory system: buffering and bridging activity, 232–3; dispersed location of partisan advisers, 232; exogenous sources of policy advice, 233*fig*, 234; intra-ministerial resource exchange, 232; nature of, 82; partisan advisers in, 233, 233*fig*; types of, 232

British Columbia Premier's Office: advisory bodies, 270n27; advisory services, 64–5; budget, 64, 65; buffering activity in, 80–1, 82, 83–4; central administrative units, 62; centralized model of, 61; chief of staff responsibilities, 66; during the Clark administration, 62; expenses, 63*t*; formal and informal advisory activity, 81–2; functions of, 65; moving activity in, 117–18, 119; organizational structure, 65–6; policy work in, 156; political staff, 63*t*, 64, 67; reorganization of, 61–2, 64–5; role of partisan advisers, 65–6, 80–1, 130–1; senior coordinator responsibilities, 66; shaping activity in, 130–1

British Columbia Premier's Office bridging activity: conducted by phone, 94; during daily meetings, 93; gatekeeping, 93–4, 102; informal nature of, 94; interactions with ministers, 92, 93; interaction with stakeholders, 94, 95; partisan advisers' view of, 92–3; policy formulation, 116–17; role of deputy ministers, 95; use of external sources of policy expertise, 94–6

Brodie, Ian: appointment as PMO chief of staff, 57; on interactions with PCO, 87; on mandate letter process, 125; on priority settings in PMO, 124; on process management, 107; on written briefing system, 77

Brown, Martyn, 64, 83, 95, 270n26

buffering activity: actors involved in, 181; at British Columbia ministers' office, 154–9; in comparative perspective, 101–2, 178, 180; concept of, 25, 27, 28, 71; core executive resource exchange and, 36–7; definition of, 145;

on federal level, 178; at federal ministers' office level, 146–54; at New Brunswick ministers' office, 159–62; political control and, 36; as provision of policy advice, 178; *vs.* shaping activity, 128–9, 136, 211
Burney, Derek, 50

Cabinet committees, 111–12, 113–14
Cabinet governance, 42
Cabinet of Canada: annex item to agenda, 271n35; committee report submitted to, 271n25; decision-making system, 113; growth of, 51; importance of process, 107; moving activity in relation to, 113; partisan advisers' work with, 110; reduction of, 55; role of committees in, 113–14
Cameron, Mark, 58, 72, 77
Campbell, Colin, 20, 50, 191, 267n1
Campbell, Gordon, 270n29
Canada: partisanship in system of responsible government, 21; policy advisory system in, 12, 13–14, 16; policymaking in, 16; study of influence of partisan advisers, 37
Canadian governance: centralization of, 16–17; concerns over power of ministers in, 16; contemporary trends in, 11; core executives and, 18; displacement of Parliament by Cabinet, 16
chiefs of staff in ministerial offices: engagement in policy formulation, 189–90; longest serving, 270n26; policy work, 148, 188; responsibilities of, 51, 52; role and functions in Quebec, 268n7
Chrétien, Jean, 55, 271n34

Civil Service Act (1963), 46
Clark, Christina, 270n24, 270n29
core executive actors: characteristic of, 18; definition of, 268n6; resources, 18*t*, 244*t*; resources and power, 19
core executive resource exchange: comparison of federal and provincial cases, 248; configuration of advisers and, 246; importance of sequencing variables for, 249–50; instrumentality of, 249; operational features, 247–8, 247*t*, 249; partisan advisers engagement in, 246–7, 248; structural features, 246–7, 247*t*; types and variations of, 102–3, 245, 248
court government, 16, 17

Day, Stockwell, 91, 115, 150
deputy ministers: appointments of, 272n38; as non-partisan policy advisers, 152; perspective on public service policy advice, 151–3; as policy arbiters, 245; view of role of partisan advisers, 149, 152
deputy prime minister, 270n15
Deputy Prime Minister's Office (DPMO), 51
Doyle, Arthur, 68
Duffy, John, 56
Duffy, Mike, 58
Dunn, Christopher, 69

Eichbaum, Christopher, 10, 27, 167
Emerson, David, 115, 150, 168, 186, 212
executive assistants, 268n3

federal government, 42, 70, 102
federal ministers. *See* ministers
federal ministers' offices: advisory
    role of deputy ministers, 163–4;
    bridging activity in, 162, 163, 164–
    5, 166–7, 169; buffering activity
    in, 181; day-to-day practices,
    165–6; external sources of policy
    advice, 166–7; gatekeeping, 167–8;
    interactions between officials and
    ministerial staff, 164; mandate
    letters, 185–6; moving activity in,
    185; policy work, 185, 208, 212;
    resource exchanges, 165; role of
    chiefs of staff, 168–9, 207–8; role
    of directors of policy, 209; shaping
    activity in, 207, 208–9, 211; signal-
    checking, 162–3
federal ministers' offices partisan
    advisers: bridging duties of,
    168; engagement in policy
    development, 195, 210;
    interactions with officials, 193,
    209, 214; interactions with
    PMO partisan advisers, 208;
    involvement in policy work, 187,
    189, 211–12; moving activity,
    187–8, 190, 194, 195–6; policy
    experiences of, 192; policy
    formulation functions, 184, 185,
    189–90, 213–14; policy interactions
    of, 193–4; as procedural
    transmitters, 195; shaping activity,
    207, 208–9, 210–11, 213–14, 221
federal partisan-political briefing
    note system: genesis of written,
    73, 77
formulation. *See* policy formulation
Fox, Graham, 59
Frenette, Ray, 67

Gallant, Brian, 67
gatekeeping: in British Columbia
    Premier's Office, 93–4, 102; in
    comparative perspective, 181–2;
    as form of bridging, 30, 90, 167; in
    ministers' offices, 62, 100–1, 102,
    166–7; in Prime Minister's Office,
    90, 102
Giorno, Guy: communication with
    ministers, 87; on dealings with
    PCO, 78–9; on engagement in
    gatekeeping, 90–1; interactions
    with senior officials, 87; on
    mandate letter process, 125; on
    PMO advisory practices, 77;
    as PMO chief of staff, 57; on
    stakeholder relations, 89; on
    Stephen Harper's top adviser, 91
Goldenberg, Edward, 53, 54, 76
governance: challenges of, 250;
    definition of, 268n4; partisan
    politics in, 31–2
Graham, Alan R., 67

Harper, Stephen: communication
    with ministers, 116; perception of
    Cabinet, 113; political staff of, 57;
    preference to PMO-PCO advisory
    system, 74; reliance on Cabinet
    committees, 114; as top policy
    adviser to himself, 91; written
    advisory system under, 73, 76, 78,
    270n21
Hatfield, Richard, 67, 69
Herle, David, 56

junior partisan advisers: bridging
    activity, 87, 88, 90, 109;
    engagement with PCO officials,
    242; expertise of, 194; general

policy functions, 111; interactions between PMO and ministerial, 72–3, 87, 88, 109, 208, 229; interactions with senior-level partisan advisers, 214, 229; involvement in partisan-political analysis, 230; in ministers' offices, 42, 193, 194, 208, 229, 230; moving activity, 194; policy coordination, 58; policy formulation activity, 127, 194; in Prime Minister's Office, 42, 58, 72–3, 75–6, 111, 127, 147, 208, 230; use of formal briefing system, 75; work on drfting policy advice, 76

Kemp, David Alistair, 31, 34
Kent, Tom, 46
Kernaghan, Ken, 30
King, Simon, 246, 267n1

Lalonde, Marc, 50
Lenoski, Gerald, 45, 48, 49
Lord, Bernard, 67
Lynch, Kevin, 78, 271n36

machinery of government: models of, 25t
MacKay, Peter, 59
Mallory, James, 6, 7, 9, 49, 224
mandate letters, 108, 125, 126, 186
Martin, Paul, 55–6, 57
Mazankowski, Donald, 51
McKenna, Frank, 67, 69
ministerial office budget, 46, 269n14
ministerial staff, 45, 47, 48, 51–2, 269n12
ministers: advisory preferences of, 77–8; budget increase, 49; departmental officials as advisers to, 49; policy advice practices, 11–12, 148, 149–50, 151, 227; policy-related interactions, 91, 115–16; resources of, 244t; responsibilities of, 9, 48; salaries, 49; view of role of partisan advisers by, 149, 150. See also ministers' offices
ministers' office partisan advisers: as advisory system participants, 177; diversity of activities of, 222; four principles of policy advice, 146; involvement in policy development, 222; moving activities of, 183–4, 220–1, 222; policy advice provided by, 148–9, 179–80; policy formulation work, 183, 184–5, 220, 225; political control and, 223; as primary source for policy council, 147–8
ministers' offices: expenditures for personnel, 60, 60t; introduction of chief of staff position in, 51, 52; policy work in, 190–1; resource exchange in, 148, 232; role of directors of policy in, 32, 37–8, 147, 190, 193; size of staff, 49–50, 53t; staff's budget, 55, 57; work on policy proposal in, 128
Morley, Terence, 61
moving activity: in British Columbia government, 117–19; categories of, 39t; characteristics of, 190; concept of, 26, 27, 28; horizontal, 105–6, 109, 110–11; impact on political control, 38–9; in New Brunswick, 119–23; signal-checking, 111, 116; vertical, 105–6
Mulroney, Brian, 50–1
Murphy, Tim, 56

neutral competence: definition of, 9
New Brunswick: characteristic of
    governments, 41, 42, 67–8; Civil
    Service Act, 69; development of
    public service, 67, 68–9; Graham
    majority government, 42; partisan
    advisers in, 66, 69; policy advisory
    system in, 234–7, 235*fig*; political
    staff in, 68–9
New Brunswick ministers' office
    partisan advisers: bridging
    with external stakeholders, 176,
    177; buffering activity of, 162;
    engagement in policy formulation,
    184, 219–20; influence of, 176–7;
    moving activity of, 203, 204,
    205, 206–7; non-involvement
    in policy development, 219–20;
    policymaking, 205–6; policy-
    related interactions, 161, 175–6,
    204; policy work, 204, 206, 218–19;
    role of, 159–60, 161, 219; shaping
    activity of, 218–20, 221
New Brunswick ministers' offices:
    absence of buffering in, 178;
    bridging activity, 174–5, 179, 181;
    communications on policy advice,
    203, 206; partisan advisers in,
    160–1, 175; policymaking in, 204;
    role of departmental officials in,
    176, 177
New Brunswick Premier's
    Office: accessibility of, 100–1;
    bridging activity in, 96–101;
    buffering activity in, 84–6; direct
    policy advice, 86; division of
    labour in, 119–20; formulation
    activity, 119–23; functions of
    partisan advisers, 84–5, 120–1,
    122–3, 136–8, 139–41; moving
    activity, 120–3; policy-related
    interactions, 86, 120–1; role of
    chief of staff, 69; shaping activity,
    136–7, 138, 139, 140
New Political Governance (NPG),
    17, 268n5
Nielson, Eric, 51
Novak, Ray, 57, 58

O'Connor, Loretta J., 52
Organization for Economic
    Cooperation and Development
    (OECD), 11, 25

partisan advisers: as arbiters in
    conflicts, 245; bridging activities,
    23, 34, 35–6, 35*t*, 101–2, 145, 166–7;
    buffering activities, 23, 34, 35*t*,
    101–2, 145–6; in Canada, historical
    evolution of, 44; as component
    of political arm of government,
    224; concept of policy work,
    27*t*; core executive approach
    in analysis of, 19; definition of,
    5–6, 267–8n2; document written
    by, 271n34; effectiveness of,
    243; evolution of, 70; exercise of
    political control, 103; formulation
    activities, 37–40, 127, 130, 141,
    143, 144, 243; governance and, 11,
    16; inappropriate actions of, 246;
    influence of, 17, 37, 40, 101, 104,
    224; institutionalization of, 44–5,
    46, 47; moving activities, 104–5,
    143–4; at national and provincial
    level, 45, 141; as non-dominant
    policy actors, 250; in partisan-
    political process management,
    142; policy advisory activities, 32,
    35*t*, 71–2, 74, 75, 80, 149, 225, 230;
    policy advisory system and, 12,
    226, 231*fig*; policy development

and, 195; policy practices, 20;
policy-related interactions of,
129–30, 153; as policy workers,
19–20, 21, 23, 187, 224, 236–7,
245–6, 249, 250, 251; in premiers'
offices, 225, 231, 245, 248–9;
privileged position of, 243–4;
as procedural transmitters, 195;
public servants' perspective
on, 182; public service and, 37;
reinforcement bureaucracy, 127;
resource exchange and, 243, 246–7;
as resources for core executives,
19; resources of, 244*t*; role in
policymaking, 250–1; scrutiny
of policy documents by, 128,
129; shaping activities, 104–5,
143–4; specialization of, 44–5, 240,
272n41; study of, 23, 40–1, 269n10;
in Westminster systems, use of,
10, 12. *See also* British Columbia
ministers' office partisan advisers;
federal ministers' offices partisan
advisers; New Brunswick
ministers' office partisan advisers
partisan advisers' formulation
activity: process dimension of,
238–40
partisan-political policy advice,
33–4, 50, 72, 147, 182, 213
partisan politics, 30–1
partisanship: in political science
literature, use of term, 268–9n8;
in Westminster-style systems,
manifestations of, 21
Pearson, Lester, 46
Plassé, Micheline, 52
PMO/PCO advisory system, 73–4
policy advice: actors in, 34; in
Canadian government, models
of, 14–15*t*; in comparative

perspective, 179–80; direct
and indirect suppliers of, 23;
globalization and changes in,
15; models of, 14–15*t*, 226*fig*;
partisan-political form of, 33–4,
50, 72, 147, 182, 213; philosophical
dimension of, 15–16; recognition
of public service in, 236; sources
of, 145, 228
policy advisory system: in
Canada, 12, 13–14; concepts of,
12–14; configuration of federal
dynamic, 229–30, 232; "dynamic"
ideal-type mode, 227–8, 228*fig*;
federal partisan advisers and,
231*fig*; government control
over, 12–13; influence of, 177;
interactions in, 229; key trends
in Anglo-American, 13, 16; in
New Brunswick, 234–7; partisan
advisers as part of, 12; spatial
foundations of, 228; types of, 13*t*
policy formulation: actors,
183; characteristic of, 30; in
comparative perspective, 184;
context of, 222; at national *vs.*
provincial level, 142; procedural
aspects in, 107, 112; role of
partisan advisers in, 104, 127,
130, 141, 182, 220; role of political
staff in, 212; studies of, 104–5;
sub-phases of, 29–30; vertical
and horizontal dimensions of, 38,
105–6. *See also* procedural policy
work
policymaking, 28–30, 31
policy work: arbiters in, 245;
characteristic of, 28; concepts
of, 20; non-partisan, 20; notion
of amphibians in, 191; role of
partisan advisers in, 22, 24–5,

27–8, 27*t*, 192, 212, 236–7, 249;
vertical intra-ministerial, 193
political advisers: collaborative
type, 25, 25*t*, 226–7; gatekeeper
type, 25*t*, 26, 226*fig*; "hybrids
and outliers" ideal type, 26;
triangulated type, 25*t*, 26, 226*fig*
political arm of government, 20, 83,
224, 250, 251
political control, 36
political staff: accountability of, 3;
appointments of, 6; characteristics
of, 4, 5; growth of, 45; influence
of, 3–4; ministers and, 7; as policy
workers, 267n1; responsibilities of,
6–7; studies of, 3–4, 267n1
Prasser, Scott, 33
Premier's Office partisan advisers
(British Columbia): buffering
activity, 154; Cabinet committee
involvement, 133, 135, 136;
departmental service plans
functions, 131; engagement in
strategic direction-setting, 134–5;
involvement in drafting party
platform, 131; policy formulation,
133–4, 135; provision of policy
advice to ministers, 154–5;
shaping activity, 130–1, 132–3, 136;
work with policy documents, 132
Prime Minister's Office (PMO):
access to scheduling agenda,
271n34; advisory practices,
78; appraisal and dialogue
activities, 124; approach to
mandate letters, 125–6; authority
to veto ministers' chiefs of staff
selection, 55; bridging activities,
86–90, 88, 92, 102; budget of,
47, 50, 59; buffering activities,

72–3; chief of staff's role in,
108, 115–16; under Chrétien
government, 53; creation of,
45; email leak, 4; formulation
activity, 143; "four corner
meetings," 190, 272n39; growth
of, 47, 50, 51; increase of cost of,
51; influence of, 45; interactions
with PCO, 78–9, 108, 114,
231–2, 271n36; junior partisan
advisers' role in, 45, 58, 72–3,
75–6, 111, 127, 147, 208, 230; main
functions of, 46; management
of, 45; oral policy advice, 54, 77;
organizational structure of, 56,
57; partisan-political advisory
system, 75–6; planning and
prioritizing, 124; policy advisory
activities, 54–5, 56–7, 58, 74–5;
policy-briefing note system, 58,
129; policymaking practices,
55–6; policy movers in, 106–16;
political staff and expenses for,
48*t*; process management, 107,
115; reorganization of, 47, 50,
57–9; role and responsibilities of,
59, 109, 111; role of director of
policy in, 58, 72–3, 74–5, 78, 88,
90, 108, 129, 193, 194; shaping
activities, 124; size of staff, 53*t*,
59; verbal culture in, 76; written
policy advice, 58, 73, 76–7
Prime Minister's Office partisan
advisers: interactions with public
service officials, 110–11; moving
activities, 106, 109–11, 113; policy
formulation activities, 112, 114,
143–4; priorities sorting, 111;
signal-checking, 108
Prince, Michael, 13, 16

Privy Council Office (PCO): appraisal and dialogue activities, 124; bridging activities, 90; guidelines on advisory activity, 32, 165; *Guide to Ministers and Ministers of State*, 6, 34; interactions with PMO, 78–9, 108, 114, 129–30, 231–2, 271n36; involvement in policy formulation, 110; policy advice practices, 75, 78–9, 87; role in policy advice, 7, 73–4; signal-checking, 130; studies of, 42–3; work on mandate letters, 125, 126; written briefing system, 73

procedural policy work: actors in, 188, 193; advisers' engagement in, 186, 187; chiefs of staff's involvement in, 188; consolidation activity, 194; dialogue activity within departments, 192; horizontal and vertical, 193–4; ministers' offices and, 185; sub-phases of, 186–7

public administration, 18

public servants, 24, 182, 197, 269n9

public service: criticism of, 8; as guardian of public interest, 9; neutral competence of, 9–10; perception of, 8, 10; political control and, 8; political purpose of, 9; as primary adviser to government, 11; responsive competence of, 10; role in policy advice, 150–1, 237

Public Service Employment Act (1967), 46

Public Service Employment Act (2003), 268n3

public service policy advice, 149, 152–3

resource exchange, 223, 226. *See also* core executive resource exchange

responsible government: principle of, 8–9

responsive competence, 10

Rhodes, R.A.W., 19, 268n6

Robichaud, Lois, 67

Roy, Bernard, 50

Ruff, Norman, 66

Savoie, Donald: on court government, 16, 17, 47; on development of public service in New Brunswick, 67; on ministerial executive assistants, 267n1; on Mulroney's reorganization of political staff, 51; on relations between politicians and administrators, 68

Schacter, Mark, 271n35

Seckel, Allan, 83, 95

shaping activity: as attempt to secure political control over policy agenda, 126–7; in British Columbia first ministers' office, 130–1; *vs.* buffering activity, 128–9, 136, 211; categories of, 39t; characteristic of, 124, 242–3; concept of, 26, 27, 28; at federal and subnational levels, 242; horizontal, 105–6, 241; impact on governmental policy formulation, 39–40; link to policy proposal, 210; policy formulation and, 143, 241; role of first ministers in, 241; studies of, 105; sub-phases of, 207; vertical, 105–6, 241–2

Shaw, Richard, 10, 27, 167

sponsorship scandal, 3

Tellier, Paul, 7, 49, 224
Thériault, Camille, 67
Thomas, Paul, 267n1
Treasury Board Secretariat (TBS):
  guidelines for ministers on
  advisory activity, 32, 35, 37–8; on
  partisan advisers' activities and
  interactions, 34, 165; *Policies for
  Ministers' Offices* (2011), 59–60
triangulated model of political
  advisers, 26, 226–7, 226*fig*,
  268n7
Trudeau, Pierre, 46–7, 48, 50, 270n15

Vander Zalm, William, 270n24

Wallace, Lawrence James, 61
Walter, James, 167
Wanna, John, 9
Westminster systems of government:
  concerns over power of
  ministers, 16; countries with, 10;
  executive advisory landscape, 12;
  partisanship in, 21; public service
  in, 10
Wright, Nigel, 58, 77, 127

Young, Walter D., 61

Zussman, David, 11, 25, 26, 34–5,
  226, 267n1

The Institute of Public Administration of Canada Series in Public Management and Governance

Networks of Knowledge: Collaborative Innovation in International Learning, Janice Stein, Richard Stren, Joy Fitzgibbon, and Melissa Maclean

The National Research Council in the Innovative Policy Era: Changing Hierarchies, Networks, and Markets, G. Bruce Doern and Richard Levesque

Beyond Service: State Workers, Public Policy, and the Prospects for Democratic Administration, Greg McElligott

A Law unto Itself: How the Ontario Municipal Board Has Developed and Applied Land Use Planning Policy, John G. Chipman

Health Care, Entitlement, and Citizenship, Candace Redden

Between Colliding Worlds: The Ambiguous Existence of Government Agencies for Aboriginal and Women's Policy, Jonathan Malloy

The Politics of Public Management: The HRDC Audit of Grants and Contributions, David A. Good

Dream No Little Dreams: A Biography of the Douglas Government of Saskatchewan, 1944–1961, Albert W. Johnson

Governing Education, Ben Levin

Executive Styles in Canada: Cabinet Structures and Leadership Practices in Canadian Government, edited by Luc Bernier, Keith Brownsey, and Michael Howlett

The Roles of Public Opinion Research in Canadian Government, Christopher Page

The Politics of CANDU Exports, Duane Bratt

Policy Analysis in Canada: The State of the Art, edited by Laurent Dobuzinskis, Michael Howlett, and David Laycock

Digital State at the Leading Edge: Lessons from Canada, Sanford Borins, Kenneth Kernaghan, David Brown, Nick Bontis, Perri 6, and Fred Thompson

The Politics of Public Money: Spenders, Guardians, Priority Setters, and Financial Watchdogs inside the Canadian Government, David A. Good

Court Government and the Collapse of Accountability in Canada and the UK, Donald Savoie

Professionalism and Public Service: Essays in Honour of Kenneth Kernaghan, edited by David Siegel and Ken Rasmussen

Searching for Leadership: Secretaries to Cabinet in Canada, edited by Patrice Dutil

Foundations of Governance: Municipal Government in Canada's Provinces, edited by Andrew Sancton and Robert Young

Provincial and Territorial Ombudsman Offices in Canada, edited by Stewart Hyson

Local Government in a Global World: Australia and Canada in Comparative Perspective, edited by Emmanuel Brunet-Jailly and John F. Martin

Behind the Scenes: The Life and Work of William Clifford Clark, Robert A. Wardhaugh

The Guardian: Perspectives on the Ministry of Finance of Ontario, edited by Patrice Dutil

Making Medicare: New Perspectives on the History of Medicare in Canada, edited by Gregory P. Marchildon

Overpromising and Underperforming? Understanding and Evaluating New Intergovernmental Accountability Regimes, edited by Peter Graefe, Julie M. Simmons, and Linda A. White

Governance in Northern Ontario: Economic Development and Policy Making, edited by Charles Conteh and Bob Segsworth

Off and Running: The Prospects and Pitfalls of Government Transitions in Canada, David Zussman

Deputy Ministers in Canada: Comparative and Jurisdictional Perspectives, edited by Jacques Bourgault and Christopher Dunn

The Politics of Public Money, Second Edition, David A. Good

Commissions of Inquiry and Policy Change: A Comparative Analysis, edited by Gregory J. Inwood and Carolyn M. Johns

Leaders in the Shadows: The Leadership Qualities of Municipal Chief Administrative Officers, David Siegel

Funding Policies and the Nonprofit Sector in Western Canada: Evolving Relationships in a Changing Environment, edited by Peter R. Elson

Backrooms and Beyond: Partisan Advisers and the Politics of Policy Work in Canada, Jonathan Craft